Teaching History, Learning Citizenship

Teaching History, Learning Citizenship

Tools for Civic Engagement

Jeffery D. Nokes

Foreword by Laura Wakefield

TEACHERS COLLEGE PRESS

TEACHERS COLLEGE | COLUMBIA UNIVERSITY

NEW YORK AND LONDON

Published by Teachers College Press, 1234 Amsterdam Avenue, New York, NY 10027

Cover design by Patricia Palao. Cover images (clockwise from top left): Protesting teens by Rawpixel / iStock by Getty Images. Freedom Rider Winonah Beamer, public domain mugshot courtesy of Wikimedia Commons. Volunteer group by nautiluz56 / iStock by Getty Images. Portrait of Abraham Lincoln by Alexander Gardner, courtesy of the Prints and Photographs Online Catalog of the Library of Congress. Colin Kaepernik courtesy of Daniel Hartwig under a creative commons attribution license via Flickr. Suffragette, 1914, public domain via Wikimedia Commons. Portrait of Susan B. Anthony by Frances Benjamin Johnston, public domain via Wikimedia Commons. Pride parade attendees by FG Trade / iStock by Getty Images. Portrait of Harriet Tubman by Benjamin F. Powelson, courtesy of the Prints and Photographs Online Catalog of the Library of Congress.

Photograph of Olympic Demonstration (Chapter 11, Document 2) taken by Angelo Cozzi (Mondadori Publishers), Getty Images.

Library of Congress Cataloging-in-Publication Data

Names: Nokes, Jeffery D., author. | Wakefield, Laura, writer of foreword.
Title: Teaching history, learning citizenship : tools for civic engagement
  / Jeffery D. Nokes ; foreword by Laura Wakefield.
Description: New York, NY : Teachers College Press, [2019] | Includes
  bibliographical references and index. | Summary: "Teaching History,
  Learning Citizenship: Tools for Civic Engagement stands out from other
  books for several reasons. First, it provides ready-to-use lesson
  materials on important historical topics, already likely to be part of
  the history curriculum. Primary sources are modified for young readers,
  with graphic organizers and ideas for other instructional support.
  Lesson materials are presented in a way that allows teachers flexibility
  in the way lessons are designed"— Provided by publisher.
Identifiers: LCCN 2019020476 | ISBN 9780807761939 (hardcover) | ISBN
  9780807761922 (paperback) | ISBN 9780807778029 (ebook)
Subjects: LCSH: Service learning—Study and teaching—United States. |
  Education—Curricula—United States. | United States—History—Study and
  teaching.
Classification: LCC E175.8 .N64 2019 | DDC 973/.071—dc23
LC record available at lccn.loc.gov/2019020476

ISBN 978-0-8077-6192-2 (paper)
ISBN 978-0-8077-6193-9 (hardcover)
ISBN 978-0-8077-7802-9 (ebook)

Printed on acid-free paper
Manufactured in the United States of America

Contents

To Raelynn, Grace, and Emery

Foreword

At a time when intense political debate divides the nation, as public trust in government and voter turnout is at an all-time low, it is easy to think that our nearly 250-year-old civic experiment is on the precipice. In *Democracy in America*, Alexis de Tocqueville wrote about his travels in America in the 1830s. The French writer pointed out that self-centered individualism had the potential to destroy civic connections in a democracy. To counter this tendency, Tocqueville recognized something unique to American democracy. He cited the crucial work of America's intellectual and moral associations such as families, churches, and schools in teaching each generation the values and skills required for self-governance to work. As educators, we believe our role is crucial in this endeavor to instill the habits and attitudes of democracy in a new generation of citizens.

But do teachers have the knowledge, experience, and skills to engage students in civic activities? Jeff Nokes knows that teaching civics must be more than understanding the structures and functions of government. In *Teaching History, Learning Citizenship* Nokes proposes that America's history classrooms are where citizens can be prepared "to ensure the survival of democracy." Rightly claiming that teaching civics without a historical underpinning is fruitless, he asks if how students learn about the past might play a role in how they interact as citizens. Throughout American history, civic engagement has required a willingness to do difficult things such as uniting for a common cause, compromising, standing up for another's rights, sacrificing for the common good, and maintaining an open mind. Practically speaking, this book reimagines history classrooms as places where students practice these civic engagement skills and collaboratively seek insight on modern problems from historic events.

Our history is so rich and the curriculum so broad that teachers risk tedious instruction by trying to "cover" everything. Instead, Nokes shows teachers how to focus on depth over breadth. Without ignoring the pertinent stories of American history, he strategically chooses topics best suited for case studies on civic engagement. Each case illustrates a strategy applicable for civic engagement and historical inquiry. Through this process, the vital habits of mind that dispose us to responsible civic behavior are practiced. For example, Nokes introduces two case studies that exemplify the principle of "sacrifice for the common good," and each uses a different historical inquiry strategy. In the first Nokes shows teachers that historical perspective can help students better understand the Great Compromise—the founders' struggle over determining representation in Congress at the Constitutional Convention. In the second case, he shows how to teach about continuity and change by exploring the political difficulties surrounding passage of the Civil Rights Act of 1964.

Teachers will appreciate the adaptability of the unscripted lessons in this book. Each reading provides background historical context for the teacher and the resources to expose students to themes of civic engagement that cut across historical time periods and current events. Every chapter begins with relatable examples of individuals actively engaging as citizens that are so timely they could have been ripped from the headlines. Through the case studies skills used by historians such as sourcing, corroboration, contextualization, and historiography teach students how to evaluate evidence. Graphic organizers are provided throughout to help students organize and critically analyze evidence in developing an argument. Nokes also includes objectives and a historical inquiry question to frame each investigation. (Educators will find the inclusion of primary sources for each case study especially helpful.) The wide range of sources, including letters, speeches, videos, photographs, and political cartoons are one of the best things about *Teaching History, Learning Citizenship*.

Some of my favorite case studies are those that look at individuals who demonstrated disapproval while courageously taking a stand. One is a case study on Alice Paul and the Silent Sentinels, women who fought for their suffrage at great cost in the early 1900s. Another compares the 1968 Olympic Protest by Tommie Smith and John Carlos to the recent protests by Colin Kaepernick and NFL athletes. These are especially timely considering the anniversary of women's suffrage in 2020.

Perhaps most important, in each section and chapter Jeff Nokes gives specific ideas for action so teachers can find ways to help students apply the knowledge and skills in their schools and community. With the case studies, ideas, and sources in this book, teachers can instill the dispositions of democratic citizens in students. This book is a primer that can be used in schools to counteract the destruction of civic ideals that Tocqueville warned of over 180 years ago.

—Laura Wakefield,
National Council for History Education

Acknowledgments

Many individuals have been instrumental in helping me produce this text. I am grateful to my colleagues in the History Department, the McKay School of Education, and the Office of Civic Engagement at Brigham Young University, who have pointed me in the right direction and made many helpful recommendations as my ideas took shape. I express gratitude to the College of Family, Home, and Social Sciences at BYU, which granted me a professional development leave to conduct research for this book. I am grateful to research assistants, in particular Michaela Griffiths and Chad Weight, who provided feedback on early drafts of chapters and helped secure permissions. I thank the many teachers and students who have field tested lessons and provided feedback, in particular Tasha Salisbury at South Cache Middle School, and Wendi Nielson and Jesse Roberts at Spanish Fork High. Many people at Teacher's College Press have been a pleasure to work with throughout this process. I thank my parents, grandparents, and great-grandparents who have served as models of civic engagement for me in their communities, nation, and overseas. Finally, I thank my wife Gina and my children for their love and support.

Introduction

History instruction is under attack from all sides. Americans' lack of historical knowledge is ridiculed in popular culture. Conservative groups decry the "revisionist history" that they see seeping into the mainstream curriculum. Minority groups complain that secondary history courses continue to focus on the "grand historical narrative," to the exclusion of minority perspectives. Elementary principals divert time and resources away from teaching history toward language arts and STEM programs (VanFossen, 2005). Educational researchers criticize traditional instructional methods that rely too much on lecture and history textbooks. Parents sometimes complain when history classes do not look like the ones they attended, with healthy doses of lecture and textbook reading. And secondary students regularly label history as one of the most boring subjects (Shaver, Davis, & Helburn, 1980). History, as a core subject, appears to be in trouble.

At the same time, the United States and many other nations are passing through perilous political times. Disagreements between partisan rivals make American constituents long for the "good old days" when questions of honor were settled by duels rather than through elections tainted by rumors of voter fraud, foreign interference, and fake news. Civil dialogue and collaboration have been eclipsed by obscene tirades, uncompromising executive orders, and legal and political maneuvering that shocks citizens and raises questions about the future of democracy. The civil rights of some appear to be incompatible with the civil rights of others without any signs of compromise. Some assert that Black Lives Matter, others yell back (correctly though mockingly) that All Lives Matter, while foreign dictators, violent gang members, and mass shooters act as if no lives matter. Citizens are left wondering whether the problems of the nation and world are beyond repair.

Could it be that the solutions to these perplexing problems—in the history classroom and in the world—are linked? Is it possible that the manner in which students learn history might play a role in how they interact as citizens of communities, nations, and the world? Thomas Jefferson certainly valued public education as a key to constitutional government. In a letter to William C. Jarvis, Jefferson (1820) wrote,

> I know no safe depository of the ultimate powers of the society but the people themselves; and if we think them not enlightened enough to exercise their control with a wholesome discretion, the remedy is not to take it from them, but to inform their discretion by education. This is the true corrective of abuses of constitutional power.

According to Jefferson, education is central to protecting citizens from government abuses. My assumption throughout this book is that history classrooms play a vital role in preparing citizens who have the *knowledge, skills,* and *dispositions* necessary to ensure the survival of democracy.

Central to Jefferson's idea of a citizen, and fundamental to the theme of this book, is the concept of *civic engagement*. Citizens become involved in civic engagement when they identify a problem or need in their community, school, nation, or the world and take corrective action. Further, *informed civic engagement* occurs when citizens possess the knowledge and skills necessary to achieve positive outcomes. Actions are not enough, one must act in an appropriate manner if one is to get results. The concept of a knowledgeable and skilled citizen with the dispositions needed to observe problems and to take action to solve them is revisited throughout this book. Informed civic engagement includes enlightened voting, wise jury service, persuasive public speaking, and useful community volunteerism. It includes an awareness of rights and their limitations, whom to speak to about needed reform, and historical precedents in policies and laws. For students, whose days are spent in venues different than those of most adults, civic engagement also includes standing up for a classmate who is being bullied, suggesting to a local official a way to accommodate someone with a disability, and working with administrators and peers to improve school conditions. The role of history teachers in preparing students for a lifetime of informed civic engagement is highlighted throughout this book.

The history classrooms that educated the current generation appear to have fallen short in preparing individuals for the demands of informed civic engagement. These classrooms, with few exceptions, were places where the development of historical *knowledge* was emphasized, while skills and dispositions were neglected. Students in these classrooms typically listened to their teachers lecture, read textbook passages, watched documentary videos, rehearsed information in study sessions, repeated it back to their teachers on tests, then forgot it (Shaver et al., 1980). Judging from the current state of American politics, it appears that students who memorized where the "Star-Spangled Banner" was penned were no more prepared for citizenship than those who memorized the atomic symbol for copper. Memorizing was memorizing, whether it was done in history or chemistry. Memorizing the names of founding fathers, the geographic features of battlefields, or other historical information, as important as it might seem, has not adequately prepared citizens for informed civic engagement.

Over the past 20 years, there has been increasing emphasis on teaching historical *knowledge* and historical thinking *skills* concurrently. The Common Core State Standards (2010) and the C-3 Framework, published by the National Council for the Social Studies (NCSS, 2013), integrate skill and content instruction. Teachers who teach historical reading, thinking, and writing skills find that such instruction leads not only to improved skills that are vital in an age of fake news and propaganda-laced websites, but also results in greater retention of historical content knowledge (Nokes, Dole, & Hacker, 2007; Reisman, 2012). Despite these successes, many teachers continue to teach history in conventional ways that build historical knowledge (temporarily) but do little to prepare citizens with the skills they need for informed civic engagement.

History teachers have given even less emphasis to nurturing *dispositions* for civic engagement than they have to teaching skills. Dispositions include character traits, tendencies, habits, and values—personal attributes even more important than knowledge or skills. Consider, for example, the oft-quoted statement "Ask not what your country can do for you but ask what you can do for your country." Students with historical knowledge and skills could recall John F. Kennedy as the speaker and explain the historical context that led him to include this statement in his inaugural address in 1961. But only those who have developed dispositions for civic engagement will ponder Kennedy's challenge, then do something to improve their country or community. Knowledge and skills alone will not correct the course of democracy; civic dispositions are needed. But because dispositions are difficult to evaluate in classroom settings, they will likely continue to be neglected in standards documents and assessments. Yet, history teachers place the future of American democracy at jeopardy when they instruct solely on historical knowledge and skills.

My purpose in writing this book is to promote history instruction that nurtures knowledge, skills, and dispositions as tools for civic engagement. My writing is based upon the assumptions that *historical knowledge* provides the background within which to understand current conditions and supplies models of historical problem solving to draw upon. *Historical skills* help citizens think critically about the information they hear, distinguish between reliable and unreliable sources, use evidence to develop an interpretation, acknowledge alternative perspectives, and collaboratively and deliberatively reach evidence-based conclusions. *Historical dispositions* include the tendency to withhold judgment until after analyzing evidence, to invite multiple perspectives, to voice an opinion on matters of importance, to seek the common good through compromise and sacrifice, and to take action when a problem is observed. Students in reimagined history classrooms are expected to develop the ability to engage civilly with one another, even those of different races, religions, or political persuasions, as they collaboratively seek insights on modern problems

from historic events. In this book, I show that history provides a plethora of cases in which citizens successfully took on challenges every bit as daunting as those we face today. Students who analyze cases involving civic engagement, and who are encouraged to apply their knowledge and skills to current events, are more likely to develop the dispositions needed to recognize, research, and solve problems facing communities, nations, and the world.

This book is organized around principles of civic engagement that individuals have demonstrated in the past. It provides students with a range of specific actions they might take should they observe problems in their communities. Chapter 1 frames the rest of the book by establishing the need to rethink history instruction. I document the futility of traditional history instruction and call for teaching methods that reflect what we now know about how people learn. I consider the conceptual knowledge, the historical thinking skills, and the democratic dispositions that can be nurtured as students engage in historical investigations.

The remaining chapters address case studies involving civic engagement. Chapters 2–13 provide historical cases highlighting principles such as defending others' civil rights, compromise, and civil disobedience. Each chapter includes (1) background information about a case, written for middle school or high school students; (2) a series of documents modified for middle school or high school readers (with information about how to access them online in their original form); and (3) graphic organizers and other instructional materials. Additionally, each section's introduction includes suggestions for additional historic and current cases that could be used to repeatedly teach the same principles of civic engagement throughout a U.S. history course. Research shows that teaching concepts across contexts increases the likelihood of transfer (Bransford, Brown, & Cocking, 2000)—in this case, into the civic arena.

Part I explores the need to defend our own civil rights and those of others. Within this section, Chapter 2 investigates John Adams's and Josiah Quincy's unpopular choice to defend the British soldiers involved in the Boston Massacre. The material in this chapter highlights Adams' belief that both friend and foe were entitled to a fair trial. Chapter 3 includes a document-based lesson on Harriet Tubman, showing her willingness to risk her own freedom to lead enslaved individuals out of bondage. Lesson ideas in this and other sections are meant to either be taught when they fit into the historical chronology at different times during the school year, or in two consecutive lessons if a teacher organizes a course thematically around civic engagement.

Part II addresses collaborative problem solving and citizens' ability to make a difference by coming together with like-minded individuals. In Chapter 4, I explore the Committees of Correspondence that were vital in building revolutionary momentum in the years leading up to American independence. Chapter 5 reflects on the formation of labor unions with a case study of Samuel Gompers and the

American Federation of Labor. Both chapters demonstrate the political power that comes from joining with others to solve problems or to promote important causes.

Part III deals with compromises and the sacrifices individuals and groups sometimes make to advance their goals and promote the common good. Chapter 6 refers to an investigation of the Great Compromise that saved the Constitutional Convention. Chapter 7 explores the Civil Rights Act of 1964, a landmark legislation that was significantly less than what civil rights leaders were hoping for, but helped them achieve some of their objectives. The lesson materials in Chapters 6 and 7 allow students to explore questions surrounding the decisions of individuals to compromise in order to achieve some of their objectives.

Part IV elaborates on the theme of compromise by considering historical efforts of individuals or groups to work together even during periods of intense disagreement. In Chapter 8, the reader considers Abraham Lincoln's plan to reconstruct the Union. The chapter includes Lincoln's second inaugural address where he called for mercy toward the Confederates, who, at the time, continued to wage war that tore the nation apart. Chapter 9 investigates the collaboration of Ronald Reagan and Mikhail Gorbachev, bitter Cold War adversaries, who forged a friendship that changed the world.

Part V explores the use of public demonstrations in civic engagement. Chapter 10 highlights the Silent Sentinels who, fighting for women's right to vote, picketed the Wilson White House for over 2 years. Chapter 11 analyzes the iconic image from the 1968 Olympics, when Tommie Smith and John Carlos raised their fists in the Black Power salute. This investigation compares Smith and Carlos's act with the 2016 protests against police violence led by Colin Kaepernick and other players in the National Football League.

Finally, Part VI considers civil disobedience as a tool for promoting reform used by those who lack political power when working within the legal system fails to yield results. Two cases help students consider the strategies associated with civil disobedience, the risks involved for the disobedient, and the immediate and long-range effects of their actions. Chapter 12 reviews Susan B. Anthony's act of civil disobedience, voting illegally in the 1872 election. Chapter 13 presents a lesson on James Farmer and the Freedom Riders, who protested the failure of southern states to enforce Supreme Court decisions that declared the segregation of public buses unconstitutional. Across chapters, teachers receive materials for lessons designed to prepare students for informed civic engagement. Figure I.1 lists the knowledge, skills, and dispositions that are the focus of each chapter.

Figure I.1: Knowledge, skills, and dispositions that are the focus of each chapter

Chapter	Knowledge	Skills	Dispositions
1	Knowledge introduced	Skills introduced	Dispositions introduced
2	Adams, Quincy, and the Boston Massacre trial	Corroboration	Defending the rights of others
3	Harriet Tubman	Historiography	
4	Committees of Correspondence	Contextualization	Uniting with like-minded peers
5	Samuel Gompers and the American Federation of Labor	Historical empathy	
6	The Great Compromise	Historical perspective taking	Compromise
7	The Civil Rights Act of 1965	Change and continuity	
8	Abraham Lincoln's plans for Reconstruction	Ethical judgment	Diplomacy and working with adversaries
9	Ronald Reagan and Mikhail Gorbachev's friendship	Argumentative writing	
10	Silent Sentinels	Analyzing photographs	Demonstrating disapproval
11	The 1968 Olympic demonstration	Contextualization through analogy	
12	Susan B. Anthony and the election of 1872	Identifying historical significance	Civil disobedience
13	James Farmer and the Freedom Riders	Sourcing	

CHAPTER 1

A New Vision of History Teaching

On February 14, 2018, the unimaginable occurred at Marjory Stoneman Douglas High School in suburban coastal Florida. A former student entered the school with a loaded assault rifle and opened fire on his classmates. He killed 17 young people and adults. Many surviving students, compelled by sorrow and rage, and recognizing an opportunity to channel nationwide sympathy into more lasting legal reforms, contacted lawmakers, organized protests, and debated politicians on national television. Students traveled to Tallahassee, Florida, their state's capital, where they met with members of the state legislature, pleading with them to revise Florida's gun laws. Others traveled to Washington DC to meet with national lawmakers and the president, asking for more sweeping reforms. They demanded that legislators refuse campaign donations from the National Rifle Association, a powerful special interest group. Many of them, too young to vote, urged their older classmates to register to vote and demanded that in the next election adults boot out members of Congress who would not act on gun control. This type of tragedy could never happen again.

Soon, young people around the nation followed their example, becoming leaders within their own communities. Showing solidarity with their young compatriots, students organized similar walkouts during what became known as the "March for Our Lives" protest. The activism and leadership of students in Florida and across the nation drew the attention of adults. In March 2018, Florida's governor signed into law the first gun control measures in decades in that state (Mazzei, 2018).

The activism of young people from Marjory Stoneman Douglas High School shows that active and informed citizenship requires *knowledge*, *skills*, and *dispositions*. For instance, understanding federalism, students addressed lawmakers at both the national and state levels. An awareness of rights protected by the Bill of Rights allowed them to coordinate protests in a manner that would not bring legal or academic penalties. Understanding campaign finance and the power of special interest groups helped students identify and criticize the National Rifle Association, a well-financed national organization that promotes gun-friendly candidates. Students hoped to make voters more aware of the political influence of this group in order to counteract its power. Knowing voting processes led them to encourage older peers to register to vote

and prompted them to call upon voters to hold officers accountable for their inaction. In addition to this knowledge, students' *skills* in public speaking, communicating with peers through social media, and using evidence to support an argument were vital to their work. Perhaps most important, the tragedy created a *disposition* in students to act. It gave them the courage to speak to powerful adults and before huge audiences. It increased their curiosity about current laws and lawmaking processes. It deepened their empathy toward other victims of gun violence. A thoughtless and tragic act revealed a problem in society, and students were motivated to learn about it, propose solutions to it, and hold adults accountable for responding to it.

In 2013, the Center on Adolescence at Stanford University hosted a conference on youth civic engagement, inviting the nation's leading experts to speak. At the conclusion of the conference, these researchers prepared a consensus report, capturing the highlights and points of agreement of these speakers. In this report, the panelists suggested:

> Civic development has three dimensions that are important to cultivate in order to educate young people for citizenship. The first dimension—knowledge—comprises the facts and ideas of democracy, citizenship, the U.S. government, and global concerns that students need to know to be informed participants in civic life. The second dimension—skills—includes the ability to navigate the rules and processes of citizenship and governance in our society. The third dimension—values—includes the democratic ideals and commitment to those ideals that motivate civic commitment. (Malin, Ballard, Attai, Colby, & Damon, 2014, p. 9)

Preparing young people for civic engagement requires a new vision of history teaching that includes knowledge, skill, and dispositional objectives. In the past, the primary purpose of history classes has been to transmit historical information. But knowing facts is not enough. Civic engagement also requires skills and dispositions. I propose that history classrooms are ideal locations to prepare young people with knowledge, skills, and dispositions for citizenship. The remainder of this chapter explores those three dimensions of civic development—knowledge, skills, and dispositions—and then previews how the lessons in the chapters that follow address each.

KNOWLEDGE

History classrooms are essential for nurturing the knowledge necessary for civic engagement. Informed civic engagement requires knowledge of important concepts, governmental processes, historical precedents, and current events. History provides opportunities to consider concepts such as democracy, power, inequality, due process, civil rights, federalism, civil disobedience, imperialism, and others that are essential for understanding historical and current events. Without an understanding of these concepts, students fail to grasp current problems, miss access to a full range of solutions, lack the vocabulary needed to communicate important ideas, and do not possess the cognitive framework necessary for thinking about civic action.

For instance, a conceptual understanding of *reform* includes such factors as the conditions that necessitate reform; avenues to pursue reform; sources of opposition to reform; and the role of government, nongovernmental organizations, and individuals in pursuing reform. Numerous reform movements, such as the democratic reforms of the Jackson era or Jane Addams's housing reforms, serve as case studies by providing concrete examples of the abstract concept of reform. A conceptual understanding of reform does not require a comprehensive understanding of every reform movement in U.S. history. Instead, teachers can strategically choose case studies through which to nurture the conceptual understanding. I propose that some of the traditional historical narrative might be eliminated from the curriculum to make room for carefully selected case studies.

For example, a teacher may want to help students understand the role of *compromise* in civic engagement. To do so, he/she may need to spend less time lecturing on the differences between Massachusetts', Maryland's, and the other 11 colonies' exports to make time for an in-depth lesson on the Great Compromise. Later, he/she may need to sacrifice lectures on troop movements during Civil War battles, Civil War generals, and other Civil War trivia in order to carve out time for a lesson on the compromises associated with Lincoln's plan for Reconstruction. Less time spent lecturing on the polling outcomes of the presidential elections of 1956 and 1960 and on the makeup of Kennedy's cabinet might make room for a document-based lesson on the compromises embedded in the Civil Rights Act of 1964. By cutting some historical content the teacher would create time to revisit the concept of compromise, an important idea associated with informed civic engagement, multiple times across a school year. Even as I write about reducing the amount of historical content, the history lover in me cringes a bit—do we really need to sacrifice our favorite lectures on George McClellan's timidity or the burial of Stonewall Jackson's left arm? Research supports such changes for several reasons.

First, abundant evidence shows that most students forget most of the historical details that they are taught (McKeown & Beck, 1990), retaining only vague understandings of historical trends and changes (Barton, 2008). Thus, arguments for the inclusion of mountains of historical facts are largely arguments over what adults want young people to hear about and forget. Americans' inability to recall basic historical facts, so well documented in scholarly articles and popular media (Romano, 2011), demonstrates the fleeting nature of historical knowledge. Studies of the past century show that the majority of Americans cannot remember history well enough to distinguish between the Battles of Fredericksburg and Chancellorsville, or between William Taft's and Calvin Coolidge's foreign policies, or between the Works Progress Administration and the Public Works Administration (see, for example, Bell & McCollum, 1917; Paxton, 2003; Romano, 2011; Wineburg, 2018). Americans' inability to remember these details is not so much a matter of laziness or a symptom of poor teaching as it is a natural phenomenon related to how human brains function. Stated simply, people have difficulty retrieving from memory details that they seldom use (Bransford, Brown, & Cocking, 2000), and obscure historical facts are rarely needed. In contrast, concepts such as *reform*, once understood, can be used to frame current issues, such as gun reform, immigration reform, or campaign finance reform.

Second, historical information, along with so much other information, is readily available to anyone carrying a cellphone (Wineburg, 2018). In a matter of seconds, the most minute historical trivia can be accessed on hand-held devices. The ability to do so raises the question: How essential is it to expose students to all of the traditional historical narrative? Would it not be more useful to help students understand important concepts that, once understood, would allow them to comprehend the historical information they pull up on their cellphones when curiosity arises? Certainly, facts, events, people, and trends in history are useful—even necessary—in nurturing an understanding of concepts. However, these details should be viewed as a means to teach concepts rather than as the ultimate ends of history teaching. To do otherwise would relegate history to an interesting pursuit with little long-term impact.

Third, it is futile to try to teach everything of importance (Wiggins, 1989). Particularly within the discipline of history, teachers often pressure themselves to cover mountains of information. They feel they are doing their students a disservice if those students have not heard of (and been tested on) things like the XYZ Affair, Pickett's Charge, the Bull Moose Party, Oliver North, and hundreds of similar people, policies, and events. Indeed, these stories are interesting, inspiring, and even important. Most history teachers enjoy telling students about these things. However, when one considers the fleeting nature of historical details in memory, one must reconsider the inclusion of so much information. The reality is that history teachers cannot teach everything that is worth hearing about—nor should they try. Instead, they need to be strategic about the history they teach—remembering that unlike historical information, historical concepts, once understood well, are likely to be retained and applied (Bransford et al., 2000). There is a place for some of the great stories of history. But that place is to serve as case studies illustrating concepts that are essential for civic engagement. Some of the great (and boring) stories of history must be sacrificed as teachers nurture conceptual knowledge, skills, and dispositions.

SKILLS

Effective civic engagement requires a number of cognitive and social skills. Public schools in general (Hess & McAvoy, 2015) and history classrooms in particular (NCSS, 2013) have long been viewed as the ideal locations to nurture these skills. And history teachers are increasingly encouraged to teach skills. The Common Core State Standards (2010) establish learning outcomes that include literacy skills. The National Council for the Social Studies' (2013) C-3 Framework lists skills vital in social studies, history, and civic engagement. Several states have recently revised their standards documents, establishing skill objectives for history. The skills that are central to historical thinking are often vital in civic engagement.

For example, history students are expected to identify the source of documents, using information about the source to think critically about the documents' content. This skill of *sourcing* includes seeking information about the source, identifying the author and genre, and considering the author's motives and audience—factors basic to historical thinking (Wineburg, 1991). The strategy of sourcing is as essential for civic engagement as it is for historical inquiry. Televised political advertisements are less manipulative when viewers consider the source. News—whether in print, digital, or video formats—is more effectively vetted and understood when consumers acknowledge the source and sponsors. Voters, consumers, jurors, and citizens, working together to solve issues, serve effectively only when they use sourcing to evaluate the information they receive. This skill of sourcing is highlighted in Chapter 13.

Some might question whether historical thinking skills transfer into the arena of civic engagement: Do students who have been taught strategies for historical reading, thinking, and writing really demonstrate superior citizenship? There is little research to show that such is the case. However, there is a great deal of research that shows that teachers increase the likelihood of the transfer of skills from one setting to another when they provide students with instruction in multiple contexts (Bransford et al., 2000). An additional instructional method that greatly increases the likelihood of transfer is teaching students directly about the potential applications of a skill. For example, as a history teacher introduces the idea of sourcing to students, he/she might talk about the usefulness of sourcing when engaging in online reading. The teacher might demonstrate by showing students how to identify the source of a webpage, then how to investigate that source using independent Internet sites (McGrew, Ortega, Breakstone, & Wineburg, 2017). Although research on the impact of classroom instruction on long-term preparation for civic engagement is lacking, it seems likely that nurturing historical thinking strategies in class and modeling their application within the civic arena will help students become more skillful citizens.

DISPOSITIONS

In 1831, Frenchman Alexis de Tocqueville toured the United States, investigating American institutions. The culmination of his 9 months of observations and years of subsequent research was the book *Democracy in America* (1900). In it, de Tocqueville highlighted, among other things, the democratic training of American citizens. He observed, "The American learns to know the laws by participating in the act of legislation; and he takes a lesson in the forms of government from governing. The great work of society is ever going on before his eyes and as, it were, under his hands" (1900, p. 324). Tocqueville's conclusion was that Americans learned how to be citizens by actively engaging in the work of citizens. It follows that American citizens' disposition to assume responsibility for governance, problem solving, and the defense of rights is central to American democracy. These dispositions for citizenship represent the third part of the trinity of instructional objectives outlined in this book.

Unlike conceptual knowledge and historical thinking skills, dispositions are rarely included in standards documents. There are a number of reasons for this. Dispositions are hard to assess. How does a teacher measure a student's curiosity, tolerance, or tendency to take action and solve a problem once it has been identified? How do teachers grade students on their willingness to stand up for another's civil rights, to sacrifice their will for the common good, or to maintain an open mind? In an era of measurable instructional outcomes and standards-based assessments, is there room for objectives associated with unquantifiable student dispositions? Unfortunately, the lack of assessment often translates into a lack of incentive for dedicating time and resources to the development of civic dispositions.

Additionally, members of society might disagree on the values and dispositions that should be nurtured. For instance, though some view compromise as essential for civic engagement, others might see compromise as the abandonment of principles. Some view patriotism as the most fundamental of civic dispositions. Others argue that there is no room for patriotism in a nation that has oppressed so many. Can dispositions be agreed upon by liberals, conservatives, minorities, and majorities, alike?

A good place to find a list of such dispositions is among those who have rigorously researched the preparation of young people for civic engagement. In the report of the

Center on Adolescence at Stanford University mentioned above, researchers described a number of dispositions they thought were essential for citizenship. These included "pro-social virtues such as tolerance, open-mindedness, truthfulness, responsibility, diligence, self-control, empathy, and cooperation" (Malin et al., 2014, p. 17). These same researchers contended that an acceptance of civic duty and a willingness to sacrifice for the common good were essential. Individuals must be inclined to actively fight for equality, liberty, justice, and civil rights. Young people must be prepared to deal with tensions and controversies in rational and productive ways. They must pursue their own political interests and the interests of others in their communities with the same gusto. Students must be willing to learn from peers who do not share their political perspectives in addition to the familiar outlets of information to which they are exposed at home. Civic engagement requires individuals who are willing to work with people they disagree with, who can compromise, and who can engage in reasoned deliberation using evidence. These researchers promoted "discerning patriotism," which acknowledges the shortfalls of a beloved country and commits to its improvement.

I contend that many dispositions shape both historical thinking and civic engagement. For example, in a recent study, a colleague of mine and I found that historians were remarkably humble in acknowledging the limitations of their interpretations. They recognized the flaws in the evidence they used and their own fallibility. They were willing to entertain multiple conflicting interpretations and to change their minds in the face of superior evidence or arguments (Nokes & Kesler-Lund, 2019). Such humility might remedy a great many of the problems confronting democracy today.

SECTION AND CHAPTER ORGANIZATION

The teaching resources included in this book are not scripted lessons but ideas and resources that teachers can use to help students develop historical knowledge, skills, and dispositions as tools for civic engagement. Section introductions provide ideas for exposing students to themes of civic engagement that cut across historical time periods and current events. These introductions end with questions intended to help students apply skills, dispositions, and conceptual understandings to solve problems that they, their schools, and their communities face today—problems such as bullying, discrimination, clashing wills, and the silencing of voices. Within each section, two chapters provide resources for two investigations of a theme of civic engagement.

Like the section introductions, chapters do not provide scripted lessons but give ideas and materials for historical investigations. Each chapter has the following structure:

1. *Introduction.* The topic of the investigation is briefly introduced.

2. *Students' Background Knowledge.* I address students' background knowledge, acknowledging what students often know as well as common gaps in students' background knowledge. Admittedly, each student brings unique experiences and culture to the classroom. But trends often exist in what students know coming into a lesson. This section reminds teachers to consider students' background knowledge when planning instruction.

3. *Historical Background for Teachers and Students.* This section includes two subsections. The first is an essay on the broad historical context of the investigation. The second is an essay that describes the immediate context. Familiarizing students with the broad context through the first essay allows the teacher to use this lesson outside of the general historical narrative. In other words, when this broad background knowledge has been reviewed, students are prepared to conduct the investigation even if they possessed little background knowledge on the topic before. For instance, a language arts teacher could teach this lesson using the first essay to build students' historical background knowledge. This essay gives students what they need to know in order to use the documents to consider the historical question raised in the investigation. The second essay was written with the specific documents of the investigation in mind. It provides students with some background on the people, organizations, and events referenced in the documents. Both essays are written between a 7th- and 8th-grade level (according to a Flesch-Kincaid readability test.) Both essays are intended to be used in one of three ways. Teachers could photocopy them for students and have students read them independently prior to the investigation. Alternatively, teachers could read them out loud with students at the start of the investigation. Instead, teachers could use the essays themselves to prepare a mini-lecture on the topic.

4. *Historical Thinking Skills.* Within this section, I provide a brief description of a historical thinking skill or metaconcept. This description is intended to prepare the teacher to talk about a skill with students. Some history teachers may have had little exposure to the reading, thinking, or writing of historians. This section gives teachers a more in-depth understanding of the skill or concept so that they can, with greater confidence, model this skill for their students. References within this section point teachers to research and other sources that discuss the skill in greater detail.

5. ***Lesson Ideas.*** This section includes a brief introduction and possible objectives for a lesson, a reminder to build students' background knowledge prior to the investigation, and a historical question or series of questions that might be the focus of an investigation. A longer subsection includes ideas for modeling for students the skill that is the focus of the chapter, with specific references to the documents that are provided. Because modeling is such an essential part of these lessons and is an instructional strategy less familiar to many teachers, I have scripted part of this stage of some lessons, with examples of things that a teacher might say to reveal the thinking that goes into document analysis. It is important that during modeling the teacher describe his/her thinking process to students by using phrases such as "I *wonder* where I can find who wrote this," "I *notice* that he doesn't talk about . . ." and "I *remember* that the last document I read said. . . ." Within the Lesson Ideas section, I also give some suggestions for group-work, during which peers support one another's analysis of the documents. Finally, I provide a number of questions that could be used during a debriefing session to help students reflect on the content knowledge, skills, and dispositions that are relevant to the investigation.

6. ***Instructional Materials.*** After listing the document set, I provide eight to 10 documents in a modified format, written between a 7th- and 8th-grade level. The note "Changed for easier reading," is included in each source (if it has been modified), along with a link to an Internet site where the original document can be found. (For an explanation of how the documents have been modified, see Wineburg & Martin, 2009.) The source is listed at the bottom of the documents, so students must become purposeful in locating source information. A handful of documents that are included cannot be found conveniently online; in those cases, the original documents are included in the chapter. Some chapters also include a sample poster that a teacher might display to help students remember the elements of a historical thinking skill. Instructional materials include a graphic organizer intended to give students a place to record evidence as they collect it from the documents. Teachers are encouraged to adapt these lesson materials to their specific circumstances. For instance, they may choose to limit the investigation to two or three of the documents rather than all of them. The teacher might provide all of the documents in a mini-archive and allow students to choose which to use in their investigation. They might choose to help students annotate the documents instead of using the graphic organizer. Or they might provide a graphic organizer that is partially completed for the students, as shown on the graphic organizers in some chapters. If students need a great deal of support, teachers might engage in an entire investigation as a class, with a few brief opportunities for students to work independently. If the opposite is true, teachers might give little support to students, letting them grapple with the evidence on their own.

KNOWING AND DOING CITIZENSHIP

Teachers are encouraged to find ways to help students apply the knowledge, skills, and dispositions highlighted throughout this book within their own relationships, in their school, and in their community. One of the purposes of this book is to demonstrate how history teachers can engage students in lessons that are rich in content while nurturing historical thinking skills, using illustrative case studies on civic dispositions that are vital for the survival of democracy. A second goal is to place students on the lookout for opportunities to act. Parker (2008) argued that "citizens need to both *know* democratic things and to *do* democratic things" (p. 65, emphasis in original). History classrooms that teach conceptual knowledge, skills, and dispositions prepare young people to be those citizens. However, teachers may need to remind students about the roles of citizens and help them find opportunities to assume those roles. Debriefing questions in sections and chapters give specific ideas for action. The following questions might be used throughout a history course to help students conceptualize their roles as citizens and to apply concepts learned in specific lessons to solve current issues:

- What are our rights and who is entitled to them?
- What does it mean to be free?
- How can we work with people who are different from us to achieve the common good?
- What can we do to promote needed reform?
- How can we collaborate with like-minded people to access political power?
- What can we do when government ignores our legitimate concerns?
- What are the best ways to achieve compromise?
- What responsibilities do we bear in solving problems we see in our school, community, nation, and the world?

DEFENDING CIVIL RIGHTS:
Looking Out for One Another

On March 23, 1777, members of a convention in Virginia debated the involvement of that colony in the escalating war with Great Britain. According to a biographer years later, Patrick Henry roused the convention with a powerful oration. Henry summed up his demands in the speech's final sentence: "Give me liberty or give me death." This phrase has resonated with Americans, who since before the Revolutionary War have demanded these liberties. In fact, the Revolutionary War was fought, first, in defense of the rights Americans possessed as British subjects, before it was waged for independence. Since that time, many Americans such as Dred Scott, Susan B. Anthony, and John F. Tinker have likewise fought for their rights. The focus of the two chapters in this section are on the ongoing struggle for rights. However, unlike Patrick Henry's concern for his own rights, these chapters highlight individuals who have pursued the rights of others. The featured individuals understood that the rights and freedoms of all Americans are interconnected. They viewed an assault on anyone's rights as an attack on their own liberties.

In 1906, Evelyn Beatrice Hall put into words a concept Voltaire had explained centuries earlier: "I disapprove of what you say, but I will defend to the death your right to say it" (Tallentyre, 1906). This attitude of defending the rights of others—even those with whom we disagree—is essential for the survival of democracy. Abraham Lincoln (1953) once said, "Those who deny freedom to others deserve it not for themselves, and under a just God cannot long retain it." In today's divisive political climate and self-interested partisan environment, it can be valuable and refreshing to consider times when individuals defended the rights of someone else.

John Adams understood this principle when he agreed to defend the British soldiers who had killed American colonists during the Boston Massacre. At first, the defendants' requests for legal counsel were rejected. No attorney would take their case. In the city of Boston, which was on fire with revolutionary rhetoric in 1770, to accept such an unpopular assignment might not only ruin one's reputation and jeopardize a law practice, but might place at risk one's life and family. Though some historians have suggested that Adams had selfish motives, almost all conclude that he accepted

the assignment because he believed that everyone, friend or enemy, was entitled to a fair trial. Chapter 2 includes materials for an investigation of the decision of Adams and his colleague Josiah Quincy Jr. to defend the British soldiers.

Almost 80 years later, in 1849, young Harriet Tubman escaped from the bondage of slavery in Maryland and made her way to Pennsylvania, a free state. Unable to fully enjoy her freedom while others were enslaved, Tubman returned to Maryland on 13 different occasions to lead others on the Underground Railroad to freedom. Even after the passage of the Fugitive Slave Act of 1850, which increased the risks and punishments for helping runaway slaves, Tubman imperiled her own life and freedom to help secure the basic civil rights of enslaved family members, friends, and even strangers. Chapter 3 provides materials for an investigation of Tubman's work on the Underground Railroad.

History provides countless other examples of individuals in full possession of their rights who worked for the civil liberties of others. In 1964, Andrew Goodman, James Chaney, and Michael Schwerner were murdered while registering African Americans to vote. William Lloyd Garrison, a White abolitionist in full possession of his rights, fought against slavery. Dorothea Dix worked for prison reform. Jacob Riis used photography and graphic descriptions to raise sympathy for the destitute. In one of the most surprising examples, the American Civil Liberties Union (ACLU) defended the right of the National Socialist Party of America, formerly the American Nazi Party, to peaceably assemble in Skokie, Illinois, a largely Jewish neighborhood. Each of these cases provides teachers with opportunities to encourage students to take a stand in defense of their own rights and the rights of others.

U.S. history is also rich with counterexamples, cases where individuals intentionally fought against the rights of others. Greed and bigotry prompted the passage and enforcement of the Indian Removal Act, in spite of the Supreme Court's finding that the law was unconstitutional. Perhaps the most blatant example of one group withholding the rights of another was the institution of slavery. Even after slavery ended, Black Codes and Jim Crow laws continued to trample upon the liberties of African Americans. Most White Americans turned a blind eye to the injustice.

Religious minorities faced persecution from time to time. Racist and exclusionary immigration policies denied the human rights of the Chinese and Eastern Europeans. Later, Jews attempting to escape the Holocaust were turned away from U.S. borders. Counterexamples juxtaposed with examples can help students better grasp the concept of looking out for the rights of others.

Current issues provide opportunities for students to apply these dispositions in real-world situations—some rife with controversy. Perhaps the most difficult might be allowing people who have different opinions—even ugly opinions—to engage in speech protected by the First Amendment. John Adams's defense of the British soldiers is better understood as students consider defending the right of someone with racist opinions to share his/her viewpoints in a public forum. The disposition to stand up for another's rights is a basic tool of civic engagement.

In connection with the lessons included in Chapters 2 and 3, the teacher might encourage students to take action by leading the class in a discussion on the following questions:

- Who is oppressed in our community or world today? What actions might we take to defend their rights?
- What violations of rights might we observe in our school or community? What can and should we do when we witness bullying or other forms of abuse?
- Could we provide leadership in promoting school policies that accommodate the rights of others, such as providing a place and release time for Muslim students to pray or increasing the number of gender-neutral bathrooms?

CHAPTER 2

John Adams, Josiah Quincy Jr., and the Boston Massacre Trial

Why would someone in full possession of their rights work to secure someone else's rights? Why would an individual risk ridicule, persecution, or even his/her safety to protect another's liberties? This chapter provides materials for an investigation of John Adams and Josiah Quincy Jr., two lawyers from Boston who defended the British soldiers who had been involved in the Boston Massacre as they stood trial for murder.

STUDENTS' BACKGROUND KNOWLEDGE

Students' understanding of the events leading up to the American Revolutionary War creates an ideal setting for a lesson on the defense of rights. Most students view patriot leaders, such as Paul Revere and Patrick Henry, as American heroes. In contrast, most students stereotype British officials and soldiers as abusive, blundering, and immoral. The Loyalists who supported them are perceived with even greater contempt. Such an unsophisticated understanding of the revolutionary movement, with heroic patriots and villainous redcoats, oversimplifies the complex interactions among patriots, Loyalists, British officials, British soldiers, and the many unaffiliated Americans who were uncertain about where their loyalties should rest and were primarily concerned with their family's survival. Students can gain a more nuanced understanding of relationships in revolutionary Boston by considering John Adams and Josiah Quincy Jr., two patriot leaders who decided to defend in court the British soldiers charged with murder for their involvement in the Boston Massacre. With this background knowledge, today's students, who are living in a time when partisanship seems to outweigh the rights of political opponents, might find it surprising that some patriot leaders understood that every person, even the hated redcoats, possessed civil rights worth defending.

HISTORICAL BACKGROUND FOR TEACHERS AND STUDENTS

Background of the Boston Massacre

In 1754, most American colonists were proud to be part of the British Empire. They felt loyal to the king of England. They felt they had the same rights as other British subjects. They felt protected by the powerful British Army and Navy. They felt threatened by France, which also had colonies in North America. When a war started between Britain and France, they helped the British. Many American colonists, including George Washington, volunteered to fight against the French in North America. After the British won, the colonists did not feel threatened by France anymore.

But the war was expensive and the British had borrowed money to pay for it. The British thought that the war had helped the colonists, so they should help pay for it. The British Parliament passed laws that made the colonists pay taxes on different things. Americans had not had to pay many taxes in the past. Some colonists became angry. They argued that they had helped win the war against France just as much as the British had. They had already sacrificed for the war. Other Englishmen could not be taxed unless their representatives in Parliament agreed to it. Colonists said that because they did not have representatives in Parliament, they could not be taxed at all. They thought they should have the same rights as other Englishmen.

From 1764 until 1770, many taxes were passed. Some Americans felt that each one violated their rights as English subjects. When many Americans became angry, Parliament got rid of one tax and passed another. The Sugar Act collected taxes on molasses, sugar, and other goods that merchants shipped. Colonists became mad and threatened to hurt tax collectors. The British sent warships to watch American cities and make sure people paid the tax. The tax hurt businesses. This made many Americans even angrier. The British decided to get rid of that tax. But in 1765, Americans became even madder when Parliament passed the Stamp Act, a tax on paper goods. All across the colonies, Americans protested the Stamp Act. Many colonists stopped buying British goods. They sent petitions to the king of England to get rid of the tax. Parliament listened to the colonists and ended the tax in 1766. But Parliament argued that England could still collect taxes from the colonists. Colonists argued that any tax violated their rights as long as they were not represented in Parliament. In 1767 and 1768, new taxes were passed that charged money for buying glass, paper, tea, and other things. Many Americans became angry again. The people of Boston were influenced by popular leaders who hated the taxes. They became especially mad. When they threatened to hurt tax collectors, British soldiers were sent to their city. British warships were sent to Boston Harbor. The British soldiers in Boston who protected the tax collectors upset many colonists.

Not all of the colonists agreed about what should be done. Some colonists, called *patriots*, were angriest about the violations of their rights. They protested the taxes and hated having British soldiers in their city. Other colonists, called *Loyalists*, felt the patriots were overreacting. They were loyal to the king. They were willing to pay the taxes. Having soldiers around was no problem for them. Other colonists were not very concerned about things with Britain. They wanted to keep their farms and businesses going.

On March 5, 1770, an incident called the Boston Massacre happened near the Boston Customs House. This was where taxes were paid and the money was kept. Historians still don't know all the details about what happened, but there are a few facts that they are sure about. There was an angry clash between a crowd of patriots and some British soldiers. As the disagreement became worse, some British soldiers fired their guns and five Americans were killed. Propaganda that was passed around made many patriots think the British soldiers were cold-blooded killers. John Adams called it a "bloody butchery." He helped pass around a picture of the massacre made by Paul Revere. Patriots demanded that the soldiers who had fired their guns be punished. Rumors spread that Captain Preston, the leader of the soldiers, had ordered the troops to shoot into the Boston crowd. Some patriots wanted to kill Captain Preston and his soldiers. Preston, eight British soldiers, and a few British civilians were arrested and charged with murder.

But the Loyalists thought the British soldiers had done what they needed to do. They thought the patriots who threatened the soldiers were the ones to blame for the massacre. They thought that Preston and the soldiers should have a chance to defend themselves in a fair trial. After all, a trial by jury was also a right of every Englishman.

John Adams, Josiah Quincy Jr., and the Boston Massacre Trial

The day after the massacre, a merchant who was loyal to the king visited John Adams. He begged Adams, a lawyer, to help Captain Preston in his trial. Earlier, this merchant had asked another lawyer, Josiah Quincy Jr., to help Preston. Quincy told him that he would only help if John Adams would, too. Adams and Quincy were as patriotic as anyone in Boston. But they thought that a person accused of a crime had the right to a fair trial. They believed that all of the patriots' talk about rights included all Englishmen, even the soldiers who were their enemies. Both agreed to take Preston's case. They also agreed to help the other British soldiers who had been accused of murder. These soldiers would have been hanged if they were found guilty.

There is evidence that Adams and Quincy thought that their decision would be unpopular with some of the other patriots. They were afraid of what people might think about them. They thought it might make people harm them or their families. They thought it might cost them business and hurt them financially. Still, they worked hard to help Preston and the British soldiers in their trial. At the trial, they argued that some of the other patriots were not honest when they told about what happened. They called the crowd of patriots who threatened the soldiers a "mob." They demanded that the American jurors look carefully at the evidence and the law. They asked the jurors not to let their emotions or propaganda influence them. In the end, Preston and most of the soldiers were found not guilty. Two of the men were found guilty of a lesser crime and were branded on the thumb as punishment.

Instead of having their reputation or law businesses ruined, Adams and Quincy were respected even more by most colonists. They had shown that they believed everyone had rights, whether they agreed with them or not. They both gained strong reputations as lawyers. Even though they helped the British, they later showed that they were true patriots. Quincy was a member of the Sons of Liberty, and he wrote papers about the rights of the colonists. He traveled to England to get support for the colonists. He died of tuberculosis while sailing home from England, just after the first shots of the Revolutionary War had been fired. Adams helped write the Declaration of Independence and served as a diplomat during the Revolutionary War. After the war, he had a successful political career. He became the second president of the United States.

HISTORICAL THINKING SKILLS: CORROBORATION

The investigation that follows provides opportunities for students to practice corroboration, one of the basic strategies that historians use. Historians engage in corroboration when they cross-check information found in one source with information found in other sources (Nokes & Kesler-Lund, 2019; Wineburg, 1991). They pay attention to discrepancies between accounts. They notice when a source omits information that is contained in other accounts, understanding that omissions are sometimes purposeful. They notice when one piece of evidence contains information that is uncorroborated by other sources. Sometimes the content of one document can only be fully understood when it is read in connection with another document, such as in correspondence between letter writers. This investigation gives students an opportunity to compare and contrast across documents, and to use the content of one document to enhance their understanding of others.

There are several things a teacher can do to teach the strategy of corroboration. First, a teacher can acquaint students with the term *corroboration* or another term, such as *cross-checking*. Doing so will allow a teacher to comment on students' thinking and writing with statements such as "I appreciate the way Jamal is cross-checking," in order to point out when the strategy has been used. In addition to giving a name to the strategy, the teacher can talk to students explicitly about the elements of corroboration: looking for similarities and differences across texts, holding information as tentative until it has been supported by a second piece of evidence, thinking about strategic omissions and inclusions that create differences between texts, looking at the different wording used—words that reveal biases in sources—and using the content of one text to understand or analyze the content of another. Teachers might even display a poster that outlines the procedures for engaging in corroboration, such as that provided in the Instructional Materials for this chapter.

Corroboration is not only useful in studying historical documents, but it is also a vital strategy for civic engagement. Informed political action requires individuals to understand controversial issues. Researching controversies is complicated because opposing parties present issues in purposefully different ways in order to persuade the undecided. Corroborating across politicized information can help a citizen take an informed stance on issues. Seeking corroborating evidence can help a citizen recognize biases and root out propaganda. Individuals who cross-check information by leaving a website or television channel to investigate its accuracy against other sources are less likely to be taken in by fake news (Wineburg, 2018). In this Information Age, corroboration is not only a skill for historians but is also a useful tool for informed civic engagement. Because this skill is unlikely to be taught outside of history classrooms, it is important for history teachers to help students learn to corroborate. This skill is featured in the lesson ideas and materials in this chapter.

LESSON IDEAS

Introduction

The investigation of Adams and Quincy's decision that follows is designed to be taught during a unit on the Revolutionary War. Alternatively, if a course is organized thematically, the lesson could be taught in connection with other lessons on the defense of civil rights.

Objectives

This lesson is designed to meet three objectives associated with knowledge, skills, and dispositions:

1. Students will explore the patriots' reactions to the Boston Massacre and its role in leading to the Revolutionary War.
2. Students will engage in corroboration, making direct comparisons across documents and using

the content of one document to analyze the content of others.
3. Students will acknowledge the importance of defending the rights of others, even at the peril of one's own standing.

Build Background Knowledge

Begin the lesson by building students' background knowledge on the events leading up to the occupation of Boston by British troops and the Boston Massacre. The material presented earlier in this chapter under the headings "Background of the Boston Massacre" and "John Adams, Josiah Quincy Jr., and the Boston Massacre Trial" provides a simple overview of what students will need to know in order to work with the documents that follow.

Ask Historical Questions

Historians focus on questions as they gather and analyze evidence. The background information provided above and the documents that follow were designed to help students ask and answer the following question: Why did Adams and Quincy choose to help Preston and the British soldiers in their trial? Teachers can simplify the task for students by giving them several possible theories for why Adams and Quincy helped Preston, such as the following: (1) to gain attention and improve their reputation as attorneys, (2) to demonstrate their commitment to the principal of rule of law, (3) to earn the fees associated with representing clients, (4) to further the cause of the revolution, (5) to support the cause of the British and the Loyalists, or (6) for some other reason. The background information provided above should prepare students to use the documents below to seek evidence of Adams and Quincy's motivation.

Provide Strategy Instruction and Model Corroboration

Students may have little experience making the intertextual connections associated with corroboration. As a result, they may need repeated opportunities to hear about, observe, and practice this challenging strategy. The process of corroboration requires students not only to comprehend multiple texts, but to remember their content and hold that content in mind while concentrating on additional texts. This process can overwhelm the cognitive abilities of even the most gifted readers (Nokes, 2011). Providing a graphic organizer with space for students to take notes allows them to keep a record of the content of each document and facilitates comparisons across texts. It helps them keep track of what they read and where they read it, which is essential for corroboration. At the start of the lesson, after providing background information on Adams, Quincy, and the Boston Massacre Trial, the teacher can model the use of the graphic organizer included at the end of this chapter as corroboration is modeled for the class.

The teacher could illustrate how to engage in corroboration by thinking out loud. Doing so might require some subterfuge, as teachers should carefully plan how to model, but then act as though they are exploring the texts for the first time, just as the students would be doing. For example, projecting Document 1 for the class, the teacher might notice its source by saying something like this: "I want to know who wrote this before I read it so I am looking around and I can see here at the bottom what looks like source information. I see it was written by John Adams himself quite a few years after the Boston Massacre." The teacher could also model how to use the graphic organizer by filling in information about the source in the first column. The teacher might then read the document out loud, pausing to think out loud about insights and questions that arise.

Because corroboration involves comparing multiple texts, the teacher might proceed to read a second document, modeling the same process of analyzing the source first. After reading Document 2, the teacher could model corroboration by noticing that the tone of Documents 1 and 2 is similar. Both make Adams's decision look heroic. The teacher can then realize why the documents are so similar: They come from the same author, Adams himself. Thinking aloud, the teacher might say, "I would expect that there would be consistency in his story."

Depending upon the students' need for support, the teacher could then look at Documents 3 and 4, using the source information to realize that one is a letter to Quincy from his father and the other is Quincy's response. Looking at the dates each was written, the teacher might think aloud: "I see that the one was written on March 22 and the other was written on March 26, just 4 days later. The source of the second letter says it was written as a reply to his father's letter. It makes sense that we should read the letters in the order they were written. Reading his father's letter first should help us understand what Quincy wrote in reply." Throughout the process of modeling, the teacher should talk explicitly about the specific actions that make up corroboration, such as noticing disagreements or similarities in the documents or using one document to better understand another.

After modeling with a few documents, the teacher might ask students to work on their own with the next text, subsequently calling on some students to describe their thinking. By doing so, the students would model corroboration and other strategies for one another. Modeling, by the teacher and/or peers, should continue until the teacher is confident that students understand corroboration.

The following document collection includes several opportunities for students to use corroboration in addition to those already explained. First, the poem (Document 5) is an example of patriot propaganda. Its existence corroborates the claim made in Document 8 about the spread of propaganda that led people to unfairly condemn the British

soldiers prior to their trial. Further, the poem corroborates Adams's claims about the risk that he took in representing Preston and the soldiers, as expressed in Documents 1 and 2. Such strong animosity to any court that would acquit Preston and the soldiers (as expressed in Document 5) was likely to have spilled over to Adams and Quincy, the defendants' legal counsel. Documents 1, 2, 5, and 8 all lead to the same conclusion—that Adams and Quincy were taking a major risk in accepting the case.

However, Document 4 raises some doubt about this interpretation. In Quincy's letter to his father, he claims that before he agreed to take the case, he sought the opinion of the leading men of the colony. If, indeed, Quincy spoke with many of the elite families in Boston, gaining their approval, as he reported, it is likely that Adams would have known that they sanctioned his choice to defend the British. If such were the case, his lamentation 3 years later was exaggerated. The following documents have been chosen to allow students to practice the skills of corroboration, comparing and contrasting across documents, and using the content of one document to enrich their understanding of others.

Group-Work

When the teacher is confident students understand how to engage in corroboration and how to use the graphic organizer to gather and compare evidence from the documents, he/she can have them analyze the remaining documents independently or in small groups. The teacher can circulate, give suggestions to groups, and provide feedback on their emerging interpretations. If the teacher discovers common problems with historical thinking or common gaps in background knowledge, he/she can provide additional whole-class instruction to try to resolve these issues. It can be helpful during groupwork or independent work to remind students about their objective: to use evidence from the documents to identify why Adams and Quincy defended the British soldiers.

Debriefing

Teachers are more likely to achieve the objectives of this lesson if they conclude it with a debriefing—a discussion of the students' work, thinking, and interpretations. The debriefing holds three purposes associated with the three objectives of the lesson. First, students can discuss the *knowledge* they have gained about the Boston Massacre and its role in leading to the American Revolution with questions such as the following:

1. How did the people of Boston react to the Boston Massacre? How was their reaction different based upon their opinions about the colony's relationship with Britain?
2. Why might it have been difficult for Adams and Quincy to choose to defend the British soldiers?

What motivated them to do so? Which evidence helped you understand their main motives?

3. Why might it have been difficult for the soldiers to choose Adams and Quincy as their attorneys?

Second, students can discuss the historical thinking *skills* associated with this investigation, particularly corroboration. The following questions could be used.

1. Which documents did you trust the most? Which did you doubt? How did you determine how reliable they were? How did corroboration help in this process?
2. What were similar messages given across documents? How did the documents disagree? How did reading one text help you understand other documents?
3. How might corroboration help you use the Internet better? How could you cross-check information found on a webpage?

Third, students can consider the *dispositions* of civic engagement highlighted in this lesson. The following questions could structure this discussion.

1. Though Voltaire didn't use these words, he is often quoted as saying, "I disapprove of what you say, but I will defend to the death your right to say it." Do you agree with this idea? Why or why not? Did Adams and Quincy?
2. Why is it important for people to watch out for others' rights, even when they might disagree with them? Why is it difficult to do this?
3. What are current examples of efforts to limit individuals' rights to express themselves, to assemble, to own a firearm, to have an abortion, or to exercise other rights? Should a person defend these rights even if he/she disagrees with what people are saying or doing?

INSTRUCTIONAL MATERIALS

Eight primary source documents are included in the pages that follow in a format that is modified for students. The originals of these documents can be found online at the links provided. Instructional materials include a graphic organizer that could support students' use of corroboration. In addition, a sample poster is provided at the end of the chapter that a teacher might display in his/her classroom, with guidelines for engaging in corroboration.

Document Set

1. An excerpt from *John Adams' Autobiography*, written between 1802 and 1807 (Adams, n.d.)
2. An excerpt from John Adams's diary entry for

March 5, 1773, the third anniversary of the Boston Massacre (Adams, 1815/1961)

3. A letter written on March 22, 1770, by Josiah Quincy Sr., the father of Josiah Quincy Jr., to his son upon hearing that he had agreed to defend the British soldiers (J. Quincy, 1965)
4. A letter written March 26, 1770, by Josiah Quincy Jr. in reply to his father's letter (J. Quincy Jr., 1965)
5. A poem included on the broadside entitled *The Bloody Massacre perpetrated in King Street, Boston on March 5th 1770 by a party of the 29th Regiment*, by Paul Revere and Henry Pelham (Revere, 1832)
6. An excerpt from John Adams's speech at the end of the trial (Adams, 1965)
7. An excerpt from John Adams's closing statement (Adams, 1909)
8. An excerpt from a letter written under the pseudonym "Philanthrop" to the *Boston Evening Post*, published Monday, December 24, 1770, shortly after the acquittal of Captain Preston (Philanthrop, 1770)

Simplified Evidence

Document 1: Adams's Autobiography

I think it was the next morning [while I was] sitting in my office, by the steps of the townhouse stairs, [that] Mr. Forrest came in. . . . With tears streaming from his eyes, he said he had come with a very important message from a very unlucky man, Captain Preston, who was in prison. He wanted an attorney, and could not find one. "I have asked Mr. Quincy, who says he will help [Preston] if you will help him, but if you won't help him he definitely won't." . . . I quickly answered that a lawyer should be the very last thing that an accused person should have trouble finding in a free country. That I thought the courts should always be free and fair. And that people whose lives were at risk should have the lawyer they wanted. He had to know that this would be as important a trial as was ever tried in any court or country of the world. That every lawyer served not only his country, but the highest and most perfect of all judges [God] in the things he did. So, he shouldn't expect me to use any tricks or speeches, no lies or deception in this case. Nothing but facts, evidence and the law would be fair. He said that was what Captain Preston wanted. Because of what everyone had said about me he believed that he could happily trust his life with me, based on those principles. "And," said Mr. Forrest, "as God almighty is my judge I believe that he is an innocent man." I said, "that must be decided by his trial. And if he doesn't think he can have a fair trial without my help, I will help him immediately."

Source: Part 1 of John Adams's autobiography, "John Adams" through 1776, written years later between 1802 and 1807. [Changed for easier reading.] Found at www.masshist.org/digitaladams/archive/doc?id=A1_12

Document 2: Adams's Diary

I did not stop working and worrying almost to death, only for what is most important—my duty. In the evening, I told my wife about my worries. That excellent lady, who always helped me, started to weep. She said she knew how dangerous it was for her, our children, and me. She thought I was doing what was right. She was ready to accept what came and trust in God.

Before the trial, Captain Preston sent me a little money and at the trial of the soldiers a little bit more. That was all that I was paid for fourteen or fifteen days of work, in the most tiring court cases I ever tried. I risked my popularity that I had worked hard for. I faced the anger, doubts, and unfairness that are still going on and will be as long as people read about this history and time. It was soon talked about all over that I had helped Preston and the soldiers, which caused a lot of anger.

The help I gave to defend Captain Preston and the soldiers gave me a lot of worries and criticism. But it was one of the most heroic, kind, brave, and selfless acts of my whole life. It was one of the best services I gave my country. Executing those soldiers would have been as bad for this country as killing the Quakers or witches anciently. From the evidence, the verdict of the jury was exactly right.

This does not mean that the town should not call what happened that night a massacre. Nor does it mean that the governor or minister was right to send [the troops to Boston]. But it shows the danger of standing armies [keeping armies in the city].

Source: Part of John Adams's diary entry for March 5, 1773, the third anniversary of the Boston Massacre. [Changed for easier reading.] Found at law2.umkc.edu/faculty/projects/FTrials/bostonmassacre/diaryentries.html

Document 3: Quincy Sr.'s Letter

22 March, 1770
My dear son,

I am very sad to hear people saying the meanest things about you, because you have become an attorney for those criminals who are accused of murdering their fellow citizens. Good God! Is it possible? I cannot believe it.

Just before I returned home from Boston, I knew that on the day those criminals were thrown in prison a sergeant had visited you at your brother's house. But I had no idea that it was possible they would ask you to defend them. Since then, I have been told that you have actually agreed to defend Captain Preston. And I have heard these things from men who had shown the most respect for you as someone who would be a savior of your country.

I must tell you, it has given your old and sick parent worries, and suffering, in case these rumors are not only true, but that they will ruin your reputation and business. And I repeat, I will not believe it unless I hear it from your own mouth or your own hand.

Your worried and suffering parent,
Josiah Quincy

Source: Letter written on March 22, 1770, by Josiah Quincy Sr., the father of Josiah Quincy Jr., who defended the British with John Adams, upon hearing that his son had agreed to defend the men. [Changed for easier reading.] Found at www.masshist.org/publications/adams-papers/index.php/view/ADMS-05-03-02-0001-0001

Document 4: Quincy Jr.'s Letter

26 March 1770
Honored Sir,

I do not have the time or desire to know or pay attention to those uninformed liars, who have dared to say the "meanest things" you heard about me. And this because I have become a lawyer for criminals accused of murder. But criticism, when based only on jealousy and lies will not hurt me. Before saying these things to an old and sick man, if they had been friends, they would have thought a little about an attorney's oath and duty. Just a little thought about how he works and a little patience to think about what I have done and will do.

Someone should tell these people that these criminals charged with murder have not yet been proven guilty. So even if they are criminals, the laws of God and man, make them deserve a lawyer's help. My duty as a man made me to agree to help them, and my duty as a lawyer strengthened the agreement. Being careful, I first said I would not help, but after I got the best advice and thought carefully about it, I told Captain Preston that I would help him. But before this, with two of his friends watching, I told him how I really felt about the struggle [between Boston and the soldiers]. I told him that my heart and hand worked for my country. Finally, I refused to help him until I was told that I should by [many important families of Boston].
. . .

I promise you that one day you and this whole country will be happy that I became an attorney for these "criminals" accused of murdering their fellow citizens.

I never thought or wanted everybody to say good things about me. I just want to understand my duty and do it. . . .

I am truly, and affectionately your son
Josiah Quincy Junior

Source: Letter written March 26, 1770, by Josiah Quincy Jr. in reply to his father's letter that criticized his decision to defend in court Captain Preston and the British. [Changed for easier reading.] Found at www.masshist.org/publications/adams-papers/index.php/view/ADMS-05-03-02-0001-0001

Document 5: Revere Poem

ORIGINAL POEM	TRANSLATION OF POEM

ORIGINAL POEM

Unhappy BOSTON! see thy Sons deplore,
Thy hallowe'd Walks besmear'd with guiltless Gore:
While faithless P--n and his savage Bands,
With murd'rous Rancour stretch their bloody Hands;
Like fierce Barbarians grinning o'er their Prey,
Approve the Carnage, and enjoy the Day.

If scalding drops from Rage from Anguish Wrung
If speechless Sorrows lab' ring for a Tongue,
Or if a weeping World can ought appease
The plaintive Ghosts of Victims such as these;
The Patriot's copious Tears for each are shed,
A glorious Tribute which embalms the Dead.

But know, FATE summons to that awful Goal,
Where JUSTICE strips the Murd'rer of his Soul:
Should venal C-ts the scandal of the Land,
Snatch the relentless Villain from her Hand,
Keen Execrations on this Plate inscrib'd,
Shall reach a JUDGE who never can be brib'd.

The unhappy Sufferers were Messs. SAM. L GRAY, SAM.L MAVERICK, JAM.S CALDWELL, CRISPUS ATTUCKS & PAT.K CARR Killed. Six wounded two of them (CHRIST.R MONK & JOHN CLARK) Mortally

TRANSLATION OF POEM

Sad Boston! Your people are angry and sad,
Your sacred streets are covered with innocent blood;
While evil Captain Preston and his cruel soldiers,
With deadly hatred reach out their bloody hands;
As wild monsters smiling over the ones they killed,
Enjoy the bloodshed and what they have done.

If the heat of anger and suffering,
Or the sadness that we can't begin to say,
Or if a world that is crying can help
The sad spirits of those who were killed;
The patriot's many tears are shed for all of them,
As a great honor for those who died.

But remember, everyone is going to die,
And after we are dead, those who commit murder receive justice by having their soul taken away.
If dishonest courts, the shame of this land,
Do not do justice by punishing the terrible villains,
The curses written on this paper,
Will go to God, a judge who cannot be bribed.

The sad victims were MR. SAMUEL GRAY, SAMUEL MAVERICK, JAMES CALDWELL, CRISPUS ATTUCKS and PATRICK CARR killed. Six wounded with two of them dying (CHRISTOPHER MONK and JOHN CLARK)

Source: Poem written on the broadside entitled The BLOODY MASSACRE Perpetrated in King Street, BOSTON on March 5th 1770 by a party of the 29th REG by Paul Revere and Henry Pelham. [With a translation of the difficult phrases on the right.] When authors criticized individuals or institutions, they often included only the first and last letters of their name. Found at www.indiana.edu/~lib-lilly/cartoon/revere.html

Document 6: Adams's Speech

I will not say anything more about the evidence, but turn it over to you. Facts are stubborn things; and no matter what we might wish, like, or feel strongly about, we cannot change the facts and evidence; nor can we change the laws any more than we can the facts. If an attack was made that endangered [the British soldiers'] lives, the law is clear. They had a right to kill in their own defense. If [the attack] did not threaten their lives, but they were attacked at all, hit in any way by any kind of snowballs, oyster shells, cinders, clubs, or sticks, this caused them [to fight back] and the law reduces the killing down to manslaughter [a lesser crime] . . . I turn these prisoners and this case over to your honesty and justice.

Even though governments and strong feelings change, the law does not change. It will not change to meet what people want, imagine, or based on their cruel moods. To use the words of a great and worthy patriot, a hero, and friend of mankind, who died for liberty, I mean Algernon Sidney,

. . . "The law (says he) has no feelings. It has no desire, fear, or anger. It is the mind without feeling. . . . The law does not make weak people happy but treats everyone the same, makes people do good and punishes evil in everyone, rich or poor, high or low. It does not hear, stop, or bend. On one hand, it does not hear the cries or howls of prisoners. On the other hand, it does not hear (is deaf as a snake) to the shouting of the people."

Source: Part of John Adams's speech at the end of the court case *Rex v. Wemms*, the trial of the soldiers involved in the Boston Massacre, from the Legal Papers of John Adams, No. 64. [Changed for easier reading.] Found at law2.umkc.edu/faculty/projects/ftrials/bostonmassacre/adamssummation.html

Document 7: Adams's Closing Arguments

People have used many different phrases, to avoid calling this sort of people [the crowd of patriots] a mob. Some call them shavers [boys]. Some call them geniuses. The plain English is, gentlemen, they were most probably, a mixed gang of rude boys, negroes and mulattoes, Irish rascals, and odd sailors. And why we should worry about calling such a group of people a mob I cannot understand, unless the name is too good for them. The sun won't stand still or go out, nor the rivers dry up, because there was a mob in Boston, on the 5th of March, that attacked a party of soldiers. Such things are not new in the world, nor in the British colonies. Though they are rare and unusual in this town.... It's just the way things are, soldiers living in a big town will always cause two mobs for every one they stop. They are bad keepers of the peace.

Source: Part of John Adams's closing statement during his defense of the British soldiers involved in the Boston Massacre. [Changed for easier reading.] Found at archive.org/stream/selectorationsi-00clapgoog/selectorationsi00clapgoog_djvu.txt

---

Document 8: Newspaper Editorial

Everyone who watched the trials saw the great care, patience, fairness, honor, and understanding of the judges. They saw the patience and thought of the jurors. And they saw the honesty of most of the witnesses. Before the trial, bias had influenced almost everyone. They jumped to conclusions in public prayers, sermons, newspapers, papers, stories, and accounts told outside of the courtroom. Everyone who compares the trial with what people were saying before it will see that the trial was as fair as God's final judgment. There was a time when all of these things made most of the good people of this area ready, if they needed to, to find all of the accused murderers guilty. But now I think everyone who heard the trials thinks, in his heart, that the courts and juries were fair. When the trials are published, I think everyone will be satisfied [with the outcome].

Source: Part of a letter written under the pseudonym [pretend name] "Philanthrop" to the *Boston Evening Post*, published Monday, December 24, 1770, shortly after Captain Preston and most of those who stood trial for the Boston Massacre were found not guilty. [Changed for easier reading.] Found at www.masshist.org/dorr/volume/3/sequence/377

Graphic Organizer

John Adams, Josiah Quincy Jr., and the Boston Massacre Trial

Why did John Adams and Josiah Quincy Jr. represent Preston and the British soldiers? Was it to (1) gain attention in order to improve their reputation as attorneys, (2) demonstrate their commitment to the principal of rule of law, (3) earn the fees associated with representing clients, (4) further the cause of the revolution in some way, or (5) secretly support the cause of the British and the Loyalists? Use the graphic organizer to record evidence in the documents that supports or weakens these theories. Then use this worksheet to answer the questions below.

Doc	Source information (genre, author, purpose, audience)	Summary (what are the main ideas from this source?)	Theories supported or weakened	Evidence suggests … (clues about their motives)	Corroboration (how this document compares with others)
1					
2					
3					
4					
5					
6					
7					
8					

1. According to your interpretation of the evidence, why did John Adams and Josiah Quincy Jr. choose to represent the British soldiers involved in the Boston Massacre?
2. What are the main pieces of evidence that support your interpretation? How do you explain the evidence that goes against your interpretation?
3. What lessons can be learned from this incident about our duty to defend the rights of others?

Sample Classroom Poster

QUESTIONS TO ASK WHEN CORROBORATING EVIDENCE

1. How are these accounts similar?
2. How are these accounts different?
3. What was left out of any of the accounts? Why was it left out?
4. How did the authors of the different documents choose different words?
5. What details does one account include that are not corroborated in any other account?
6. What do the differences in the accounts show us about the authors' perspectives, purposes, biases, insights, and values?
7. What other evidence might we look for to corroborate evidence in these accounts?

CHAPTER 3

Harriet Tubman and the Underground Railroad

John Adams and Josiah Quincy risked their business, reputation, and economic status to defend the rights of their adversaries, the British soldiers. In contrast, this chapter deals with an individual who risked her freedom, safety, and life to liberate enslaved family members, friends, and strangers. Harriet Tubman is one of the historical characters most familiar to Americans. Her fame is a result of the courage with which she guided enslaved individuals to freedom, risking her own liberty in the process. In this chapter, I provide information on the context within which Tubman labored and lesson materials for conducting a document-based investigation of her evolving celebrity status.

STUDENTS' BACKGROUND KNOWLEDGE

Most students have heard of Harriet Tubman and her role in guiding enslaved individuals to freedom through the Underground Railroad. Much of what students think they know may be inaccurate. Tubman's story has been told and retold in many ways, with each retelling being spun by an author for unique audiences and purposes. To abolitionists, Tubman exhibited superhuman ingenuity and courage. To religious leaders, she represented one who received direct divine guidance. To Southerners, she was the face of evil, stirring up insurrection and leading away their property. Even among historians, Tubman's story has evolved through the years. Considering the way her story has been told and retold provides a suitable opportunity to introduce students to historiography—the study of how historical research is conducted and how historical narratives on particular topics have changed over time. Reflecting on Tubman's heroism, regardless of how her story is told, is a moving case study on the importance of standing up for the rights of others.

HISTORICAL BACKGROUND FOR TEACHERS AND STUDENTS

Background of the Runaway Slaves

No group in American history has suffered more abuse than those enslaved. Many people were taken from their homes in Africa and brought to America in chains. They and their descendants were enslaved from colonial times until the 1860s. The rights protected by the Bill of Rights did not apply to them. Instead, the people held in slavery were beaten and abused in many ways. The U.S. government had racist policies. Slavery was approved by the Constitution. Very few laws protected the enslaved. They were treated as property by the laws of the colonies and states. Still, enslaved people resisted slavery by working slowly, breaking tools, meeting with other slaves illegally, and in many other ways. After slavery died out in the northern states, some of the millions of slaves in southern states gained their freedom by escaping to the North. Many others tried to escape but were caught, severely punished, and returned to slavery.

Not all White Americans approved of slavery. In the early and mid-1800s, more people, Black and White, began to fight against it. They were called abolitionists because they wanted to abolish, or end, slavery. Abolitionist William Lloyd Garrison published *The Liberator*, a newspaper that told about the evils of slavery. Many Quakers, members of a religion that had opposed slavery for many years, began to help fugitive slaves who tried to escape. With the help of other abolitionists, they organized a system of homes and hiding places where runaway slaves could find food, support, and a place to rest. This network of hiding places became known as the Underground Railroad.

In 1850, the U.S. Congress passed the Fugitive Slave Act. This law forced Northerners to help catch runaway slaves. Abolitionists who helped with the Underground Railroad could pay fines or go to jail if they were caught. But many still helped slaves escape. The law forced their neighbors who thought they were helping slaves to turn them in. The law divided Americans over the issue of slavery. Americans who had not thought much about slavery before were now forced to take a side. They had to either support their abolitionist neighbors or turn them in.

The Fugitive Slave Act of 1850 made life more dangerous for slaves who escaped into the North. They could be caught and sent back into slavery. Some of them fled to Canada. There, they were safe from bounty hunters who searched the cities of the North for runaways. Others stayed in hiding in the United States. They were always afraid of being captured and returned to slavery. A few, like Frederick Douglass, stayed in the northern states and openly fought against slavery. Douglass became a powerful speaker and famous abolitionist. He met with Abraham Lincoln many times. Not very many slaves who escaped dared to go back to the southern states to help others escape. If they were caught, they knew they would be severely punished, killed, or forced into slavery again.

Harriet Tubman and the Underground Railroad

Harriet Tubman was born Araminta (Minty) Ross about the year 1822. Raised in slavery in Dorchester County, Maryland, Minty learned as a child how terrible slavery could be. She was whipped, beaten, and abused by her masters. When she was little, her master hurt her head. The injury caused her pain, dizziness, and unusually deep sleep throughout her life. In 1849, Tubman's master died. She believed his death was an answer to her prayers. But she became afraid that his widow would sell her away from her family. So, she and two of her brothers, Ben and Henry (Harry), escaped to Philadelphia. But her brothers loved and missed their families so much that they returned to them—and to slavery. Tubman, who was 27 years old, returned with them.

But Tubman was determined to be free. She soon escaped again. She found her way north through the network of hideouts and trails known as the Underground Railroad. Those who were running away through the Underground Railroad were called *passengers*. Those who helped, fed, and guided the runaways were called *conductors*. The safe places along the route were called *stations*. Tubman traveled mostly at night, hiding in the woods, marshes, or stations during the day. Eventually, she made her way back into Pennsylvania, a free state.

Tubman loved freedom enough to have risked her life to gain it. But she could not rest knowing that many of her loved ones were still enslaved. Even though the harsh Fugitive Slave Act had been passed, she returned to help her family members to freedom. With the help of many others, she returned to Baltimore, near her original home. There, she led her niece and her niece's children to Pennsylvania. Tubman returned again and again, leading a brother, her parents, and many other slaves to freedom. During each trip, she became more familiar with the Underground Railroad and learned new ways to avoid being caught. She sometimes led runaways all the way to Canada to evade the slave catchers who patrolled the northern states.

Tubman became a hero of not only those she helped escape but to free Blacks and abolitionists alike. She developed friendships with many conductors of the Underground Railroad. She became friends with other abolitionists, such as Frederick Douglass, Thomas Garrett, William Lloyd Garrison, and John Brown. As stories of her bravery were told and retold, her adventures became legendary and her reputation became larger than life. She was often compared with Moses, the prophet in the Bible who led the slaves of the Egyptian pharaoh to freedom.

Tubman continued to fight against slavery and for civil rights during and after the Civil War. She served as a Union nurse during the early years of the war. After the Emancipation Proclamation freed the slaves in rebel territory, she led a group of Union raiders through several plantations on the Combahee River. The soldiers she led helped hundreds of slaves gain their freedom. Following the war and the end of slavery, Tubman worked to end the mistreatment of African Americans and women.

In 2016, the secretary of the treasury announced plans to replace the picture of Andrew Jackson on the $20 bill with an image of Harriet Tubman. Jackson's picture would be moved to the back of the bill. This decision was made after seeking input from people across the country. The vote shows how popular Harriet Tubman has become. One of the challenges of studying legendary people like her is that it can be hard to separate myths from accurate history. This is especially true of Harriet Tubman. In some stories that were told, she prayed her master to death. She survived exposure to smallpox without becoming ill. She walked past former masters without them recognizing her. She was guided by a still, small voice. And she was never captured and never lost any of the fugitives she helped during her many expeditions. Which of these stories are true?

HISTORICAL THINKING SKILLS: HISTORIOGRAPHY

Historiography has two meanings. First, it is the skillful assembling and critical evaluation of evidence in the process of constructing historical interpretations. The skills presented throughout the chapters of this book, such as *corroboration* discussed in Chapter 1, are the building blocks of historiography. Historiography also has to do with the historical writing on a particular topic. In the lesson materials that follow, students can be introduced to this second notion of historiography by tracing the way historians and nonhistorians have written about Harriet Tubman, both during her life and in modern times. Studying historiography in this manner can help students better understand the nature of history as a discipline and the process of constructing historical knowledge. Students can see that history not only reflects the individual or event that is being studied, but also the time period during which it is written. Historical accounts, including the writing of historians, are produced for particular audiences at unique times. They are written by individuals who view evidence through certain lenses and within political and social contexts.

Understanding the concept of historiography is essential for understanding the nature of history; however, its application also deepens one's understanding of the world. Exposure to the concept of historiography can prepare young people for civic engagement by helping them be more critical consumers of the information to which they are exposed. Exploring historiography can help students see how perspectives influence perceptions, how the same evidence can be interpreted differently, and how new evidence can enhance interpretations. Understanding historiography might encourage open-mindedness, as students see that all historical interpretations are works in progress, open to revision, refinement, or even recantation. Familiarity with historiography primes individuals to remain humble, acknowledging that current views and opinions are tentative and can and should be modified in the face of new evidence. Transferred into the political arena, understanding historiography can facilitate cognitive and social maturity that enhances an individual's positive interaction with those whose perspectives are different though their intentions are as sincere in their search for solutions to society's ills.

The documents in this chapter include descriptions of Harriet Tubman from her contemporaries, from a biographer in 1886, and from a biographer in 2016. From these accounts, students can trace Tubman's superhuman status during her lifetime to modern historians' efforts to debunk some of the myths about her. For instance, the number of enslaved individuals she helped directly was scaled back from 300 in 1886 to 50 or 60 in 2016. Yet modern biographers claim that the risk she took in undertaking the work was greater than earlier biographers understood. Discrepancies between the following documents are a result of differences in biographers' evaluation of the trustworthiness of evidence, with a modern historian using Tubman's early speeches, and earlier biographers using Tubman's later speeches. In spite of the more modest estimates of Tubman's work produced by recent scholarship, her fame has not waned, as evidenced by the recent decision to place her on the $20 bill. With an understanding of historiography, and based upon an analysis of the documents included in this chapter, students can trace the evolving story of Harriet Tubman as told and retold by her contemporaries and historians, then and now.

LESSON IDEAS

Introduction

The following materials could be used in a lesson taught during a unit on sectionalism, slavery, and abolition in antebellum America. Alternatively, if the course is organized thematically, the lesson could be taught in connection with other lessons on the defense of civil rights.

Objectives

This lesson is designed to meet three objectives associated with knowledge, skills, and dispositions:

1. Students will analyze the effects of Harriet Tubman, other enslaved individuals, and abolitionists' resistance to the institution of slavery, and the role of the Underground Railroad.
2. Students will define *historiography* and will trace the evolving history of Harriet Tubman from her lifetime until modern times.
3. Students will express the importance of defending the rights of others, even at the risk of one's own security.

Build Background Knowledge

Begin the lesson by building students' background knowledge on the Underground Railroad and Harriet Tubman. The essay "Background of the Runaway Slaves" describes the broad historical context of the topic. The essay "Harriet Tubman and the Underground Railroad" gives a specific overview of what students will need to know in order to work with the documents that follow.

Ask Historical Questions

The background information provided above and the documents that follow were designed to help students ask and answer the following questions: How does each individual's telling of the story of Harriet Tubman reflect his/her perspective, purpose, audience, and time? How can students today distinguish between myths and accurate accounts when studying someone like Tubman who has legendary status?

Talk About Historiography

The evidence included in this chapter for the investigation of Harriet Tubman provides an opportunity to help students understand the interpretative nature of history and to learn about the concept of historiography. Teachers can teach students about historiography by contrasting the tone of the accounts and biography written during Tubman's lifetime with those produced more recently. The teacher might want to first define *historiography* for students as the body of historical writing done on a particular topic. The teacher might also help students understand that this body of work often evolves over time. Changes in the way historians think and write about a topic are a result of a number of factors. For example, sometimes the discovery of a new piece of evidence revolutionizes the way historians think about an event. More often, current events influence the way historians view the world and shape the way they interpret the past. Standards for historical investigation have also changed over time, influencing the way historians analyze and use evidence.

After defining and explaining historiography for students, the teacher might show how the documents, particularly Documents 3, 7, and 8, reflect changes in the body of historical work. Looking at the sources of all the documents first, the teacher might sort the documents into those produced during Tubman's lifetime and those produced later. The teacher might categorize documents as primary or secondary sources. For example, thinking out loud, the teacher might say something like this: "Looking at all of the sources first, I see that Documents 3, 7, and 8 were produced by historians and biographers at different times. They will probably be most helpful in identifying shifts in the way Tubman's story has been told." Having looked at all of the sources with the students, the teacher might point out that the other documents, as primary sources, give a sense of the type of evidence historians have worked with, both then and now.

The teacher might explain that differences in the interpretations of biographers in Tubman's day (found in Documents 3 and 7) and a modern historian (found in Document 8) reflect changes in the way history is written. Modern researchers, unlike those who wrote 150 years ago, are expected to take a relatively neutral position and to think more critically about evidence. They take an academic stance and avoid attributing events to supernatural forces. Documents 2–7, all produced during or shortly after Tubman's lifetime, tell the story of the superhuman Tubman who hears the voice of God, sacrifices her own comforts, never asks for a penny, and assumes the persona of Moses in liberating her people. In contrast, Document 8 challenges one of the myths about Tubman, using different evidence from that used by Tubman's contemporary biographers. Larson, the author of Document 8, claims that earlier writers relied upon the legends that were produced after Tubman had become a celebrity. She claims, instead, that the speeches given by Tubman early in her life more accurately reflect what she had actually accomplished. Students facing conflicting historians' accounts, Document 7 and Document 8, are led to acknowledge that the historical record has changed. And against students' intuition, the most recently produced accounts may be more accurate than those produced by historians during her lifetime. This realization can be a helpful step in the process of learning about historiography and the nature of history as a discipline. The graphic organizer at the end of the chapter facilitates students' direct comparison of document sources and content.

Finally, Document 9 reveals that Americans today continue to revere Tubman, hinting that perhaps the mythological Tubman survives in spite of the work of modern historians. Depending on the skill level and sophistication of the students' thinking, a teacher can either model the process of thinking about the documents in order to identify the changing historical record contained in them or can allow students to discover the changing historical record on their own. Whichever approach the teacher takes, this lesson can introduce students to the nature of history as a constructed body of knowledge that continues to evolve with new evidence, new methods of looking at old evidence, new interests and concerns, and new perspectives.

Group-Work

When the teacher is confident students understand the concept of historiography, how to use the graphic organizer to gather evidence from the documents, and how to consider why each author included in his/her account what he/she did, the teacher can have students work in small groups analyzing the remaining documents and completing the graphic organizer. During group-work or independent work, the teacher should remind students about their objective: to try to identify how each individual's telling of the story of Harriet Tubman reflects his/her perspective, purpose, audience, and time, and to attempt to distinguish between myths and accurate accounts when studying someone with legendary status, like Tubman.

Debriefing

After the students have had ample time in groups to analyze the documents, the teacher might regroup the entire class for a debriefing session. The debriefing holds three purposes associated with the three objectives of the lesson. First, students can discuss the *knowledge* they have gained about Harriet Tubman and the Underground Railroad, responding to the following questions:

1. What were some of the legends about Harriet Tubman that you now think are inaccurate because of evidence in the documents or the background information?
2. What were some of Tubman's most remarkable accomplishments?

A second phase of the debriefing can focus on the *skill* of historiography using the following questions:

1. How can a person distinguish between legends and accurate information about Tubman?
2. How have the histories associated with Tubman changed over time? Why do you think they have changed the way they have?
3. Do you think the recent efforts to dispel some of the myths about Tubman have tarnished her reputation? Why or why not?
4. Why is it important to consider the speaker/writer's perspective when studying both historical and current events?

The third phase of the debriefing can focus on the importance of the *disposition* to defend the rights of others using the following questions (it might be necessary to review Adams's defense of the perpetrators of the Boston Massacre from the previous chapter before engaging in this discussion):

1. How were Tubman and Adams similar and different in their defense of the rights of others?
2. What makes Tubman particularly remarkable in seeking the rights of others?
3. What are current examples of efforts to limit individuals' rights? Should we take a stand to defend these rights even if we do not feel that our own rights are in jeopardy?

INSTRUCTIONAL MATERIALS

Nine primary source documents are included in the pages that follow in a format that is modified for students. Original documents, except Document 4, can be found online using the links included in the source information. Document 4 is provided in its original format. In addition, a graphic organizer is included for compiling information from the various sources.

Document Set

1. A newspaper advertisement for escaped slaves Minty (Harriet Tubman) and her brothers placed by Eliza Ann Brodess in October 1849. (Brodess, October 1849)
2. An excerpt from a letter sent by Thomas Garrett, an abolitionist and friend of Harriet Tubman, to colleague James Miller McKim on December 29, 1854 (Garrett, 1854)
3. An excerpt from the book *The Underground Rail Road* published by William Still in 1872 documenting Harriet Tubman's arrival at his station in 1854 (Still, 1872)
4. An excerpt from an article, "The Fourth at Framingham," which appeared in the abolitionist newspaper *The Liberator*, telling about one of Tubman's speeches (Horton, 2013)
5. An excerpt of a letter written by Thomas Garrett, friend of Harriet Tubman, to Sarah Bradford, Tubman biographer (Garrett, 1868)
6. An excerpt from a letter written from Frederick Douglass to Harriet Tubman on August 29, 1868, as an endorsement of her soon-to-be-published biography (Douglass, 1868)
7. An excerpt from the introduction of Sarah H. Bradford's biography *Harriet: The Moses of Her People*, published in 1886 (Bradford, 1886)
8. A statement written by historian and Tubman biographer Kate Clifford Larson entitled "Myths and facts about Harriet Tubman, and selected quotes and misquotes," published at www.harriettubmanbiography.com/harriet-tubman-myths-and-facts.html (Larson, n.d.).
9. A possible design for the new $20 bill, created by Women on 20s and published at www.womenon20s.org/presskit (Women on 20s, 2015)

Simplified Evidence

Document 1: Runaway Ad

THREE HUNDRED DOLLARS REWARD.

RANAWAY from the subscriber on Monday the 17th ult., three negroes, named as follows: HARRY, aged about 19 years, has on one side of his neck a wen, just under the ear, he is of a dark chestnut color, about 5 feet 8 or 9 inches hight; BEN, aged aged about 25 years, is very quick to speak when spoken to, he is of a chestnut color, about six feet high; MINTY, aged about 27 years, is of a chestnut color, fine looking, and about 5 feet high. One hundred dollars reward will be given for each of the above named negroes, if taken out of the State, and $50 each if taken in the State. They must be lodged in Baltimore, Easton or Cambridge Jail, in Maryland.

ELIZA ANN BRODESS,
Near Bucktown, Dorchester county, Md.
Oct. 3d, 1849.

☞The Delaware Gazette will please copy the above three weeks, and charge this office.

Vocabulary:

subscriber = the person who placed the ad
ult. (ultimate) = this month
wen = cyst or growth
lodged = held
Md. = Maryland

Source: Newspaper advertisement for escaped slaves Minty (Harriet Tubman) and her brothers Ben and Henry (called Harry in the ad), placed by Eliza Ann Brodess in Maryland's *Cambridge Democrat* and the *Delaware Gazette* in October 1849. Found at harriettubmanbyway.org/harriet-tubman/

Document 2: Garrett Letter to McKim

WILMINGTON, December 29th, 1854

Dear Friend, J. Miller McKim: —

We helped Harriet Tubman and sent her away with six men and one woman to Allen Agnew's. They will be taken across the country to the city. Harriet, and one of the men had worn the shoes off their feet. I gave them two dollars to help them get new ones. I also paid for a carriage to take them, but I don't know how much it cost yet. Now I have two more [runaway slaves] from the lowest county in Maryland on the peninsula, about one hundred miles [from here]. I will try to get one of our reliable African American men to take them tomorrow morning to the anti-slavery office. Then you can pass them on.

THOMAS GARRETT

Source: Letter sent by Thomas Garrett, an abolitionist friend of Harriet Tubman's and operator of one of the stations on the Underground Railroad in Wilmington, Delaware, to colleague James Miller McKim of Philadelphia on December 29, 1854. [Changed for easier reading.] Found at housedivided.dickinson.edu/ugrr/letter_dec1854.htm

Document 3: Still Book

Harriet Tubman had been their "Moses." . . . She had faithfully gone down into Egypt [Maryland], and had helped these six slaves by being a hero. Harriet was a humble woman. She was as ordinary as any of the unlucky slaves of the South. But, she showed more courage, smartness, and selflessness in her work of rescuing others, by making visits to Maryland among the slaves, than anyone else.

Her success was wonderful. Again and again she made successful visits to Maryland on the Underground Railroad. She would be gone for weeks at a time, taking risks every day while caring for herself and her passengers. We were very afraid for her safety, but she did not seem to ever be afraid. She never thought about being captured by slave-hunters or slave-holders. . . . Though she didn't care about herself, she was much more careful of the runaways she was guiding. Half of the time, she looked like she was asleep, and would actually sit down by the side of the road and go fast asleep. When helping runaways escape from the South, she would not let any of them whimper once, about "giving out and going back," no matter how tired they might be from the hard travel day and night. She had a very strict rule or law of her own: death to anyone who talked about giving up and going back. When things got hard she would let everyone know that "just because times were very hard she wouldn't let anyone be foolish on the road." Several runaways who were nervous and scared were encouraged by Harriet's honest and positive actions and her threat of severe punishment. . . .

It is clear that her success in going into Maryland as she did, was because of her adventurous spirit. She didn't think about the consequences. There has probably never been anyone like her, or will ever be anyone like her in the future.

Source: Part of the book *The Underground Rail Road* published by William Still in 1872 documenting Harriet Tubman's arrival at his station in 1854. Still had been one of Tubman's contacts and an important recordkeeper of the fugitives who passed on the Underground Railroad through his "station." [Changed for easier reading.] Found at nyhistory.com/harriettubman/life.htm

Document 4: Speech Account

Then "Moses," the deliverer, stood up in front of the audience, who cheered for her with excitement. She spoke for a short time, telling the story of her hard life as a slave, her escape, and her work on the Underground Railroad. She spoke in a simple way, which made those who heard her very interested. It would not be enough to say what she said, so we won't write her words. But we think all of our readers should see and hear her as soon as they can.

Mr. Higginson said that this brave woman had never asked for a penny from the abolitionists. She had paid for all of her work herself with money earned by herself. But now, with her father and mother out of slavery, the work she had to do to support them made it so she couldn't do any work in the way of business [helping runaways]. So she wanted to raise a few hundred dollars so that she could buy a little place where her father and mother could take care of themselves. That would let her to go back to doing her profession [helping runaways]! (Laughter and applause.)

Source: Part of an article, "The Fourth at Framingham," which appeared in the abolitionist newspaper *The Liberator*, telling about one of Tubman's speeches (though using the pseudonym of Moses), published July 8, 1859. [Changed for easier reading.] Found in Horton, L. E. (2013). *Harriet Tubman and the fight for freedom: A brief history with documents* (p. 126). Boston, MA: Bedford/St. Martin's.

Document 5: Garrett Letter to Bradford

MY FRIEND:

. . . I never met with any person, white or black, who was more sure about the voice of God, as spoken direct to her soul. She has told me many times that she talked with God, and he talked with her every day of her life. She has told me that she was not afraid of being arrested by her former master, or any other person, whether she was in his neighborhood, or in the state of New York, or Canada, for she said she only went where God sent her, and her faith in a Supreme Power truly was great.

I'm not exactly sure when she started her work, but I think it must have been about 1845. From then until 1860,

I think she must have brought from the place where she had been a slave, in Maryland, about 80 miles from here, between 60 and 80 people. No slave who she cared for was ever arrested that I have heard of; she mostly had her regular stopping places on her way. But once, when she had two large men with her, about 30 miles below here, she said that God told her to stop, which she did. Then she asked him what she must do.

He told her to leave the road, and turn to the left. She obeyed, and soon they came to a small stream of tide water. There was no boat, or bridge. She again inquired of her Guide [God] what she was to do. She was told to wade through the stream. It was cold, in the month of March; but having confidence in her Guide [God], she went in. The water went up to her arm-pits. The men would not follow her until they saw her safe on the opposite shore. Then they followed. If I am not mistaken, she soon had to wade across a second stream. Soon after that she came to a cabin of colored people, who took them all in, put them to bed, and dried their clothes. They were ready to continue on their journey the next night.

Harriet ran out of money, and gave them some of her underclothing to pay for their kindness. When she called on me two days later, she was so sick she could hardly speak, and was also hurting with a very bad toothache. The strange part of the story, we found out later, was that the master of these two men had hung up the previous day, at the railroad station by the place where she had left the road, an advertisement for them [the men], offering a large reward for their capture. But they made a safe exit.

Etc., etc. Your friend,
THOMAS GARRETT

Source: Part of a letter written in June 1868 by Thomas Garrett, friend of Harriet Tubman's, devout Quaker, and "station" operator on the Underground Railroad. The letter was written to Sarah Bradford in response to Bradford's request to learn more about Tubman, as she was writing a biography of her. The letter was published in Bradford's biography *Harriet: The Moses of her People*. [Changed for easier reading.] Found at www.harriet-tubman.org/letter-by-thomas-garrett/

Document 6: Douglas Letter

ROCHESTER, August 29, 1868.

DEAR HARRIET: I am glad to know that a kind lady has written the story of your important life, and that it will be published soon. You don't really need what you have asked for from me, a word of commendation [a recommendation for her book]. I need a commendation from you much more than you need one from me, especially because of your better work and your love of the cause of the slaves of our land.

The difference between us is very clear. Most of what I have done and suffered in the service of our cause has been in public. And I have been given a lot of help all the time. You on the other hand have worked in a private way. I have worked in the day. You have worked in the night. I have had the applause of the crowd and the happiness that comes of being loved by many people. While most of what you have done has been seen by a few trembling, scared, and tired slaves, whom you have led out of slavery, and whose heartfelt "God bless you" has been your only reward.

The midnight sky and the silent stars have watched your love of freedom and your heroism. Only John Brown—who passed away—has had more dangers and suffering to serve slaves than you have.

A lot of what you have done would seem unbelievable to those who don't know you like I know you. It is a great pleasure and a great privilege for me to tell people about your character and your works, and to say to people who see you [or your book], that I think that you are, in every way, truthful and trustworthy.

Your friend,
FREDERICK DOUGLASS.

Source: Letter written from former slave and abolitionist Frederick Douglass to Harriet Tubman on August 29, 1868, as an endorsement of her soon-to-be-published biography. [Changed for easier reading.] Found at www.accessible-archives.com/2012/02/scenes-in-the-life-of-harriet-tubman-part-3/

Document 7: Bradford Book

I have given my black hero the title "THE MOSES OF HER PEOPLE." This might seem a little ambitious. After all, this Moses was a woman and she only guided three or four hundred slaves from the land of bondage to the land of freedom. But I only give her the name that she used to be called, both in the North and the South. She was called it during the years of terror of the Fugitive Slave Law, and during the Civil War....

[She didn't] free a whole nation of enslaved men and women. But this goal was the desire of her heart, as it was of that of the great leader of Israel [Moses]. She said to the slave-holders, like Moses did to Pharaoh, "Let my people go!" And not even Moses risked his life and limb more happily than our brave and unselfish friend did.

Her name should be passed down forever, along with the names of Joan of Arc, Grace Darling, and Florence Nightingale. Not one of these noble and brave women has shown more courage and strength in facing danger and death to help human suffering, than this poor black woman, whose story I am trying in a most imperfect way to give you....

For those who don't believe me (and there will probably be many of them, when I tell them a story as strange as this), I will say that when possible, I have checked out every story told to me by my heroic friend [Tubman]. I did this to satisfy others, not me. No one can hear Harriet talk and not believe every word she says. As Mr. Sanborn says about her, "she is too real a person, not to be true."

I have not told many stories just as wonderful as the ones that I tell because I had no way to find people who could verify them....

After her almost superhuman efforts in escaping from slavery herself, she returned to the South nineteen times bringing back with her over three hundred fugitives. Then she was sent by Governor Andrew of Massachusetts to the South at the beginning of the Civil War, to be a spy and scout for our armies. She also worked as a hospital nurse when needed.

Source: Part of the introduction of Sarah H. Bradford's biography, *Harriet: The Moses of Her People*, published in 1886. Bradford gathered letters from Tubman's friends and worked with Tubman herself in preparing the biography. [Changed for easier reading.] Found at www.docsouth.unc.edu/neh/harriet/harriet.html

Document 8: Larson Account

Myth: Harriet Tubman rescued 300 people in 19 trips.

Fact: According to Tubman's own words, and the many records of her rescue missions, we know that **she rescued about 70 people. They were her family and friends. She made about 13 trips to Maryland.** During public and private meetings in 1858 and 1859, Tubman repeatedly told people that she had rescued 50 to 60 people in 8 or 9 trips. This was before her last mission, in December 1860, when she brought away 7 people. Sarah Bradford exaggerated the numbers in her 1868 biography. Bradford never said that Tubman gave her those numbers. But Bradford guessed that was the number. Other friends who were close to Tubman went against those numbers. We can name almost every person Tubman helped. Besides her family and friends, Tubman also gave instructions to another 70 or so slaves on the East Coast. They found their way to freedom on their own.

Source: A statement written by historian and Tubman biographer Kate Clifford Larson called "Myths and facts about Harriet Tubman, and selected quotes and misquotes." Larson wrote a book, *Bound for the Promised Land: Harriet Tubman, Portrait of an American Hero.* [Changed for easier reading.] Article found at www. harriettubmanbiography.com/harriet-tubman-myths-and-facts. html

Document 9: Proposed $20 Bill

Source: Possible design for the new $20 bill Found on a website created by *Women on 20s* at www.womenon20s.org/presskit

Original Evidence

The following material appears in a modified format in the document set. It is not easily retrievable online, as the other documents in the text set are.

Document 4: Speech Account

"Moses," the deliverer, then stood up before the audience, who greeted her with enthusiastic cheers. She spoke briefly, telling the story of her suffering as a slave, her escape, and her achievements on the Underground Railroad, in a style of quaint simplicity, which excited the most profound interest in her hearers. The mere words could not do justice to the speaker, and therefore we do not undertake to give them; but we advise all our readers to take the earliest opportunity to see and hear her.

Mr. Higginson stated that this brave woman had never asked for a cent from the Abolitionists, but that all her operations had been conducted at her own cost, with money earned by herself. Now, however, having brought her father and mother out of slavery, she found that the labor required for their support rendered her incapable of doing anything in the way of business, and she therefore desired to raise a few hundred dollars to enable her to buy a little place where her father and mother could support themselves, and enable her to resume the practice of her profession! (Laughter and applause.)

Source: Excerpt from an article, "The Fourth at Framingham," which appeared in the abolitionist newspaper *The Liberator*, telling about one of Tubman's speeches (though using the pseudonym of Moses), published July 8, 1859. Found in Horton, L. E. (2013). *Harriet Tubman and the fight for freedom: A brief history with documents* (p. 126). Boston, MA: Bedford/St. Martin's.

Graphic Organizer

Harriet Tubman and the Underground Railroad

Harriet Tubman is one of the most famous women in U.S. history. The U.S. Treasury Department plans to place her portrait on the $20 bill. Individuals have often become confused about Tubman's history. For instance, did she invent the Underground Railroad? Is it true that none of the enslaved individuals whom she helped escape ever got caught? Did she possess other supernatural powers? Did she free hundreds or even thousands of slaves? The fame she achieved during her lifetime makes it difficult to distinguish between the truth and legends about her today. Use the graphic organizer to trace the historiography of writing on Tubman and to distinguish between myths that developed about her during her lifetime and facts about her life. Then answer the questions below.

Doc	Source information (genre, author, purpose, audience)	Summary (what are the main ideas/ stories from this source?)	How reliable do you find this source? Less More	How does this document reflect the values of the author and time when it was produced?
1			1 2 3 4 5 6 7 8 9 10	
2			1 2 3 4 5 6 7 8 9 10	
3			1 2 3 4 5 6 7 8 9 10	
4			1 2 3 4 5 6 7 8 9 10	
5			1 2 3 4 5 6 7 8 9 10	
6			1 2 3 4 5 6 7 8 9 10	
7			1 2 3 4 5 6 7 8 9 10	
8			1 2 3 4 5 6 7 8 9 10	
9			1 2 3 4 5 6 7 8 9 10	

1. What would you say are documented facts about Harriet Tubman found in the strongest accounts you have reviewed?
2. How was Tubman talked about in her time? How is that different from current historical research on her? What does this change show about historiography?
3. Is it a good choice to place Tubman on the $20 bill? Why or why not?

COLLABORATIVE PROBLEM-SOLVING:
Making a Difference by Coming Together

On September 8, 1965, farm workers in Delano, California, walked off of their jobs harvesting grapes in demand of higher wages and better working conditions. A week later, the National Farmworkers Association joined the strike. Soon, more than 2,000 workers, primarily Filipino and Latino, were striking. They were joined by dock workers who refused to load harvested grapes for shipment, causing grapes to spoil. Consumers across North America who became aware of the plight of the farm workers soon joined in a boycott. Cesar Chavez and other union leaders traveled across the United States asking labor organizations, religious congregations, and university students to support the boycott. Grape producers refused to budge, so the strike and boycott continued. The owners of the fields were confident that the strikers would be unable to continue for long. Many of those on strike lost their homes, cars, and other possessions. Chavez called on the residents of American cities to become involved in the boycott, suggesting that change would come if "vast numbers [did] little things" (Levy, 1975, pp. 269–270). Millions of Americans stopped eating grapes. It took 5 years, but by 1970, grape growers had signed union contracts raising the wages for farm workers and improving their working conditions.

The Delano Grape Strike is one of many times in U.S. history when people have united behind a common cause. Each incident illustrates the power of collective action to elect officials, enact laws, or promote reform. Collective action can come in many forms. Labor unions, like the United Farm Workers that grew out of the Delano Grape Strike, increase the power of employees to place demands on their employers. Political parties unite like-minded voters to elect officials who represent their priorities. Special interest groups pool resources to support particular causes. Consumers unite in boycotts to change business practices or government policies. Websites like GoFundMe draw small financial donations from large numbers of sympathetic strangers in order to cover the financial burdens of a worthy applicant. In each case of collective action, groups of people unite to achieve a common cause with outcomes that individuals would be unable to produce on their own.

Patriots in Boston and other colonial cities understood that greater pressure could be placed on Great Britain to change its policies if individuals across the colonies united in their demands for reform. Patriot leaders created "Committees of Correspondence," a network of like-minded reformers who shared information (with a patriotic slant) and coordinated resistance to unpopular British policies between cities and the countryside and from one colony to the next. Committees of Correspondence organized boycotts, planned the Stamp Act Congress, and arranged the First Continental Congress, setting in motion events that would lead to war and American independence. Chapter 4 includes materials for an investigation of the unifying tactics of Committees of Correspondence.

Samuel Gompers, too, understood the power that common people could have when they united. In 1881, Gompers helped found the Federation of Organized Trades and Labor Unions, a coalition of trade unions that would later be known as the American Federation of Labor (AFL). Under Gompers's leadership, membership in the AFL grew to more than 4 million members, solidifying its position among unions. Gompers's work demonstrated the power that united workers could have in improving working conditions and raising wages. Chapter 5 provides materials for an investigation of Gompers and the power of, and opposition to, the American Federation of Labor.

U.S. history is filled with other examples of people uniting to work for a common cause. During colonial times, residents of Boston pooled their resources to create the Boston Latin School, the first public school in America. Benjamin Franklin, a dropout of that school, created the Union Fire Company, volunteers who worked together to battle Philadelphia's fires. Firefighters understood that a fire in any home in their neighborhood posed a threat to their own homes. During George Washington's presidential administration, individuals formed political coalitions behind Thomas Jefferson and Alexander Hamilton that evolved into political parties, which have become central to the U.S. government system. Throughout U.S. history, special interest groups have formed to support various agendas. For example, in 1909, W. E. B. Du Bois and others created the National Association for the Advancement of Colored People (NAACP) in order to pool the resources of justice-oriented individuals who sought civil rights for African Americans. Over a century later, the Black Lives Matter movement brought together individuals who were concerned about the mistreatment of African American men by police officers. In the 1980s, Americans united in a boycott of tuna fish, resulting in fishing practices that were safer for dolphins. Today, other special interest groups and political action committees have found that when individuals pool their resources, they gain significant political power.

In contrast to these stories of Americans uniting to work for a common cause are stories that highlight "rugged individualism." Even as teachers share examples of unions, political parties, and special interest groups, they might share counterexamples of so-called "self-made" men and women in order to help students gain a more nuanced understanding of collective action. American history provides examples of individuals who claim to have "pulled themselves up by their bootstraps," being solely responsible for their success. Many of these individuals, such as Andrew Carnegie and John D. Rockefeller, opposed labor unions as

un-American. Still, some problems are too large for an individual to solve and instead require collective action. The strategy of joining with others to maximize political power is a useful tool for civic engagement.

In addition to the lessons provided in Chapters 4 and 5, a teacher might help students think about specific actions they might take to form coalitions dedicated to solving current problems using the following questions:

- How might a new school club address one of the problems you see at school?
- How might you use social media to pool resources or unite people to solve a problem?
- How could you join or support a political party or special interest group that promotes your interests?

CHAPTER 4

Committees of Correspondence

Thousands of disgruntled citizens, individually complaining to their families or friends, are unlikely to cause reform. Yet, if they were to unite, they might attract attention, put pressure on policymakers, and cause change. The organization of unassociated unhappy citizens into a united force for change requires leadership, vision, and, in the topic of this chapter, a little propaganda. "Committees of Correspondence," formed in the years leading up to the Revolutionary War, united patriots from across the colonies in their demands for reform and independence. In this chapter, I provide materials for an investigation of the collaborative efforts used by committees to build support for the patriot cause.

STUDENTS' BACKGROUND KNOWLEDGE

The current grand historical narrative might give students the impression that the American Revolution was largely the work of powerful individuals such as Samuel Adams and Benjamin Franklin. Certainly, patriot leaders were vital in promoting the revolution. However, they could not accomplish this work alone. Instead, much of the success of the revolution was the result of the efforts of thousands of independent farmers, merchants, housewives, lawyers, and laborers from New Hampshire to Georgia, united behind the patriot cause. Students may have heard of Committees of Correspondence, a vocabulary term often included in a textbook chapter on the revolution. But few of them understand the irreplaceable role these committees played in fostering cooperation among disgruntled citizens, sharing information across colonies, and coordinating strategic resistance to British policies and redcoat armies.

Students who view the United States as a single unified nation today may find it difficult to imagine the 13 colonies as unaffiliated neighbors. A modern perspective of the United States might interfere with students recognizing the innovative impact of the Committees of Correspondence, which began to unite the colonies behind a single cause and organized the First Continental Congress and a more formal confederacy. Moreover, few students understand the lessons that can be drawn from the Committees of Correspondence in terms of engaged citizenship today. This investigation provides a suitable case study on the power of united, like-minded individuals to promote a cause.

HISTORICAL BACKGROUND FOR TEACHERS AND STUDENTS

Background of Colonial Unity

Before the American Revolution, the colonies were not united. But in the summer of 1754, during the French and Indian War, a gathering was held in Albany, New York. Representatives from several North American colonies attended. The French and their Native American friends were a threat to the British colonists. The delegates talked about how the colonies could work together to defend themselves. At the meeting, Benjamin Franklin proposed a plan to unite the British colonies under one government. However, the colonial government of every colony rejected his plan. They saw themselves as different from their neighboring colonies. They were nervous about giving up any power to a central authority. The failure of Franklin's "Albany Plan of Union" shows the thinking within each colony. Most of Britain's North American colonies traded more with Great Britain than with one another. Their economies, cultures, and people were different from those of the other colonies. Virginia's imports and exports were not like those of Massachusetts. The cultural diversity of New York made it different from the colonies north and south of it. Geographic differences between the colonies added to their uniqueness. Most colonists did not want strong ties with other colonies.

After the French and Indian War, the British imposed taxes on colonists to pay for the war. These taxes hurt merchants in New York, Boston, Philadelphia, and Charleston. People across the colonies now had something in common. Many of them hated the taxes. Patriots thought that taxes violated the rights of British subjects. They thought the taxes violated the British constitution (a collection of documents and acts). Angry colonists protested taxes through boycotts. They published papers explaining their rights. They threatened violence.

Many residents of Boston became patriot leaders. But Virginians, New Yorkers, and others demanded their rights, too. Threats to British soldiers by an angry Boston mob led to violence. In the Boston Massacre, British troops fired on a crowd, killing five people. In Virginia, Patrick Henry declared that only the colonial assemblies had the power to tax the colonies. Patriots threatened tax collectors in New

York and other places. Protests led British Parliament to get rid of some taxes. But each time they did, they replaced the tax with a new one. Parliament passed a law called the Stamp Act. It was a tax that made colonists pay for a stamp on important papers. Representatives from nine colonies met in New York in 1765 to decide what to do. Together, they planned a boycott. It hurt British merchants in the colonies. The Stamp Act was dropped after less than a year. Their success fighting the Stamp Act showed colonists what could happen when they worked together.

Problems between patriots and the British agents grew. The passage of the Tea Act resulted in the "Boston Tea Party." There patriots destroyed over a million dollars' worth of tea to stop British agents from collecting a tax. The king of England was furious. The British Navy closed Boston Harbor. Boston relied on the harbor for trade, so its economy was ruined. British troops were placed in Boston. Britain's harsh punishment of Boston made many people of other colonies feel sorry for Boston. They wanted to help.

Committees of Correspondence

A few years before the Boston Tea Party, the first Committees of Correspondence were created. *Correspondence* means to communicate back and forth. Committees of Correspondence were groups of people in different colonies who sent messages to one another about important events. (There were no telephones at that time, so people could only speak in person or through writing.)

The first Committee of Correspondence was set up in Boston during a town meeting in 1772. The committee was formed because of a change in British policy. Instead of having the colonists pay colonial leaders, the king would pay them. This may not seem like a big change. But it made the leaders obey the king instead of the colonists. The people of Boston were upset. At Boston's town meeting, they formed a committee. City leaders asked the committee to write a report on British abuses. They asked it to send a letter to the people of nearby towns seeking their help. The committee's report was called the *Boston Pamphlet*. It told people about the many wrongs done by the king.

This first committee was an example for other towns and colonies. Soon, committees were organized by patriot leaders everywhere. They shared information about British abuses. They spread patriotism. They planned protests and boycotts. They shared ideas for fighting British policies. Committees published the names of people who did not follow boycotts. They printed papers that told patriots to live a simple life without imported British luxuries. They harassed Loyalists, people who were loyal to the king. At first, people thought the committees would only be temporary. But after patriot leaders found that the British went from one abuse to another, they made more permanent committees. By 1774, many towns linked their committee to those of other towns. After the British closed Boston

Harbor in 1774, committees planned the First Continental Congress in Philadelphia. After the Revolutionary War started, they sent supplies to armies. They spread unity across the colonies.

Committees of Correspondence included the loudest patriots. They spread information from a patriot point of view. People who were loyal to the king were not allowed to join. Through pamphlets, letters, and newspapers, committee members spread information. Patriot leaders urged people to be united and help their abused neighbors. Committees allowed patriots to discuss what to do before acting. They changed individual responses into collective action. Historian William Warner (2013) argued that the Revolutionary War was mostly a war of communication. He said that the war started when Boston's first Committee of Correspondence was formed. The work of the committees in changing the hearts and minds of the people was what patriot John Adams (1856) called the real American Revolution.

Committees of Correspondence became colonial governments during the Revolutionary War, though they were no longer needed after official state governments were created. But today, the committees remind us of what can be done when people unite behind a common cause. Committees of Correspondence joined patriots across the colonies in a revolution. They created unity in what would eventually become the United States.

HISTORICAL THINKING SKILLS: CONTEXTUALIZATION

Contextualization, the skill highlighted in this chapter, is one of the most basic historical thinking skills (Wineburg, 1991). Contextualization involves cognitively placing oneself in the physical, social, political, economic, technological, material, linguistic, and historiographic context of the time and place when a primary or secondary source was created. Historians use background knowledge about historical conditions to imaginatively re-create events and to better understand evidence. Knowing, for instance, the difficulty of communication in colonial North America would help historians understand the time it took to spread news of the Battle of Lexington from Boston to other towns and colonies. Familiarity with Samuel Adams's fiery personality helps historians understand his writing. Historians acknowledge the imaginative work involved in comprehending documents that were produced by individuals who lived in times and places that were different from current conditions—individuals who saw the world differently, espoused different values, had access to different technologies, and faced challenges distinct from those of the current generation.

Though basic to historians, contextualization is among the most difficult historical thinking skills for young people (Nokes et al., 2007). Two explanations exist for the challenges they face in imagining past contexts: They do not have the background knowledge necessary to imagine those contexts, and they do not realize the importance of trying to imagine past contexts. Students often lack background knowledge on both the broad historical context and the immediate context surrounding a historical event. For this reason, background information in each chapter of this book includes the broader context as well as the immediate context of the event under investigation.

Instead of employing contextualization, students tend to project current conditions and familiar places onto the events and people of the past. As a result, they often perceive people from the past with a "deficit" perspective—thinking that the actions of historical characters resulted from their stupidity or immorality rather than from different values, priorities, resources, or awareness. For example, today, when the United States is viewed as a single nation, it is difficult to understand documents written by individuals who saw the colonies as distinct states, more like unaffiliated nations. Modern conditions pose a barrier for understanding the context of such documents. Challenges like this exist for young people in interpreting all evidence produced in contexts that differ from current conditions. In contrast, historians understand that individuals' actions and words are best understood when the context during which they spoke is kept in mind.

Though generally considered a historical thinking skill, contextualization has applications for civic engagement. The deficit perspective is not only taken when viewing the actions of people of the past, but also when considering the choices of political opponents. And just as the deficit perspective interferes with an accurate analysis of historical evidence, a deficit perspective stands in the way of positive interactions with those who differ politically. Certainly, the millions who voted differently in the most recent presidential election are not all stupid or corrupt, a point of view projected by frustrated politicians and their pundits. Is it possible that the physical, social, economic, and political contexts from which political opponents view issues play a role in their political opposition? Of course, it does. Helping students engage in contextualization during historical investigations can be a step toward helping them understand the role of context in creating diverse opinions about current actions, decisions, policies, and problem solving.

LESSON IDEAS

Introduction

The following materials could be used in a lesson during a unit on the American Revolution. Alternatively, if a course is organized thematically, this lesson could be taught with other lessons on the role of collective action as a tool for civic engagement.

Objectives

This lesson is designed to meet three objectives associated with knowledge, skills, and dispositions:

1. Students will analyze the rhetoric used by Committees of Correspondence and describe the role of committees in promoting patriotic causes.
2. Students will engage in contextualization, imagining the social and political context during which the Committees of Correspondence were formed, and use imagined contexts to make inferences about the content of primary sources.
3. Students will describe the political power that comes when like-minded individuals coordinate their efforts to promote reform. Students will be inclined to seek out or form such groups when reform is needed.

Build Background Knowledge

Begin the lesson by building students' background knowledge on the events that led to the formation of committees of correspondence. The material provided in this chapter under the headings "Background of Colonial Unity" and "Committees of Correspondence" provide a basic overview of what students will need to know in order to work with the documents that follow.

Ask Historical Questions

The background information provided above and the documents that follow were designed to address the following questions: How did Committees of Correspondence organize their actions? What tactics did they use? How did they retell stories of events to promote their cause?

Provide Strategy Instruction and Model Contextualization

As mentioned above, contextualization is one of the most difficult historical thinking strategies for students to employ. Teachers can help students engage in contextualization by (1) providing explicit instruction, and (2) providing students with the background knowledge necessary to imagine the geographic, demographic, social, economic, political, and cultural context of the formation of Committees of Correspondence. Some history teachers help their students engage in contextualization by breaking the process up into two components: an analysis of the "Big C Context," which includes events and conditions that have been building up for a long period of time before the event—the long-term context, and the "Little C Context," which includes the events and conditions that immediately surround the production of the document—the immediate context of the production of the text (Teaching Channel, n.d.).

For example, the long-term context (Big C Context) of all the documents below was a world without formal political affiliation among the American colonies. The failure of Benjamin Franklin's Albany Plan of Union in 1754 revealed that uniting the colonies would not be easy. However, the Stamp Act Congress, which brought together delegates from nine colonies for a couple of weeks in 1765, was successful in coordinating boycotts and protesting the hated stamp tax, and served as an important precedent of coordinated colonial efforts. The difficulty of travel and communication between the colonies, the strong economic ties between the colonies and Great Britain, and mixed feelings of individual colonial families about Great Britain are also part of the long-term context (Big C Context). The teacher might talk about the information in the background essays as part of the Big C Context.

Because each document below possesses a unique immediate context (Little C Context), the teacher can model for students how the context of any document influences its content. For instance, in Document 1, Samuel Adams writes under a false name, Candidus. Because pseudonyms are uncommon in newspapers today, students might be confused or make assumptions about his writing. Within the context of the 18th century, however, pseudonyms were the norm. Adams may have used a false name to protect himself from retribution by royal officials, though many readers, even in his day, knew his identity by his writing style and the content of this entry. Adams's letter was written in 1771, nearly a year before a Boston town meeting called for the formation of what would become the first of many Committees of Correspondence. It shows that Adams was considering ways to promote solidarity across the colonies before any committees were formed. Document 2, in comparison, is a resolution passed in a town meeting, calling for the formation of the first Committee of Correspondence. This meeting is a direct response to changes in British policies described above that made the royal governor and judges subject to the will of the crown. Document 3 grows out of Document 2. It is the report issued by Boston's Committee of Correspondence calling on other communities to share their opinion of the perceived British abuses. The immediate context of Documents 1–3, then, relates to the formation of the first committee. The teacher might model for students how to use the source information, blended with background information, to imagine the Little C Context of each document.

The immediate context of the other documents varies, and an understanding of the context of each improves students' ability to analyze their content. Document 4 was written shortly after the Boston Tea Party, an extremely radical act that might have alienated some of the more moderate colonial leaders and Whigs in British Parliament. (The Whigs had been somewhat sympathetic to the patriot cause prior to the

Boston Tea Party.) Patriot leaders wrote to Franklin, who was in Great Britain, in order to justify the act, suggesting that it was done in desperation by a united people. Document 5 was produced within a few months of Document 4, though in a completely different context. It is a speech given in British Parliament condemning Boston's formation of Committees of Correspondence. Unlike the other documents in this text set, it is critical of the Committees of Correspondence. Document 6 was written in New York during the British occupation of Boston, suggesting that the Committees of Correspondence were indeed promoting unity among the colonies. Document 7 represents the collaborative effort of the townships surrounding Boston to keep supplies from the British troops who occupied the city in 1775, less than 2 months prior to the first battles of the revolution at Lexington and Concord. Document 8 was a report of the battles produced shortly thereafter and circulated through Committees of Correspondence in Pennsylvania and Virginia. Finally, Document 9 is a letter written in response to news of the Battles of Lexington and Concord by a New Yorker, demonstrating the solidarity the committees of New York felt with those of Massachusetts. That it was produced 2 weeks after the battles is a result of a technological context in which news traveled much more slowly than today.

As part of the process of contextualization, students can be shown how the context can sometimes be inferred from the content of the documents. For instance, Adams makes an allusion to Massachusetts' support for New York when its legislature was censured, contextual events that students might not know. Though they may not be familiar with the New York Restraining Act of 1767, they could infer from the document that such legislation had been passed. From this inference, they could better understand why Adams would provide an example of a time when Massachusetts supported New York in the face of abuse as part of his call for solidarity under new circumstances. Teachers might discuss with students the Big C and Little C Context of one or more of these documents, showing them how to use the graphic organizer to record the relevant contextual factors.

Group-Work

Once the teacher is confident that students understand contextualization and how to use the graphic organizer to gather evidence from the documents, he/she can have them analyze the remaining documents independently or in small groups. He/she should remind students about their objective: to use evidence from the documents to identify how the Committees of Correspondence organized their actions, what tactics they used, and how they retold stories and events in order to promote their causes. In order to increase prolonged engagement with the challenging texts, the teacher might pull the small groups into a whole-class discussion at checkpoints throughout the analysis to allow them to discuss their preliminary findings and receive feedback from their peers.

Debriefing

After the students have had ample time in groups to analyze the documents, the teacher might regroup the entire class for a debriefing session. The debriefing holds three purposes associated with the three objectives of the lesson. First, students can discuss the *knowledge* they have gained about the role of Committees of Correspondence with the following questions:

1. What did evidence from the documents suggest about the tactics and effectiveness of the Committees of Correspondence?
2. How did the Committees of Correspondence promote unity among the colonists?
3. How did committees retell events in order to further their causes?

A second phase of the debriefing can focus on the *skill* of contextualization with the following questions:

1. How did knowing something about the long-term (Big C) context or the immediate (Little C) context of the documents help you understand and analyze what they included? Can you give an example of a time when the context helped you understand a document?
2. What did you infer about the contexts based upon the content of any of the documents?
3. How would contextualization be useful as a tool for civic engagement?

Using the following questions, the third phase of the debriefing can focus on the *disposition* to collaborate and the importance of solidarity and unity in promoting a cause:

1. How did Committees of Correspondence build unity among people from different colonies?
2. How might similar tactics be used today to form and inspire groups of like-minded individuals to promote a common cause?
3. What are current examples of special interest groups through which individuals have united in order to increase their political power?

INSTRUCTIONAL MATERIALS

Nine primary source documents are included in the pages that follow, modified for students with links to the originals. Document 5 is not easily accessible online, so it is also included here in its original format. A graphic organizer, provided at the end of the chapter, gives structure for students as they engage in contextualization and formulate an interpretation to the historical questions. A sample classroom poster is also included, which teachers might display in class in order to remind students about the different elements of contextualization.

Document Set

1. An excerpt from an essay written by Samuel Adams in the *Boston Gazette*, September 16, 1771, using the pseudonym of Candidus (Adams, 1906)
2. Part of a resolution passed in a Boston town meeting, November 2, 1772, in response to a new royal policy, recorded by William Cooper, town clerk (Votes and Proceedings, 1772)
3. An excerpt from a document known as the Boston Pamphlet, produced by the Boston Committee of Correspondence in 1772 (*Boston Pamphlet*, 1772)
4. An excerpt from a letter written by Thomas Cushing, Samuel Adams, John Hancock, and William Phillips to Benjamin Franklin in London on December 21, 1773 (Cushing, Adams, Hancock, & Phillips, 1773)
5. Part of British legislator Lord North's speech to Parliament on March 14, 1774, after the Boston Tea Party (Warner, 2013)
6. An excerpt from a resolution passed by the New York assembly on July 19, 1774, in response to the British occupation of Boston (Proceedings of the Committee of Correspondence, 1774)
7. An excerpt from the notes taken during a meeting of the Committees of Correspondence from Boston and eight other Massachusetts towns, February 25, 1775 (Cooper, 1775)
8. An excerpt from a note written by J. Palmer of the Worcester, Massachusetts, Committee of Correspondence and circulated through other committees (Palmer, 1775)
9. An excerpt from a letter signed by Abraham Yates Jr., chairman of the Albany, New York, Committee of Correspondence, sent to the Boston Committee of Correspondence on May 1, 1775 (Yates, 1923)

Simplified Evidence

Document 1: Adams Essay

I have often thought that in this time of shared troubles it would be wise for colonists to correspond with each other more often. They should pay more attention to the way things are in each other. It seems like lately the enemies of America point their guns at only one colony. They slyly ignore the other colonies. They want to make the one colony seem obnoxious to the others. So, one colony feels the king's hatred in order to help all of them. But I hope that the colonies will understand this trick. When the king tries to defeat one colony, we should understand that the king is trying to make all of them slaves. . . . So it is best for all of them to help each other with all their strength and power. When the legislature of the colony of New York was ended [by the king], the House of Representatives of Massachusetts thought that it was "alarming [upsetting] to all the colonies." They spoke against it. . . . Whoever really thinks about this will see that a terrible shot is aimed at the liberty of these colonies. The cause of one is the cause of all. If parliament can take away from New York any of its rights, it can take away all the other colonies' rights. And nothing encourages the king to do this, as much as the colonies not paying attention to each other. To divide and to destroy is the first rule in attacking those who are powerful when they are united. . . . And when the smallest freedom of a single colony is hurt, I truly wish, that all the rest [of the colonies] will, with equal energy, support their sister. . . . May the British American Colonies guard and take care. By not paying attention to each other they will become lazy and careless of the grand cause of American liberty. Then they would finally become a victim of the MERCILESS HAND OF TYRANNY.

Source: Part of an essay written by Samuel Adams in the *Boston Gazette*, September 16, 1771, using the pretend name of Candidus. Adams is sometimes thought to have invented the idea of Committees of Correspondence. [Changed for easier reading.] Found at www.fullbooks.com/The-Writings-of-Samuel-Adams-volume-II-1770-4.html

Document 2: Boston Resolution

MOVED, that a committee of correspondence be made with 21 people. They will explain the rights of the colonists, especially of this region. They will explain their rights as men, as Christians, and as subjects. They will communicate and share this with other towns in this region and to the world. They will explain the feelings of this town, with the harms and abuses that have been done to it, or that might be done to it in the future. They will also ask each town to freely communicate how they feel about this subject.

Source: Part of a resolution passed in a Boston town meeting, November 2, 1772, in response to a new royal policy taking away the colonial assembly's power to decide the salaries of court officials. Recorded by William Cooper, town clerk. [Changed for easier reading.] Found at www.masshist.org/revolution/image-viewer. php?item_id=609&mode=small&img_step=3&tpc=#page3

Document 3: Boston Pamphlet

These [violations of rights] are something everyone should be concerned about. So the town of Boston thought that they needed to talk with their brothers throughout the province. They created a committee to talk with others who are also suffering from this recent act of oppression. These and many other violations of our rights have made us groan [hurt us] for the past several years. . . . Tell this town how you honestly feel about the danger we all face. We would appreciate [hearing from you.] If you agree that we have talked about our rights correctly and that the acts of Parliament and the King take away our rights, you will certainly think that it is very important to stand firm together to get our rights back and support our rights. Together we should do what we need to to ask our representatives . . . to rescue our glorious Constitution from being ruined. But let us know if most people do not think we have the rights we talk about. Or if you think that the King and the Courts have not violated these rights. Or if our rights are not worth fighting to keep. If this is the opinion of the province, we will accept the terrible policies. We will forever be sorry for the death of the great love for civil and religious liberty that led our fathers to leave their native country and settle the wilderness facing every danger and even death. But we do not think this is the case. We are sure your wisdom and your care for yourself and the next generation will not allow you to sleep [ignore us]. We are sure that you will not ignore us as we sit on the edge of destruction. We are sure that you will not ignore us while we are hurt every day. And while the enemies steal the fruits of the tree of liberty that was planted by our forefathers.

Source: Part of a document known as the *Boston Pamphlet* made by the Boston Committee of Correspondence in 1772. The pamphlet first described rights, then listed the abuses of rights, before concluding with "a letter of correspondence to the other towns," from which this part comes. [Changed for easier reading.] Found at americainclass.org/sources/makingrevolution/crisis/text6/bostonpamphlet.pdf

Document 4: Letter to Franklin

[The people of Boston thought Parliament would stop abusing them. They thought they would get rid of the taxes]. But they were very surprised to find out they had been lied to. Instead they found out that Parliament created new ways to collect and increase these oppressive taxes, just when they thought the taxes would end. Parliament passed an act last session that gave the East India Company the power to ship tea to America. In this act, the colonists saw that they had no hope for the King's help. Instead they found that Parliament would not give them any relief from taxes. They thought the act was full of new problems and new taxes. So it threatened to finally destroy American liberties. Becoming desperate, the people in this province [Massachusetts], New York, Pennsylvania, and in all the colonies, united and decided that they would never allow the tea to be unloaded. They would risk any danger instead of giving in to the tax. Giving in would lead them into complete slavery. It would have been impossible for a genius or the wise King to think of a better way of making the colonies angry or of helping them feel united.

Source: Part of a letter written by Thomas Cushing, Samuel Adams, John Hancock, and William Phillips, members of Boston's Committee of Correspondence, to Benjamin Franklin in London on December 21, 1773, justifying the Boston Tea Party. [Changed for easier reading.] Found at dp.la/primary-source-sets/road-to-revolution-1763-1776/sources/11

Document 5: Lord North Speech

For five, six, or seven years the town of Boston has always been the ringleader. They are the ones to cause all of the problems, the complaining, and troubles.... In the end of 1772 ... they started holding town meetings to talk about their rights and their complaints. They started correspondence with the country towns in the area. They wanted to wake up and relight the flame [of revolution] which looked to them at that time like it was nearly going out. Since then there has been nothing but chaos and confusion. Almost all of it has started, and all at last winning out without opposition in the town of Boston.

Source: Part of a speech given by Lord North, a member of Parliament, to Parliament on March 14, 1774, after the Boston Tea Party, to introduce the Boston Port Bill that closed Boston Harbor. [Changed for easier reading.] Found in William Warner's book *Protocols of Liberty*, written in 2013.

Document 6: New York Resolution

Resolved, that all acts of the British Parliament that tax the colonies are unfair and unconstitutional. The act that closes the port of Boston is senseless and oppressive. It is the most limiting and abusive in its use of power. It goes against every idea of British liberty. So, it should be hated by all good men.

Resolved, that punishing separate colonies is more dangerous to American liberties than punishing them together. So, it is the duty of all the colonies ... to help a sister colony in trouble in every way that makes sense. They must especially help when the punishment is meant to scare others from helping....

Resolved, that delegates from the colonies meet to talk about the ways of getting help for our problems. That is the wisest thing that could be done in this upsetting crisis.

Resolved, that if congress starts a boycott of goods from Great Britain, it should be followed very carefully by everyone. A boycott that is only followed by some people, like the last boycott, will not work. That would only cause more harm to all the colonies.

Source: Part of a resolution passed by the New York assembly on July 19, 1774, in response to the British occupation of Boston

after the Boston Tea Party. Part of the resolution was to call for a Continental Congress. [Changed for easier reading.] Found at www.loc.gov/teachers/classroommaterials/presentationsandactivities/presentations/timeline/amrev/rebelln/proceed.html

Document 7: Massachusetts Resolution

If these actions are followed carefully, they will, in our opinion, have an effect. No wagons will be allowed to load in ... any town in this region on their way to Boston if their load has anything [useful to British soldiers] or oats. The only exception would be if the driver can get a paper from the committee of correspondence for the town where he loaded. The paper must show his name and the place where he lives. It must give the details of his load. The paper must also show the person who is sending the load and the person who will get the load in Boston. The paper should be shown to one or more members of the committee of correspondence of Boston before the driver starts to unload.

Source: Part of the notes taken during a meeting of the Committees of Correspondence of Boston and eight other Massachusetts towns, February 25, 1775, during the British occupation of Boston. [Changed for easier reading.] Found at dp.la/primary-source-sets/road-to-revolution-1763-1776/sources/12

Document 8: Palmer Note

To all friends of American liberty. Be it known, that this morning, before the break of day, a brigade [large group] of about 1000 or 1200 [British soldiers] landed in Cambridge. They marched to Lexington, where they found a small group of our colonial militia armed with weapons. They shot at them without any reason, killed six men, and wounded four others. In a letter from Boston, we found out another brigade is now marching from Boston, supposed to have 1000 men. The person bringing this letter, Trial Brisset, has been asked to warn the country, all the way to Connecticut. All people are desired to give him fresh horses if they are needed. I have spoken with several [people] who have seen the dead and wounded. Please let the delegates from this colony to Connecticut see this note. They know Colonel Foster, one of the delegates.

J. Palmer, one of the committee.

Source: An excerpt from a note written by J. Palmer of the Worcester, Massachusetts, Committee of Correspondence passed through the Philadelphia, Pennsylvania, Committee of Correspondence on April 24, 1775, and circulated by the Williamsburg, Virginia, Committee of Correspondence on April 29, 1775. [Changed for easier reading.] Original found at americainclass.org/sources/makingrevolution/crisis/text8/vacommlexingtoncroncord.pdf

Document 9: Albany Letter

We are sorry about the sad event which caused the blood of our brothers in Massachusetts to flow. But we feel the pride that every honest American must feel at the glorious stand you have made. We have more pride to think that this event will unite every American in feelings and unity. We hope this unity will not be broken up by our enemies. This afternoon the people of this city met and all repeated their old promise. They would cooperate with our brothers in New York and in the other American colonies. We will stop the British plan now being carried out against us.... We are completely sure that every district in this large county will follow our example. On the 22nd of this month, a provincial congress will meet and we are sure that useful help will be given to you. We will teach tyrants and their minions that we were born free and we will live and die free. We will pass on that valuable blessing to our children. Be sure, gentleman, that nothing that we do will make you doubt that we feel strongly about the need for unity. We need to cooperate with you in this hard struggle for liberty with all of our power. The person carrying this letter, Captain Barent Ten Eyck, who is sent quickly, has our orders to show it to the other committees on his way to the town where the enemy is camped. That is why it is not sealed. We ask that you give us as detailed an account of the last battle as you can. We beg you to give us directions so that we may get information about every important event as soon as possible. We are gentleman with the warmest wishes and most fervent prayers for your success, safety, and the success of the common cause.

Your most humble servant
By order of the committee
Abraham Yates Jr. Chairman

Source: Part of a letter signed by Abraham Yates Jr., chairman of the Albany, New York, Committee of Correspondence sent to the Boston Committee of Correspondence on May 1, 1775, 2 weeks after the Battles of Lexington and Concord. [Changed for easier reading.] Found at archive.org/stream/MinutesOfTheAlbany-CommitteeOfCorrespondence1775-1778Vol1/MinutesOfTheAlbanyCommitteeOfCorrespondence1775-1778Vol1_djvu.txt

Original Evidence

The following document is included earlier in a modified format. Because the original is not easily accessible online I have included the original here.

Document 5: Lord North Speech

For five, six, or seven years the town of Boston has always been the ringleader and the one to cause all of the disorders, the discontents, and disturbances .... They, Sir, in the end of 1772 ... began to hold town meetings to talk about the rights, and of their grievances. They started correspondence with the country towns in the province, to revive and rekindle the flame which looked to them at that time like it was nearly going out. Since then there has been nothing but disorder and confusion, almost all starting, and all at last winning out without opposition in the town of Boston.

Source: Lord North, speech to Parliament on March 14, 1774, after the Boston Tea Party, to introduce the Boston Port Bill that closed Boston Harbor. Found in William Warner's book *Protocols of Liberty*, written in 2013.

Graphic Organizer

Committees of Correspondence

Committees of Correspondence that were created in cities and towns of every colony used common tactics in their patriotic causes. As you analyze the documents, consider how the context of the time period (the physical environment, social values, and political events that were happening) influenced the content of the documents. Also consider the common tactics used to promote patriotic causes. Seek common language and tactics used by committees from different communities. What lessons can be drawn about the role of collaboration in promoting change? After analyzing the documents, answer the questions below.

Doc	Source information (genre, author, purpose, audience)	Summary (what are the main ideas/stories from this source?)	How does the (Big C and Little C) context influence the document?	What common tactics can be seen across the different committees?
1				
2				
3				
4				
5				
6				
7				
8				
9				

1. How did the context of these documents influence what the authors said and how they said it?
2. How did Committees of Correspondence organize their actions? What tactics did they use? What evidence did you see of their success?
3. How did they retell stories and events in order to promote their causes?
4. What lessons can be drawn about the role of uniting with like-minded peers in promoting change?

Sample Classroom Poster

IMPORTANT PARTS OF THE HISTORICAL CONTEXT
1. Physical context (land, weather, distances, other conditions)
2. Social context (how different groups interacted, norms, expectations, values)
3. Technological and material context (technologies and other things they had or didn't have)
4. Political context (who was in power, laws, policies, organizations)
5. Economic context (who had money; how things were made, moved, bought, sold)
6. Linguistic context (what words meant then)
7. Personal context (what people were like who were involved)
8. Historiographic context (how people viewed the past at the time)
9. Comparative contexts (how different contexts can help us understand this time period)

CHAPTER 5

Samuel Gompers and the American Federation of Labor

Studying the Committees of Correspondence reveals how like-minded individuals collectively sparked a political revolution that resulted in the creation of the United States of America. Seventy-five years later, serious problems threatened the safety and well-being of many of the workers in that nation. They found solutions through the formation of labor unions. This chapter includes materials for an investigation of labor unions, Samuel Gompers, and the American Federation of Labor.

STUDENTS' BACKGROUND KNOWLEDGE

Students live in a world where many employees work 8-hour shifts and have weekends off from work. Jobs are relatively hazard-free and often include benefits such as health insurance, paid vacation time, and retirement plans. Workers enjoy a minimum wage and are often paid overtime if they are asked to work more than 40 hours in a week. It might be difficult for students to imagine a time when the benefits that workers enjoy today were only a dream of laborers. Working conditions were deplorable during the Industrial Revolution.

The grand historical narrative often includes the story of industrial leaders like Andrew Carnegie, J. P. Morgan, and John D. Rockefeller. However, sometimes missing from the narrative is the story of the common men and women workers who provided the human capital behind the Industrial Revolution and who shaped the structure of labor today. In order to fully understand the impact of the Industrial Revolution and the resulting progressive reforms, students need to have a basic understanding of the role of labor unions. Some students are unfamiliar with the structure or purpose of unions or with collective bargaining, though most have a basic knowledge of strikes. Students have rarely thought deeply about the personal sacrifices involved in union membership or in striking, however. Nor have most students reflected on the controversies surrounding unions, particularly during the 19th century, or of the opposition to the reforms they promoted. These reforms seem like common sense and are taken for granted today. Students may need some basic instruction on the economic systems of socialism, communism, and capitalism and of class conflict in order to understand the different responses to labor unions both historically and today.

HISTORICAL BACKGROUND FOR TEACHERS AND STUDENTS

Background of Industrialization and Unions

The Industrial Revolution brought major changes to the United States. Before the Industrial Revolution, most Americans were farmers. Those who worked in manufacturing usually labored in a small business. Most businesses had one or two employees who were usually family members or neighbors. Goods were made by hand, one by one, in small shops near the business owner's house. Some of the most tedious tasks, spinning thread and weaving fabric, were also done by hand. Many people thought that spinning and weaving were women's work.

The Industrial Revolution changed the way things were made. Borrowing technology from England, Americans began to build mills. In mills, water-powered machines spun thread and wove fabric. Later, machines were invented that could make all kinds of things. Eventually, steam power replaced water power. This change allowed larger mills to be built. These new, more powerful factories made things even faster. Factories were built in every city. They needed lots of workers. The days when the shopkeeper worked side by side with his children or neighbors were gone. Now factory owners competed fiercely with other factory owners. And they employed strangers rather than family members or friends. The skills of building things by hand had once taken years to learn. Now workers labored on assembly lines. Their jobs could be learned in minutes.

In order to compete, factory owners had to keep their cost of making things low. One way they did this was by paying their workers low wages. And machines were expensive. When they were not running, business owners did not make any money. So, factories were opened for long hours at least 6 days each week. Safety features for machines were not used because they were expensive and slowed production. That meant factories were dangerous places. Factory workers felt the effects of the business owners' drive for efficiency. They worked many hours for low wages in unsafe places. Many business owners did not care very much about the strangers who worked in their factories. They looked at them like they looked at their machines. They cared little about their personal lives or the suffering that work created.

Over time, workers began to ask for better conditions. The factory owners usually said no. A single worker who complained to his boss or asked for a raise was fired and "blacklisted." People who were blacklisted were labeled troublemakers. Other factory owners would not hire them. Unskilled assembly-line workers who did not do what the owner wanted could easily be replaced by immigrants, who all needed jobs. It seemed like employers had every advantage. What could workers do?

In time, workers found that they could have more power if they approached their bosses in large groups. They began to form labor unions. A labor union is a group of workers, usually within the same job, who unitedly demanded higher pay and better working conditions. Bosses could not fire all of their employees. The size and number of unions grew in the United States during the late 1800s and early 1900s. Members of labor unions would stand together to place demands on factory owners. They would sometimes threaten to strike—to stop working until the employer raised their wages or reduced the hours they had to work. Sometimes they even went on strike. Most strikes ended unsuccessfully. However, sometimes union members gained some of the changes they wanted.

Fighting between factory owners and their workers led some people to think about the economy in new ways. Three ideas about the economy became important as union leaders chose their goals and tactics. In the first idea, a *capitalist* system, people or groups own factories. They compete freely with other factory owners. This system is supposed to keep wages and prices in balance without government involvement. The United States has mostly followed capitalism. In the second idea, a *socialist* system, the government has laws that control businesses. They have rules that make rich factory owners share more of their money with the poor workers. In the third idea, a *communist* system, the workers or government take control of businesses. Profits are supposed to be shared equally by the workers. Some conservative labor union leaders thought that adding some socialist ideas would improve the capitalist system in the United States. More radical union leaders favored socialism. The most extreme union leaders liked communism. As labor unions grew, many people opposed them. They were worried about the radical changes that some union leaders wanted. They did not like the violent tactics that some union members used. They confused some union members with anarchists who wanted to overthrow the government.

Samuel Gompers and the American Federation of Labor

Samuel Gompers was born in England in 1850 during the early years of the Industrial Revolution. His father was a skilled cigar maker. As a boy, Gompers learned his father's trade. Gompers came to the United States with his family in 1863. He continued to roll cigars. When he was 14 years old, he joined a cigar makers' union. He enjoyed talking with his older coworkers about socialism and unions. In 1875, Gompers was elected president of his local cigar makers' union. In 1881, he started the Federation of Organized Trades and Labor Unions. This union grew into the American Federation of Labor (AFL).

The AFL was a union of unions. It united many different unions that had the same beliefs and tactics. The AFL was for skilled workers. Unskilled workers' unions were not part of it through most of its history. Membership in the AFL grew slowly at first. It competed with other unions like the Knights of Labor. However, over time, the AFL grew in size and influence.

Unlike some other unions, AFL members did not want a socialist revolution. They supported capitalism, with some changes. They worked for better wages and working conditions. AFL members argued that workers should receive a fair share of the money that businesses earned. They thought workers should be treated well and work in safe places. They organized boycotts of some companies that were unfair to their workers. A boycott is when many people unite and stop buying things from someone. They made lists in the newspapers of companies to boycott. They called them "We Don't Patronize" lists or "Unfair" lists. By 1900, the AFL was the largest group of unions in the United States. By 1920 it had over 4 million members. Samuel Gompers was elected its president every year except one from 1886 until his death in 1924.

Gompers and the AFL were opposed by business owners, government officials, and more radical unions. Government leaders usually took the side of business owners. They sometimes used the army or police to end strikes. The courts, too, usually ruled against the workers. The Sherman Antitrust Law was used against labor unions. It was originally passed to stop businesses from forming monopolies. The courts ruled that unions were monopolies of workers. Courts ordered the AFL to stop some of its boycotts. The AFL sometimes broke the judges' orders. Gompers and other AFL leaders were charged with crimes. Opposition to the AFL and other unions grew in 1917 after the Bolshevik Revolution. In this revolution, communists took control of Russia. Some Americans were afraid that unions promoted socialism, communism, and anarchy. They thought communists might take over America. This time was called the First Red Scare. It lasted in the United States from 1917 until 1920. During the First Red Scare, Americans were even more worried about unions. In 1919, anarchists mailed bombs to government leaders. Some people thought labor unions had planned this attack.

When Gompers died in 1924, he had watched the union grow in size and importance. He had led the union through financial problems. He led the AFL through social changes and World War I. He led it as laws changed and technology grew. He led it through changing labor and market conditions and during the First Red Scare. He was one of the country's most important union leaders.

HISTORICAL THINKING SKILLS: HISTORICAL EMPATHY

What was it like to be an unskilled laborer or craftsman at the turn of the 20th century? How did it feel to be a business owner in a world of rapidly changing economic conditions and intense competition? How did rural Americans feel about the strikes and boycotts that inconvenienced their lives by disrupting access to goods they needed? Historical empathy is the ability to understand the decisions and actions of historical figures based upon their context, values, and priorities (Davis, 2001). Historical empathy has a cognitive aspect, imagining (within the constraints imposed by historical evidence) the conditions that influenced people's decisions. Historical empathy also carries an affective or emotional aspect, acknowledging the feelings resulting from historical conditions, events, and interactions (Endacott & Brooks, 2013). Historical empathy requires an understanding of the perspectives of historical figures, even those with whom one may disagree. If a student of history is to really understand past conditions and events, historical empathy has to be applied when analyzing the actions of both those individuals who they naturally empathize with, and those whose actions are more difficult to understand given 21st-century perspectives. This process is not intended to justify the evil actions of historical figures, but to try to understand why they may have considered their acts good, fair, wise, or desirable at the time.

Historical empathy is a thinking process that may have implications for civic engagement, though little has been done to research such transfer. For instance, one who engages in historical empathy acknowledges the past as a very different place from the present, weighing evidence and contextual factors in order to understand seemingly irrational actions (Foster, 2001). Such thinking requires open-mindedness and an appreciation of the sensibility of historical figures. Civic engagement is enhanced when individuals appreciate the context from which political opponents approach current issues and problems. The values, priorities, and actions of others can best be understood when considering their context and perspective. Instead of an opponent being seen as a villain, he/she can be viewed as a rational colleague, with insights and goals worthy of consideration. Practicing historical empathy might prepare young people to engage in civic empathy, which may result in greater civility in political discourse, enhanced collaboration, richer deliberation, and better governance. Students' ability to transfer historical empathy into civic empathy is likely to increase as teachers talk with them explicitly about both strategies.

LESSON IDEAS

Introduction

The following materials could be used in a lesson taught during a unit on the Industrial Revolution and Progressive Era. If a course is organized thematically, this lesson could instead be taught with other lessons about the tool of collective action, uniting with peers, in civic engagement.

Objectives

This lesson is designed to meet three objectives associated with knowledge, skills, and dispositions:

1. Students will describe the goals of labor unions, analyze their tactics, and explore the reasons that many people opposed them.
2. Students will engage in historical empathy, imagining the perspectives, feelings, and worldviews of both union leaders and those who opposed them.
3. Students will describe the political power that comes when groups of like-minded individuals coordinate their efforts to promote sound policies. Students will be inclined to seek out or create such groups when reform is needed.

Build Background Knowledge

Start the lesson by building students' background knowledge on the working conditions that led to the formation of unions in the United States. The material provided in this chapter under the headings "Background of Industrialization and Unions" and "Samuel Gompers and the American Federation of Labor" describe the broad and immediate context of this investigation. These essays provide a basic overview of the things students will need to know in order to work with the documents that follow.

Ask Historical Questions

Good questions guide historical inquiry. The background information provided above and the documents that follow were designed to help students ask and answer the following question: How did union leaders and those who opposed them demonstrate a commitment to "American values?" In order to address this question, students will consider the following questions as well: What conditions prompted the creation of unions like the AFL? Why did so many Americans oppose the work of unions? Why did government officials and courts side against workers when their demands and tactics seem so reasonable by today's standards? How did Samuel Gompers and the AFL attempt to win support for union goals? What are "American values?"

Provide Strategy Instruction and Model Historical Empathy

The following documents provide opportunities for students to evoke historical empathy toward two perspectives—that of the workers and that of those who opposed labor reforms. Students naturally feel historical empathy toward the downtrodden worker. The writing of Gompers and other union leaders in Documents 1, 6, 7, 8 and 9 will help them understand more deeply the thinking, feeling, goals, and perspectives of union members. The perspective of government officials, judges, strike breakers, and common folks who opposed labor reforms might be more difficult for students to empathize with. Yet, if students are to fully appreciate the enormity of labor reforms achieved in part by labor unions, they must understand the context in which the majority of Americans, or at least those in positions of power, opposed unions.

Document 5 provides a good example of the attitudes of mainstream Americans toward unions. The teacher might consider modeling historical empathy with this document before having students work in groups on other documents. To do so, the teacher might project an image of Document 5, including the source information, in front of the class. The teacher could then read the source, pausing to think about the author. The teacher might then do a Google search of William A. Quayle, finding that there is a biography on Wikipedia. The teacher might model for students the effective use of Wikipedia, including when it is appropriate. For example, he/she might point out that Wikipedia is usually accurate enough when the stakes are low and when someone does not want to take a lot of time to find information. Using Wikipedia, the teacher can learn or infer the following about Quayle: He was an intelligent and successful man. He had a doctoral degree and was an ordained bishop in the Methodist Episcopal church, a popular, mainstream faith. He published a dozen essays and had two honorary doctoral degrees conferred upon him.

Looking again at the source of Document 5, the teacher can recall from the background information that this speech was given during the time period now called the First Red Scare. The teacher might speculate out loud for students, "Maybe Quayle, like many Americans in 1920, was caught up in what would become known as the First Red Scare, the fear that communists might overthrow the U.S. government." After considering the source and context, the teacher might begin to read the document, pausing to analyze some statements. For instance, when Quayle argued that "it is our duty as American citizens to accept the challenge and in our strength rise up and crush the foe to our most cherished ideals," he undoubtedly believed that unions threatened

America's ideals. Events from a few years earlier in Russia demonstrated that such a revolution was a threat.

The teacher could model for students how to complete the graphic organizer at the end of the chapter while analyzing Document 5. The graphic organizer has notes included in the cells related to Quayle's 1920 speech. The partially completed graphic organizer might be given to students to model note-taking and to provide support for their thinking. Alternatively, a teacher might model how to make written annotations on the document itself and to highlight or underline evidence in the speech that is associated with the historical question being interpreted.

Students can also be shown through modeling that Quayle's speech shows that he made no distinction between Gompers's relatively conservative AFL, more radical unions, and anarchists who had engaged in a bombing campaign the previous year. Later, as students are working in groups, they might notice that Gompers's reply in Document 6 hints at his frustration with Quayle's lumping of all unions together, as he asks Quayle repeatedly to learn about the AFL. Additionally, Document 4, a political cartoon published in the *New York Evening Post*, corroborates Quayle's concerns, suggesting that other Americans held similar fears that labor unions (all lumped into the same class) were leading America step by step into chaos.

Depending on the needs of the students, the teacher could also model historical empathy using Documents 2 and 3. These documents are useful for showing the thinking and feeling of AFL leaders and court officials who opposed them. They show the cat-and-mouse play between the courts and AFL leadership. Document 2 is a court injunction banning the AFL from publishing in its newspaper, *American Federationist*, "We Don't Patronize" lists that encouraged a boycott of the Bucks Stoves and Ranges Company of St. Louis, Missouri. Document 3, from a subsequent publication of the *American Federationist*, ignored the court order by announcing the court verdict as news, with bold print subtly encouraging the boycott to continue. The courts were not amused, and Gompers and two other board members were convicted of contempt of court and sentenced to prison terms. Gompers appealed the case to the Supreme Court and was acquitted on a technicality. The documents demonstrate the perspective of the courts, Gompers, and the AFL in relation to the court verdict, which they believed was an unconstitutional violation of free speech. As students engage in historical empathy, they must attempt to imagine and feel the perspectives of union leaders, government officials, business owners frustrated by union activity, and common people, inconvenienced by boycotts and strikes.

Group-Work

After this introduction, the teacher can have students analyze the remaining documents independently or in small groups. It can be helpful during this time to remind students about their objective: to use evidence from the documents to identify how both union leaders and those who opposed them believed that their actions demonstrated a commitment to "American values."

Debriefing

At the end of the lesson a debriefing is an effective way to allow students to share their ideas and to critique their peers' interpretations. The debriefing holds three purposes associated with the three objectives of the lesson. First, students can discuss the *knowledge* they have gained about the AFL and its role in improving working conditions and raising wages with questions such as the following:

1. What working conditions prompted the formation of unions?
2. What were the main tactics of unions? Which tactics do you think were most effective? Which tactics are used by unions today?
3. Why was there opposition to unions? Why does there continue to be opposition to unions?

A second phase of the debriefing can focus on the *skill* of historical empathy with the following questions:

1. How does historical empathy help us consider how both union leaders and those who opposed them demonstrated a commitment to "American values?"
2. Why do you think it is easier to experience historical empathy for some historical characters (the workers) than others (the business owners and government officials who opposed unions)?
3. How can imaginative work like historical empathy help someone today understand the priorities of his/her political opponents and help him/her engage civilly with them?

The third phase of the debriefing can focus on the *disposition* of working together to promote a cause:

1. How did labor unions like the AFL build unity among workers? How might similar tactics be used today to form and inspire groups of like-minded individuals behind a common cause?
2. What were some of the similarities and differences between the Committees of Correspondence and labor unions?
3. What are current examples of special interest groups through which individuals have united in

order to increase their political power? What can be learned from their tactics?
4. How might modern technology have been used by unions? How do they use it today?

INSTRUCTIONAL MATERIALS

Nine primary source documents are included in the pages that follow in a format that is modified for students. Links are provided to the original documents. The graphic organizer that follows provides a place for students to record their ideas about the documents and the evidence they contain as they consider how both union leaders and those who opposed them demonstrated a commitment to "American values." Teachers could have students highlight and annotate their documents instead of using the graphic organizer.

Document Set

1. Part of *Labor's Bill of Grievances*, written by Gompers and the executive board of the AFL and sent to President Theodore Roosevelt, March 21, 1906 (Gompers et al., 1906)
2. An excerpt from a court injunction prohibiting Gompers and the AFL from boycotting, issued December 18, 1907 (*Gompers v. Bucks Stove & Range Co.*, 1911)
3. An excerpt from a newspaper article in *American Federationist*, published by the AFL in September 1908 after the court injunction (*American Federationist*, 1908, p. 686)
4. A political cartoon created by Sidney Joseph Greene for the *New York Evening Telegram*, November 1, 1919, during the First Red Scare (Greene, 1919)
5. An excerpt from a speech given by William A. Quayle, a Methodist Episcopal bishop as recorded in *Baltimore American*, February 11, 1920 (Quayle, 1920)
6. An excerpt from a letter written by Samuel Gompers to William A. Quayle, February 14, 1920 (Gompers, 1920a)
7. An excerpt from a letter written by Samuel Gompers to William A. Quayle, May 22, 1920 (Gompers, 1920b)
8. An excerpt from an article entitled "The Challenge Accepted: Labor Will Not Be Outlawed or Enslaved" in *American Federationist*, a newspaper published by the AFL, April 21, 1921 (*American Federationist*, 1921)
9. *Labor's Reward*, a silent film sponsored by the AFL in 1925 (Manning, 1925)

Simplified Evidence

Document 1: AFL Grievances

The people who signed this paper are the Executive Council [leaders] of the American Federation of Labor. We and those who support us in making this document, give to you the reasons we are upset. . . .

The eight-hour work law has been seriously and often broken. The violations have been told to the leaders of many [government] departments. They have not done things to enforce it. . . .

To help all of our people, and to do what almost all of them want, we have asked Congress for some real solution to the constantly growing evil of encouraged and unwanted immigration. But nothing has happened. . . .

Laws were passed to protect the people against monopoly in the making of goods and against unfairness in the shipping of those things. But these laws have been changed and applied to workers. These laws attack and take away workers' personal liberty as guaranteed by the Constitution. Our repeated tries to stop Congress from doing this have not worked. . . .

Labor unions tell you about these problems because you are the representatives who can make laws or not make laws. The workers ask you as your fellow-citizens. Because of their place in life, they have not only cared the same about our country as all other citizens, but are also the workers and wage-earners of America. As the workers' representatives, we ask you to fix these problems. You have the power to do so.

Very respectfully, Samuel Gompers
[followed by nine other names]

Source: Parts of *Labor's Bill of Grievances* [problems], written by the executive board of the AFL, including Samuel Gompers and submitted to President Theodore Roosevelt, the president pro tempore of the Senate, and the speaker of the House of Representatives, March 21, 1906. [Changed for easier reading.] Found at www.gompers.umd.edu/Bill%20of%20Grievances%201906.htm

Document 2: Court Order

We make an order to the American Federation of Labor. This order includes Samuel Gompers, Frank Morrison, . . . and John Mitchell. . . . This order also includes all of their representatives, lawyers, and coworkers. It includes everyone helping or working with them. With this order, they are required to stop from agreeing or planning in any way to block or hurt the business of the Bucks Stoves and Ranges company. . . . They must stop until a final decision in this

court case is made. They must stop bothering them in any way. They must not block the sale of the things made by that company. . . . And they must stop supporting any boycott. They must stop printing, publishing, or mailing any document that has or uses the name of the that company. This includes the 'We Don't Patronize,' or the 'Unfair' list. . . . They may not use the name in any other way. This order applies to copies of the *American Federationist*. It also applies to any other printed or written newspapers, magazine, letter, or other document.

Source: Part of a court injunction [demand] stopping Gompers and the AFL from boycotting the Bucks Stone and Range Company, issued December 18, 1907. The AFL would frequently boycott companies who treated union employees unfairly. [Changed for easier reading.] Found at caselaw.findlaw.com/us-supreme-court/221/418.html#f1

Document 3: AFL Boycott

UNLAWFUL BOYCOTT.
Our readers should govern themselves
accordingly and allow all to live unmolested.

Here is something smart and cute from the *Galesburg Labor News*: Whether or not the Manufacturers' Association, who started the suit for the Buck Stove and Range Company, will get what they want is difficult to say. Trade unionists don't think they will. Because no power on earth can force a man to buy something he does not want and an announcement like this is enough to indicate to a union man what not to buy:

It is unlawful for the American Federation of Labor to BOYCOTT BUCK STOVES AND RANGES.

Justice Gould, in the Equity Court of the district of Columbia, on December 17, made the decision to give the company a temporary order that stopped the Federation [AFL] from publishing this firm as

UNFAIR TO ORGANIZED LABOR.

This statement can't be thought to go against the law, because it just says the facts. . . .

Source: Excerpt from *American Federationist*, a newspaper published by the AFL for September 1908 (p. 686) after the courts had ordered an injunction preventing the publication of a "We Don't Patronize" list. [Changed for easier reading.] Found at babel.hathitrust.org/cgi/pt?id=njp.32101045284831;view=2up;seq=18

Document 4: Political Cartoon

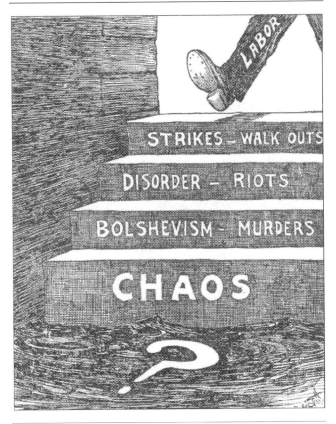

Source: Political cartoon created by Sidney Joseph Greene and published in the *New York Evening Telegram*, November 1, 1919, during the First Red Scare. Found at en.wikipedia.org/wiki/First_Red_Scare#/media/File:Step_by_step_greene.jpg

Document 5: Quayle Speech

By what right does the railroad brotherhood [union] threaten the rest of the nation with hardship, if their own requests are not granted? Who gave the coal miners the right to freeze the nation? I thank God there has risen up to defend the principles upon which our great republic is founded, men like Governor Coolidge. I thank God for the governor of Kansas who took energetic action to defeat the forces of organized labor when their activity threatened to work evil to the citizens he was sworn to protect.... The threat of labor unions is a challenge against all we have and are in government. So it is our duty as American citizens to accept the challenge and in our strength, rise up and crush the enemy to our most loved ideals. Our government is for all the people. It is not for any one class or group.... Who is this Gompers anyway? Who gave him power to tell the people of the land what they could do, or what they must not do? Was his name ever on the ballot of any political party? Did Republican or Democrat ever vote for him at the polls? Away with him and the policies he represents. They will, if continued as far as union leaders want, end political liberty in the land.

Source: Part of a speech given by William A. Quayle, a Methodist Episcopal bishop, in February 1920. The speech was given during the First Red Scare, when many Americans feared that union activity threatened America with communism. The speech was recorded in the *Baltimore American* newspaper, February 11, 1920. [Changed for easier reading.] Found at americainclass.org/sources/becomingmodern/prosperity/text5/lettersbishop.pdf

Document 6: Gompers February Letter

REVEREND SIR:

I cannot believe that you are quoted right [in the newspaper article]. You are a man whose goal in life is to make people better. You are supposed to raise hopes of a future life as a reward for pure living. You are supposed to support honor in all actions. You should not be accused of saying such things.... If you did say what it says you did, it is probably because, unfortunately, you do not know about the goals of the American Federation of Labor. You must not know about its work to raise the standard of citizenship in our country. So I am sending you some documents telling about the goals and purposes of the unions.... After you have read these documents ... will you please tell me what you think about the American Federation of Labor? Is it a danger to our country? If the American Federation of Labor was loyal during the war [World War I], how can it be accused of being a danger in peace times? Why does a citizen need to have been voted for in an election or hold office before he can be heard? The American Federation of Labor is fighting against the stealing of democracy from the people and the start of a dictatorship. Does that make it a danger? All my life I have tried to help my fellowmen and my country, men, women and children. My goal is to bring light into their lives. I have tried to take the children out of the workshop and factory and put them in schools and playgrounds. I want to make their homes more cheerful in every way. I try very hard to make life more worth living. I want to give the workers their rights as citizens. I want them to do the duties and responsibilities they owe to our country and our fellow men....

Yours truly,
SAMUEL GOMPERS
President American Federation of Labor

Source: Part of a letter written by Samuel Gompers to William A. Quayle, February 14, 1920, in response to the news report of a speech Quayle had given criticizing Gompers (see Document 5). [Changed for easier reading.] Found at americainclass.org/sources/becomingmodern/prosperity/text5/lettersbishop.pdf

Document 7: Gompers May Letter

The trade union movement started as a movement of hunger. It was made necessary by conditions. It was in the beginning formed in response to a hunger for enough to eat, enough to keep the body alive. As it became possible to get more food, other hungers needed to be met. People needed unions because they could not get what they needed through any other organization. The demands were for more and better food, for better clothes and for better homes. It required a struggle to fill these needs. A lot of the time, the struggle was most bitter in character. This was because at every step of the way it was necessary to overcome the stubborn opposition of employers who were resolved not to give in and not to give up any of the powers and privileges which they held. Through its whole history, the trade unions' only purpose was to satisfy the hungers and the needs of those who work. It is today no different than it has been. . . . Working people are not pieces of machines to be moved and given jobs or thrown out just because owners want to. The church should be the first to agree when unions say that workers are human beings. They have all of the rights that go with life. And in America the rights that go with life are in theory equal for all the people. As they use these rights, the organized workers sometimes need to strike until they get the proper conditions. I wonder what you have said to those employers [bosses] of the United States who in the past have brought to the United States year after year shipload after shipload of the poor people of southern Europe and of Russia who take the place of American citizens in their jobs, at a wage too low to live like an American. . . . Working people do not strike because they have fun striking, or because they want vacations. To strike means sacrifice. Often it means serious suffering. It always means some hardship which is never fun. The strike is a protest. It is the one argument left to workers who can't find any other way to get help. No other argument will change conditions, which are terrible. The wage-earners don't attack anyone. They attack unfair conditions and they fight to fix those conditions. They try to make life better and finer. They seek to end cruelty and to spread democracy in every possible direction, as our country is committed. I ask you to think more deeply about this and to see if after thinking you won't change your mind.

Source: Part of a letter written by Samuel Gompers to William A. Quayle, May 22, 1920, in response to a letter from Quayle March 17, 1920. [Changed for easier reading.] Found at americainclass. org/sources/becomingmodern/prosperity/text5/lettersbishop.pdf

Document 8: AFL Article

The greatest force in American life that can stop capitalists who harm people is the trade union movement. Trade unions maintain the democratic institutions of the country. The trade union movement . . . protects the values of our country. It protects the people, whose confidence it needs. It protects its own members, whose hopes it is organized to protect. It does this by working hard for the liberty and well-being of the great masses of our people. This is why unions of organized workers fight against all kinds of force. They fight against such things as so-called industrial courts [courts that settle labor disputes]. They fight against the un-American and stinking idea of forced arbitration [making workers settle disagreements outside of courts]. And they fight against the mean, cruel abuse of the writ of injunction [court orders stopping an act]. . . . Because of these things, free, democratic, and helpful labor unions are practically outlawed.

Source: Part of an article entitled "The Challenge Accepted: Labor Will Not Be Outlawed or Enslaved" in *American Federationist,* a newspaper published by the AFL, April 21, 1921, p. 294. [Changed for easier reading.] Found at babel.hathitrust.org/cgi/pt?id=mdp.39015034112923;view=2up;seq=8

Document 9: AFL Movie

Source: Clip from *Labor's Reward,* a silent film sponsored by the AFL in 1925, produced by Rothacker Film Manufacturing Co., with John J. Manning as production supervisor. Found at www. filmpreservation.org/dvds-and-books/clips/labor-s-reward-1925#

Graphic Organizer

Samuel Gompers and the AFL

Use the following graphic organizer to collect evidence as you develop an interpretation of the following question: How did both union leaders and those who opposed them demonstrate a commitment to American values? (You may not have any information to put in some of the cells of this chart. Leave them blank.) Then answer the questions below.

Evidence of priorities of <u>Gompers, the AFL, and unions</u> (and sources)		Evidence of the priorities of <u>those who opposed unions</u> (and sources)	
Evidence of priorities/values	*Source information*	*Evidence of priorities/values*	*Source information*
Selfishness, undemocratic (unelected) leadership	*Bishop Quayle's 1920 speech*	*Well-being of American people (Unions threatened neutral people with hardship)*	*Bishop Quayle's 1920 speech*
		Representation for all people (Unions threaten our government, which represents all people, not just the working class)	*Bishop Quayle's 1920 speech*

1. What conditions prompted the creation of unions like the AFL?
2. Why did so many Americans and government officials oppose the work of unions?
3. How did Samuel Gompers and the AFL attempt to win support for union goals?
4. How did both union leaders and those who opposed them demonstrate a commitment to American values?

PART III

COMPROMISE:
Sacrificing for the Common Good

On February 16, 1820, the U.S. Senate voted to combine two bills that had been debated for weeks. The first would admit Missouri as a new state. Senators from free states had not been pleased with the idea of an additional slave state, upsetting the perfect balance of senators representing northern and southern states. The second bill would shave off part of Massachusetts to create the state of Maine. Senators from southern states opposed this bill for the same reason. Combining the two bills retained the balance of slave and free states and thus maintained an equal number of senators from each region of the country. This action is known as the Missouri Compromise.

Unlike the Missouri Compromise, most compromises in our nation's history are known by titles that downplay the roll of give-and-take in the legislative process. For example, on January 1, 1863, Abraham Lincoln issued a compromise entitled the Emancipation Proclamation, freeing the people held in bondage in states that remained in rebellion. The proclamation did not free all of the slaves, as abolitionists had hoped. Nor did it maintain the status quo, as many poor Whites in the North had hoped. Instead, the proclamation was a carefully drafted compromise balancing the hopes of abolitionists and African Americans with the realities of maintaining the loyalty of border states (slave states that remained in the Union) and many northern soldiers who opposed fighting to liberate the enslaved.

The Missouri Compromise and the Emancipation Proclamation demonstrate the need for political leaders to compromise on tough issues. There has been no more divisive issue in U.S. history than that involved in these two compromises—slavery. Yet compromise was reached. The ability to compromise is a vital tool for civic engagement. It involves seeking common ground that opponents can agree upon, with both sides achieving some objectives, but neither side completely satisfied. The ability to compromise includes knowing when to relinquish some ambitions in order to achieve other goals. Compromise is not the same as surrendering or caving, as some ideologues would call it. Instead, it is a necessary social art that has allowed America to balance tradition and change, freedom and security, isolationism and intervention, and self-interest with the common good. With the diversity of backgrounds and perspectives that exist in the United States, it is unsurprising

that compromise has been essential since the nation's origins.

The founding fathers learned of the need for compromise during the Constitutional Convention. In what is now called the "Great Compromise," delegates from the large states and the small states established a legislative system with two congressional houses, one with equal representation, pleasing the small states, and one with proportional representation, pleasing the populous states. Chapter 6 provides materials for an investigation of this compromise that saved the Constitutional Convention.

Nearly 200 years later, civil rights proponents reached a compromise with conservative political leaders in the passage of the Civil Rights Act of 1964. Civil rights legislation proposed by John F. Kennedy was defeated through a Senate filibuster. A year later, Lyndon B. Johnson led a bipartisan Congress that overwhelmingly passed the Civil Rights Act. It mandated fewer changes than civil rights leaders hoped for, but it reduced discrimination in employment, voting, and public accommodations. Chapter 7 includes materials for an investigation of the process used to reach this historic deal.

U.S. history is full of other examples of compromises that have moved forward important legislation that generally, but not always, had effects that are appreciated in hindsight. For instance, the Compromise of 1850 temporarily settled the issue of slavery as the United States expanded to the Pacific Coast. Franklin D. Roosevelt's Social Security Act and Lyndon B. Johnson's Medicare plan both required compromise and bipartisan support. Some historic compromises are viewed unfavorably today, such as the Compromise of 1877, which ended Reconstruction following the Civil War, and introduced an era of extreme racial discrimination.

U.S. history also reveals times when leaders were unable to compromise, often with tragic consequences. The most obvious failure resulted in the Civil War. The 620,000 dead show the importance of compromising when faced with disagreements. Recent unilateral executive orders, gerrymandering, political power plays, government "shutdowns," and party extremism further illustrate an inability to compromise. For instance, the aptly titled "nuclear option," used by both Democrat and Republican senators in recent years to confirm presidential nominees, has eliminated the tradition of presidents nominating judges who are supported by at least some members of both political parties—compromise appointees.

The polarized political landscape of the 21st century calls for a renewed interest in compromise. The ability to negotiate and make concessions is one of today's most important tools for civic engagement. In fact, researchers at the Conference on Civic Engagement held at Stanford University in 2013 concluded, "constructive participation requires the ability to work with people one disagrees with in a respectful way and in a spirit of progress toward mutually beneficial outcomes" (Malin et al., 2014, p. 17). Democracy depends upon compromise.

A teacher can help students apply the concept of compromise by discussing with them the following questions in connection with the lessons included in Chapters 6 and 7:

- What controversies exist in our classroom, school, or community that might be settled through compromise?
- When disagreements develop within your circle of friends, how do you find a compromise solution?
- How might you convince local, state, or national leaders to compromise in this era of political gridlock?

CHAPTER 6

The Great Compromise

How could people with different backgrounds, perspectives, passions, and values, and who held different social, political, and economic priorities, collaboratively create a system of government that could achieve general approval? The Constitutional Convention brought together men who represented very different communities. Some relied on the labor of enslaved individuals. Others abhorred slavery. Delegates represented states that imported and exported different products. Some came from cities and others from rural areas. Many had completely different ideas about how government should function. Yet over several months, these men were able to create a government system that has held the United States together for over 230 years. This chapter provides materials for an investigation of the "Great Compromise," which satisfied the concerns of delegates from populous and small states, and preserved the process of creating the Constitution.

STUDENTS' BACKGROUND KNOWLEDGE

Students may or may not be familiar with the United States' current bicameral legislature. Those who understand the nature of Congress may or may not know the narrative of its origins, a result of the Great Compromise at the Constitutional Convention. The most familiar narrative goes something like this: Madison proposed the Virginia Plan with representation based on population, Paterson proposed the New Jersey Plan with representation equal, and eventually Sherman proposed the Great Compromise that blended the plans. This sanitized story misses the messiness involved in reaching compromise.

Few students understand the powerful passions of delegates to the Constitutional Convention, all of whom sought the best interests of their home states, and many of whom had been explicitly instructed not to support any change that would weaken their state's position. Few students understand the argument between those who favored a *federal* government (a U.S. government that represented a union of states) and a *national* government (a U.S. government that represented the interests of its citizens directly). These differences made it difficult for principled men, like James Madison, to accept compromise.

Nor do many students understand the context of the Great Compromise. When the compromise was finally passed on July 16, 1787, the Constitutional Convention had been in session for nearly 60 days, with the issue of representation in Congress either being debated explicitly or held in the back of delegates' minds almost every day of the convention. New York's divided delegation had left Philadelphia a week earlier in frustration. Days before the compromise was reached, an outsider read the despair in George Washington's eyes, reminiscent of his expression during the desperate months of Valley Forge (Bowen, 1966). Helping students understand this context helps them recognize the importance of the Great Compromise and of the need for compromise generally.

HISTORICAL BACKGROUND FOR TEACHERS AND STUDENTS

Background of the Constitutional Convention

The colonies declared independence from Great Britain in July 1776. When they did, they got rid of the only government that had united them. The delegates at the Second Continental Congress knew the colonies needed a central government. They wrote the United States' first federal constitution, called the *Articles of Confederation*. They were afraid of the power of the king and Parliament. So, they set up a weak government that represented the states. Each state had one vote in congress. The Articles of Confederation were still being debated and approved by states until a few months before the end of the Revolutionary War. But they held the states together during the war and the first 6 years of the new nation.

A rebellion in Massachusetts and fighting among the states soon made many Americans think that the government was too weak. Alexander Hamilton, James Madison, and many others called for a convention to change the Articles. Support for the meeting grew. The Second Continental Congress agreed that a grand convention should be held in Philadelphia. States began to choose some of the brightest political thinkers as delegates to the convention. In early May 1787, delegates began arriving in Philadelphia. Some came more prepared than others.

Among the most prepared was James Madison. He thought that the federation of states should be replaced by a national government. It would represent the people directly, not the states. Before the convention, he wrote a list of 15 rules for a new form of government. He called it the *Virginia Resolves*. His idea was to create a government different from that under the Articles of Confederation. Madison's friend introduced his plan on the second day of the convention. For the rest of the summer, delegates talked about and debated Madison's ideas and many other proposals.

Though Madison was the best prepared, the other delegates arrived with many ideas about government. Most had been leaders in their colonies and states. And most of them came with instructions from their state assemblies. Delaware's lawmakers feared that the convention might try to weaken the role of small states. They warned the delegates from their state to make sure that each state kept one vote in the new congress. Delegates remembered that they had been asked by the Second Continental Congress, the government at the time, to just fix the Articles. They were not asked to make a whole new government. It is surprising, then, that when Madison's plan was introduced, there was no shock or anger from the other delegates. They probably saw his plan as ideas that could be talked about and changed before any final decisions were made.

Not only was Madison the most prepared for the convention, he was also its best note-taker. He kept a record of almost everything said during the months of the convention. His notes show that many questions were debated and settled relatively quickly. Delegates decided that three branches of government would be best. They created two houses in the legislative branch. They decided to have one person, the president, lead the executive branch. However, they could not agree on representation in the legislature. Massachusetts, Virginia, and Pennsylvania were the states with the most people. They wanted *proportional representation*. This would give states with more residents more representatives in Congress. The new national government would represent the citizens, they argued. Most of the smaller states wanted *equal representation*. They thought that the federal government should represent states, just as it did under the Articles of Confederation. Almost half of the summer was spent talking about this one issue. When the delegates could not reach an agreement, it put the whole convention at risk. Would they give up and go home without agreeing on a new government?

The Great Compromise

The men at the convention knew that they were doing something new and important. Even though most of them understood a lot about government, they had never created a new national government before. They knew that they would need to be open-minded. They would have to think carefully about ideas. They would need to change their minds. Most of their work was done as a *committee of the whole*. Working like one big committee, they held votes that did not really count but were done just to show how people felt about an issue. They decided that even their formal voting could be done again after a new discussion. One historian thinks that maybe the background of the delegates created confident men who were "strong enough to yield" when they heard a better

idea (Bowen, 1966, p. 37). But sacrificing the desires of the states they represented made it difficult for them to give in on the issue of representation in Congress.

A month before the issue was resolved, Roger Sherman of Connecticut made a proposal. He thought Congress should have two houses: one with states equally represented and a second with proportional representation. When he shared his idea, the other delegates did not really think about it. They changed the topic and worked on other issues. When the question was brought up later, Madison's notes show that some delegates got mad. He recorded that Benjamin Franklin reminded them all to stay calm. Once again, they talked about other topics that were easier to agree on. Four days later, William Paterson proposed a new plan. His *New Jersey Plan* sounded better to the small states. But a few days later, the New Jersey Plan was voted down. The tension over representation in Congress grew. Delegates would not give in.

A reason the delegates could not agree was that they had different ideas about the role of government. Madison thought a national government represented citizens rather than states. Only proportional representation made sense if the government spoke for the people. Others thought the federal government represented states. Only equal representation made sense if the government was a federation of states. These two points of view made it hard to compromise. Some delegates were required by their state legislature to oppose proportional representation.

On June 29, Oliver Ellsworth of Connecticut proposed Sherman's idea once again. Madison strongly opposed it. Franklin pled for a compromise to be considered. The delegates became angry again. One said that small states might work with a foreign country against the large states. His statement shocked many of the others. They decided once again to talk about it later. Alexander Hamilton was so mad that he left the convention. A few days later, the others from New York did, too. Luther Martin remembered years later that the issue almost ended the convention (Bowen, 1966). Hamilton later came back as New York's only delegate.

By the time the issue was raised once again on July 14, the delegates were ready to compromise. A committee had studied the issue and liked the compromise. The delegates had worked together for so long. They had invested so much time in the process. The stakes were high. They knew the nation was at risk. Maybe the cooler weather in Philadelphia that day helped. Roger Sherman called for a vote on the compromise again. The debate went on all day. Some delegates thought that if this system turned out to have problems, they could always change it sometime in the future. The next morning, a vote was taken and the compromise passed. Madison and many representatives of the large states still opposed it. But the exhausted delegates did not talk about the issue again. The question of representation in Congress had been answered. The grand convention had been saved. The delegates finished their duty in writing the Constitution. It then went to the states to be ratified or approved.

HISTORICAL THINKING SKILLS: HISTORICAL PERSPECTIVE TAKING

Historical perspective taking is a concept similar to historical empathy, explained in Chapter 5. It consists of an imaginative effort to perceive conditions as another person would. Historical perspective taking allows one to understand the actions of historical characters, even when such actions do not seem sensible from a modern perspective. Some have preferred the use of the term *perspective acknowledgment* over *perspective taking*. *Perspective acknowledgment* suggests an understanding that others perceive things differently. Unlike *perspective taking*, the term implies that no amount of cognitive exertion by an individual will ever allow him/her to assume another's point of view. Though I agree with this assertion, I propose that the cognitive effort required to attempt to engage in perspective taking can better position students of history to understand the actions of others, even if it does not allow them to perceive things precisely as others did.

History educators have listed perspective taking as one of the most basic historical thinking skills (Lee & Ashby, 2001). And students at a young age intuitively understand that two different people who observed the same incident might describe it in distinct ways based upon their background, audience, and purposes (Nokes, 2014). What students of history may not understand is that two disagreeing descriptions of the same event might both be accurate from different points of view. For instance, an individual's perspective influences what he/she pays attention to and what goes unobserved. Perspective influences perception—those things that an individual sees and hears. Perspective impacts inferences made about an observation, such as others' intentions. Perspective influences the way accounts are recorded or shared, with most individuals customizing accounts based not only upon their understanding of the event but on their perception of their audience.

Why is perspective taking important in the study of history? Perspective taking positions students to understand descriptions of the past as *accounts* rather than as unadulterated information to be accepted at face value. Accounts are intentionally produced portrayals of the past. Accounts are found in textbook passages, letters, diaries, telephone conversations, and ranger-led tours. Accounts include political cartoons, paintings, movies, museum exhibits, photographs, video, and countless other texts. Each account represents the perspective of its creator and can be best comprehended and used when remembering that perspective. An understanding of the concept of *perspective* and *account* allows the student of history to be patient with the imperfections of evidence and to appreciate the unique insights inherent in diverse points of view. Perspective taking positions students to deal with discrepancies in accounts in productive ways, rather than in frustration. Such an understanding facilitates, and is facilitated by, the use of other historical thinking strategies, such as sourcing, corroboration, and contextualization.

Why is perspective taking important in civic engagement? Collaboration is necessary for establishing policies and programs that promote the common good. People within a democracy must work civilly with individuals who have different backgrounds, priorities, values, opinions, and needs. Research is lacking in the connection between teaching historical perspective taking and students' ability to engage in civil discourse. However, it seems reasonable that civil collaboration is more likely to take place when individuals appreciate the perspectives of others, viewing others' points of view as assets rather than barriers. It seems that such perspective taking would increase the likelihood of compromise and of individuals sacrificing personal interests for the common good. Just as biased accounts can help historians make interpretations, others' points of view, though biased, might lead to the adoption of mutually acceptable policies.

LESSON IDEAS

Introduction

The following materials could be used during a unit on the American Revolution and early government. If a course is organized thematically, this lesson could instead be taught in connection with other lessons on the role of compromise in civic engagement.

Objectives

This lesson is designed to meet three objectives associated with knowledge, skills, and dispositions:

1. Students will explain the disagreement between populous and small states that led to the Great Compromise and the structure of the United States' legislative branch.
2. Students will practice the historical thinking strategy of perspective taking, and analyze the perspectives of delegates from populous states and small states in the debate over the structure of Congress that occurred at the Constitutional Convention.
3. Students will explain how compromise is possible, even when political opposition is strong.

Build Background Knowledge

Begin the lesson by building students' background knowledge on the events leading up to the Constitutional

Convention and the Great Compromise. The essays provided in this chapter under the headings "Background of the Constitutional Convention" and "The Great Compromise" provide a basic overview of what students will need to know in order to work with the documents that follow.

Ask Historical Questions

The background information provided above and the documents that follow were designed to help students ask and answer the following question: How did the delegates at the Constitutional Convention work through their disagreements to reach a compromise? In order to address this question, students may need to consider additional questions: How did the differing perspectives of delegates from populous and small states lead to disagreements at the Constitutional Convention? What type of dialogue was likely to lead to compromise? What types of dialogue decreased the likelihood of compromise?

Provide Strategy Instruction and Model Perspective Taking

The documents that follow hold opportunities for students to consider the biases and disagreements associated with two perspectives that stood in opposition. The documents are intended to help students understand the process that produced the Great Compromise, a development that occurred in spite of the passions of delegates, which were based in large part on their perspectives. Stated simply, delegates from the small states, as represented in Documents 1 and 3, perceived the large states as a threat to their freedom and safety. In contrast, delegates from the large states, as represented in Documents 2, 4, and 7, viewed the delegates from the small states as barriers to the establishment of a national government based upon fair principles. Documents 5 and 6, from Benjamin Franklin, call for compromise, and represent a moderate perspective. Document 8 shows how battle-wearied delegates grudgingly accepted the Great Compromise.

The teacher should first introduce the concept of *perspective taking* to students. The teacher might need to define *perspective* as the way someone sees something from where he/she is located. The teacher might ask several students to describe something they can see, such as the door of the classroom or the teacher's computer, from their perspective. The teacher should selectively choose students who have a different view of the object. Next, the teacher might ask a student to describe how another student in a different location in the room sees the object. The teacher can then define this as *perspective taking*—imagining how another person sees something from a different perspective.

The teacher might next explain that perspective taking is not limited to the way we see things. It also has to do with the way we think about things that happen. To illustrate,

the teacher might ask students to think about and write down the most important thing that happened at the school in the past week. It is likely that different students in the class would write different events as the most important. For someone, it might be an AP test. For another, it might be opening night of the school play. For another, it might be an accident that happened in the school parking lot. It might be a basketball game, a choir concert, or even a surprising text message the person received. The point is that just as people see things differently based upon where they are located, they also think about things differently based upon their values, priorities, interests, friends, and background. If a student could guess what another person in the class wrote as the most important event of the week, he/she would be engaging in perspective taking—trying to understand events as someone else thinks about them. Historical perspective taking is more difficult because it involves trying to imagine the way people in the past thought about the things going on around them. Historians have to rely on the things historical actors wrote, what is known about their background, and other evidence to try to imagine their perspectives.

The perspectives of most of the delegates at the Constitutional Convention were shaped by their devotion to their home states. Most felt greater loyalty to their states than to a national government. The teacher might model perspective taking by analyzing with the class one or more of the documents, considering the point of view of the person or group who created it. For example, the teacher might project Document 1 in front of the class. It is the resolution passed by Delaware's legislature to send delegates to the Grand Convention. The teacher can then consider the perspective that this document reveals. He/she must first review the source and think about Delaware. In particular, the teacher must consider whether Delaware was a small state or a populous state, recognizing that it was a small state. After considering the source, the teacher might read the document with students. It states explicitly that the delegates from Delaware were not authorized to discuss a change to the then-current system that gave each state a single vote in Congress. This document demonstrates why Delaware's delegation was predisposed to oppose any plan that included proportional representation.

The teacher might go through the same process with Document 2, an outline of the Virginia Plan, pointing out the contrasting perspective it presents. This document shows that the second change Madison proposed was to create a proportional system where representation was based on population. Considered collectively, Documents 1 and 2 show that the issue of representation was on the mind of delegates from both the small states like Delaware and the large states like Virginia. These documents suggest the high priority placed upon this single issue, helping students acknowledge the perspectives of the delegates. The teacher might also point out that Documents 2–8 all come to us from James Madison's notes. Historians debate the degree of objectivity of his notes, though most trust his general accuracy. Students should remember that these documents represent the perspective of the speaker as captured by Madison, a delegate from Virginia.

When the teacher is confident that students understand perspective taking, the students could practice with the other documents. For instance, Documents 3 and 4 elaborate on the perspectives of delegates from small states like New Jersey (Document 3), and populous states like Pennsylvania (Document 4). They reinforce the perspectives of the delegates and demonstrate their commitment to their states' interests. Further, Documents 4 and 5 were both produced by Pennsylvanians, James Wilson and Benjamin Franklin, but show that there were disagreements within state delegations. Unlike Wilson, Franklin favored compromise. Students might consider things that shaped Franklin's perspective, such as his age, his cosmopolitan experience, his reputation of being a wise counselor, and the fact that the convention had been debating the issue for a few more days when he spoke. (He might simply have been so tired of talking about it that he was prepared to compromise.) Document 8, an excerpt of a series of speeches that come from Madison's notes, provides additional opportunities to consider the perspectives of multiple speakers.

Group-Work

Once the teacher is confident students understand perspective taking and how to use the graphic organizer to gather evidence from the documents, he/she can have them analyze the remaining documents independently or in small groups. During group-work or independent work, the teacher should remind students about their objective: to use evidence from the documents to explore the process of delegates moving from conflicting perspectives toward compromise, and to consider the type of dialogue that promoted or interfered with compromise.

Debriefing

At the end of the lesson, during a debriefing, students can discuss the *knowledge* they have gained about the Constitutional Convention and the Great Compromise with questions such as the following:

1. What were the main arguments for equal representation and for proportional representation in Congress?
2. What were the main elements of the Great Compromise? Which parts of it favored the small states and which favored the large states?
3. Why did Madison, sometimes called the Father of the Constitution, oppose the Great Compromise?

A second phase of the debriefing can focus on the *skill* of perspective taking. The following questions might help students debrief:

1. How did the perspectives of the delegates change as the convention continued, allowing them to reach the Great Compromise?
2. Why is it important to remember a person's perspective when listening to his/her account of an event?

The third phase of the debriefing can focus on the disposition to compromise and sacrifice part of what is desired in order to promote the common good:

1. When it is appropriate to compromise and when should someone stick to his/her principles?
2. What are some of the main barriers to compromise? How can these barriers be overcome?
3. How might the ability and inclination to compromise help today's elected officials?

INSTRUCTIONAL MATERIALS

Nine primary sources are included in the pages that follow in a format that is modified for students. Links are provided to the original documents, including James Madison's notes of the convention, the source of documents 2–8. The graphic organizer at the end of the chapter provides a place for students to record their ideas about the evidence the documents contain, the perspectives of delegates from the small and populous states, and the process of reaching compromise.

Document Set

1. Part of a resolution passed by the General Assembly of Delaware appointing and instructing Delaware's delegates, passed February 3, 1787 (Delaware General Assembly, 1937)
2. The first three resolutions of the Virginia Plan, proposed by Virginia delegate Edmund Randolph on May 29, 1787, as recorded in Madison's notes (Madison, 1787)
3. An excerpt from a speech given by New Jersey delegate, William Paterson, June 9, 1787, as recorded in Madison's notes (Madison, 1787)
4. An excerpt from a speech given June 9, 1787, by Pennsylvania delegate James Wilson in response to Paterson (Document 3), as recorded in Madison's notes (Madison, 1787)
5. Part of the remarks written by Pennsylvania delegate Benjamin Franklin and read by James Wilson on June 11, 1787 (Madison, 1787)

6. An excerpt from a speech given by Pennsylvania delegate Benjamin Franklin on June 30, 1787, as recorded in Madison's notes (Madison, 1787)

7. An excerpt from a speech given by Virginia delegate James Madison on July 5, 1787, as recorded in his notes (Madison, 1787)

8. Selected statements made by delegates including Roger Sherman (Connecticut), Luther Martin (Maryland), Elbridge Gerry (Massachusetts), and Caleb Strong (Massachusetts) on July 14, 1787, prior to the vote passing the Great Compromise as recorded in Madison's notes (Madison, 1787)

9. Part of Article 1 of the U.S. Constitution, the product of the Great Compromise (Constitution of the United States, 1787)

Simplified Evidence

Document 1: Delaware Resolution

An act choosing delegates from Delaware to the convention which will be held in Philadelphia. The convention is to revise the Federal Constitution [Articles of Confederation]....

The General Assembly of Delaware, chooses George Read, Gunning Bedford, John Dickinson, Richard Bassett and Jacob Broom, Esquires, delegates from this state. They are to meet in the convention of the delegates of other states, to be held in Philadelphia on May 2.... They are to join with them in creating, thinking about, and discussing, changes and additions that might be needed to make the Federal Constitution work for the way things are in the Union.... These changes must not include that part ... which declares that "in determining questions in the United States in Congress assembled each state shall have one vote."

Source: Part of a resolution passed by the General Assembly of Delaware appointing and outlining the purpose of Delaware's delegates to the Constitutional Convention, passed February 3, 1787. [Changed for easier reading.] Found at press-pubs.uchicago.edu/founders/documents/a1_3_1-2s2.html

Document 2: Virginia Plan

1. Resolved that the Articles of Confederation should be corrected & enlarged to reach the goals of our government. These goals are the "common defense, security of liberty, and general welfare."

2. Resolved therefore that voting in the national legislature should be proportioned to the amount of [each state's] contribution, or to the number of free people, whichever seems best.

3. Resolved that the national legislature ought to consist of two branches.

Source: Part of the first three resolutions of the Virginia Plan, proposed by Virginia delegate Edmund Randolph on May 29, 1787, as recorded in the notes of James Madison. [Changed for easier reading.] Found at www.nhccs.org/dfc-0529.txt

Document 3: Paterson Speech

He said that Virginia, Massachusetts, and Pennsylvania were the three large states and the other ten were small ones. He repeated what Mr. Brearly had said about the unequal votes which would happen. And he repeated that the small states would never agree to it [proportional representation]. He said that it did not make sense that a large state that paid a lot should have more votes than a small one that paid a little, any more than it did to give a rich citizen more votes than a poor one.

New Jersey will never agree with the plan before the committee. New Jersey would be swallowed up. He had rather give in to a king, to a tyrant, than to such a fate. He would not only oppose the plan here [in the convention]. But when he returned home he would do everything he could to defeat it there [during ratification].

Source: Part of a speech given by New Jersey delegate, William Paterson, June 9, 1787, as recorded in Madison's notes. [Changed for easier reading.] Found at www.nhccs.org/dfc-0609.txt

Document 4: Wilson Speech

[Wilson] spoke in detail for proportional representation. He argued that all authority came from the people. So equal numbers of people should have an equal number of representatives. Different numbers of people should have different numbers of representatives. This principle was not followed in the [Articles of] Confederation, because of how desperate they were then....

Aren't the citizens of Pennsylvania as good as those of New Jersey? Does it take 150 from Pennsylvania to equal 50 from New Jersey? Representatives of different places should have the same proportion to each other as the people they represent have to each other. The small states might not agree to this plan. But Pennsylvania and some other states would not agree to any other plan.

Source: Part of a speech given June 9, 1787, by Pennsylvania delegate James Wilson in response to Paterson (Document 3), as recorded in Madison's notes. [Changed for easier reading.] Found at www.nhccs.org/dfc-0609.txt

Document 5: Franklin Written Comments

Mr. Chairman. It has made me happy to see that until now, when we talked about the proportion of representation, our debates happened with great calmness. If anything different has happened now, I hope it will not happen again. We have been sent here to *talk with*, not to *fight with* each other. Saying that we will not change our opinion, does not teach or convince us. Being angry and sure we are right by one side, causes the same from the other side. It creates and enlarges disagreements and division on this important topic. But harmony and union are needed for our councils. It helps them to support and gain what is good for all of us.

Source: Comments written by Pennsylvania delegate Benjamin Franklin and read by James Wilson on June 11, 1787, during a heated debate at the Constitutional Convention, as recorded in Madison's notes. [Changed for easier reading.] Found at www. nhccs.org/dfc-0611.txt

Document 6: Franklin Speech

Doctor Franklin: The difference of opinions [about representation in Congress] come from two points. If proportional representation is used, the small states say that their liberties will be in danger. If equal votes are used instead, the large states say their money will be in danger. When a wide table is being built, and the edges of boards do not fit together, the carpenter trims a little off of both boards. This makes a good joint. In the same way here, both sides need to give up some of their demands. That way they may join in some cooperating plan.

Source: Part of a speech given by Pennsylvania delegate Benjamin Franklin at the Constitutional Convention on June 30, 1787, as recorded by Madison. [Changed for easier reading.] Found at www.nhccs.org/dfc-0630.txt

Document 7: Madison Speech

He thought that the convention had come down to two choices. They could either give up justice to make the smaller states and the minority of the people of the United States happy. Or they could make them angry by making the larger states and the majority of the people happy, as they should. He was sure which choice he thought should be made. The Convention, with justice and the majority of the people on their side, had nothing to fear. But with injustice and the minority on their side, they had everything to fear. It was foolish to make an agreement at the Convention that would cause disagreement among the people of the United States. The Convention should follow a plan which could be carefully looked at. They should follow a plan that would be supported by the educated and fair part of America. This is what they themselves could support and favor. He was not afraid that the people of the small states would be stubborn and refuse to agree to a government based on fair principles, and that promised to protect them. He did not think that Delaware would try to make it separated from the other states, rather than

give in to such a government. He doubted even more that Delaware would be foolish enough to try to get foreign support. This was what one of her representatives [Mr. Bedford] had angrily said. Or if Delaware should try to get foreign support, no foreign nation would be foolish enough to agree to give support.

Source: Part of a speech given by Virginia delegate James Madison July 5, 1787, as recorded in his notes. [Changed for easier reading.] Found at www.nhccs.org/dfc-0705.txt

Document 8: Final Speeches

Mr. Sherman was in favor of the compromise at once. He said it was a peace-making plan. It had been thought about in all its parts. A lot of time had been spent on it. If any part of it was changed now, they would need to go over the whole thing again.

Mr. Luther Martin urged the compromise to be accepted as it was. He did not like many parts of it. He did not like having two branches, nor the inequality of votes in the first branch. But, he was willing to try the plan out rather than not do anything.

Mr. Gerry said he would like [an alternative] plan, but had no hope of success. A change [in government] must take place. And it was apparent from what he had seen that the change [in government] could not happen with any other plan. He was strongly against a partial union, leaving some states in a union and others out, as some delegates had talked about.

Mr. Strong said the convention had been very divided in their opinions. In order to avoid the consequences of it, a compromise had been proposed. A committee had been appointed. And though some of the members of it were against an equal number of votes for the states, a report had been made in favor of the compromise. Everyone agreed that the current government was close to an end. If no compromise was reached, the union itself would soon end. It has been said that if we cannot come to any general agreement, the large states may form and recommend a type of government. But will the small states in that case ever agree to it. It is probable that the large states themselves will in that case accept and agree to it. He thought the small states had given in on the issue of money bills; and that they might naturally expect the other side to also give in on some things. From this perspective, he would vote for the compromise.

Source: Summary of some statements made by delegates including Roger Sherman (Connecticut), Luther Martin (Maryland), Elbridge Gerry (Massachusetts), and Caleb Strong (Massachusetts) on July 14, 1787, in the Constitutional Convention, prior to the vote passing the Great Compromise, as recorded in Madison's notes. [Changed for easier reading.] Found at www.nhccs.org/dfc-0714.txt

Document 9: Article 1

Section. 1.

All legislative powers are given to a Congress of the United States, which will be made up of a Senate and House of Representatives.

Section. 2.

The House of Representatives will be made up of members chosen every second year by the people of each state. . . . Representatives . . . will be numbered among the different States which may be included within this Union, according to their respective numbers [population]. . . .

Section. 3.

The Senate of the United States will be made up of two Senators from each state, chosen by the legislature of the states, for six years; and each Senator will have one vote.

Source: Part of Article 1 of the U.S. Constitution, which resulted from the Great Compromise. The Constitution has been changed so that senators are now elected by the people of each state. [Changed for easier reading.] Found at www.archives.gov/founding-docs/constitution-transcript

Graphic Organizer

The Great Compromise

Most of the delegates to the Constitutional Convention represented the perspective and interests of the states that sent them. Massachusetts, Virginia, and Pennsylvania were populous states. The others had smaller populations. Use the following graphic organizer to outline the position of the small states and the large states. Trace their discussion of the Great Compromise and use the material you have gathered on this worksheet to answer the questions below.

Document	Source	Perspective	Argument	Attitude about the compromise
1		large state small state other:		
2		large state small state other:		
3		large state small state other:		
4		large state small state other:		
5		large state small state other:		
6		large state small state other:		
7		large state small state other:		
8		large state small state other:		
9		large state small state other:		

1. How did the delegates work through their disagreements to reach a compromise?
2. What type of dialogue was likely to lead to compromise?
3. What types of dialogue decreased the likelihood of compromise?

CHAPTER 7

Compromise and the Civil Rights Act of 1964

The Great Compromise may be the most famous compromise in U.S. history, but it is only one of many important policies achieved through compromise. One of the most vital pieces of legislation to come out of the U.S. Congress in the 20th century was the Civil Rights Act of 1964 (Risen, 2014). The act prohibited discrimination in public accommodations, promoted the right of all Americans to vote, prevented discrimination in federally funded programs, and accelerated the desegregation of schools. This act was hotly contested and required a great deal of political wrangling, including bipartisan cooperation, to be passed. This chapter provides materials for an investigation of the compromises involved in the passage of the Civil Rights Act of 1964.

STUDENTS' BACKGROUND KNOWLEDGE

Students' understanding of the civil rights movement is often confined to leaders like Rosa Parks, Dr. Martin Luther King Jr., and perhaps Malcolm X. Most know something about Jim Crow laws and the segregated society that they created, though few understand the extent or the social and psychological effects of such segregation. Students may know something about sit-ins, Freedom Riders, and the March on Washington for Jobs and Freedom. However, most know little about important legislation such as the Civil Rights Acts of 1957, 1960, and 1964, the Voting Rights Act of 1965, or the Fair Housing Act of 1968. Few students understand that many civil rights leaders watched very carefully the work of federal lawmakers and were strategic in timing their protests and activities to influence the passage of laws.

Even more challenging for teachers is helping students understand the social context for civil rights legislation. From a 21st-century perspective, the civil rights movement represents a struggle between good and evil, with those who supported civil rights reform as heroes and those who opposed it as villains. Such a view results from students projecting their worldviews onto a society that saw things very differently. Because overt racism is less common today (in comparison to 20th-century realities), students might believe that there were only a handful of racist fanatics who stood in the way of the goals of civil rights leaders. Such an understanding distorts the epic work of civil rights reformers. Instead, students must understand that the conditions created by Jim Crow perpetuated a racist society. Many things that Americans saw in public reinforced the idea that Whites were superior to Blacks. And many Americans, White and even Black, often held such racist views. The devastating psychological effects of segregation were used by the Supreme Court to justify its *Brown v. Board of Education* decision in 1954. "To separate them [children in grade and high schools] from others of similar age and qualifications solely because of their race generates a feeling of inferiority as to their status in the community that may affect their hearts and minds in a way unlikely to ever be undone," Justice Earl Warren (1954) wrote. The view that Whites were superior to Blacks, now considered by so many as evil, was thought to be a fact by many Americans in 1960, with Jim Crow conditions perpetuating this bigoted view.

Rather than diminishing the success of civil rights reformers, understanding the context of the 20th century makes their successes even more incredible. Reformers were not fighting a handful of evil fanatics; instead, they waged a battle against respected and respectable men and women who were convinced that African Americans were inferior and who supported policies based upon that error. Rather than a battle between good and evil, the civil rights movement is better understood as a contest between reform and tradition, with many good, though misguided, individuals failing to understand the injustice and immorality of their opposition to reform. Throw into this mix the racist fanatics who engaged in lynching and other extreme tactics, and the work of civil rights reformers takes on an even greater dimension. Certainly, the opinions of many Americans were shifting in favor of African American civil rights by 1964, though reformers still faced formidable opposition.

Further, students might misunderstand the complexity of opposition to civil rights legislation. For example, some legislators who were sympathetic to the cause of civil rights opposed civil rights legislation because of their views on the role of government in private business enterprises. Others opposed federal civil rights legislation because of their opposition to federal overreach into state issues, including voting. Some opposed any measures that expanded the authority of the federal government, regardless of the outcome. A handful, primarily from the Midwest, felt little need to become involved in issues that were of little concern to the vast majority of their constituents. Thus, winning the support of many legislators involved not only winning them over to the cause of civil rights but convincing them of the necessity and justification of legislation at the national level that impacted the decisions of private business owners in terms of whom they could hire or accept as patrons.

HISTORICAL BACKGROUND FOR TEACHERS AND STUDENTS

Background of the Civil Rights Movement

For African Americans, the road to freedom and equality was long and difficult. The Thirteenth Amendment freed slaves. African Americans became citizens under the 14th Amendment. The 15th Amendment gave them the right to vote. All three amendments were ratified shortly after the Civil War. Still, Black Americans faced public discrimination and openly unfair treatment through most of the 20th century. Prior to the Civil War, slaves were seen as property. Slave codes made slaves behave as if they were lower than Whites. For a short time after the Civil War, Radical Republicans, who favored giving African Americans more rights, controlled Congress. Union troops in southern states protected those rights. African Americans enjoyed some freedoms and many voted. Some even held political office.

But in time, Union troops left the South. Different lawmakers were elected. African Americans were again treated as second-class citizens. Black codes were passed. They took the place of the old slave codes. The right to vote was taken away from them. Many years of violence and unfairness followed. African Americans struggled for civil rights even as those rights were being taken away. However, racism and tradition worked against them. Some White Americans were not aware of how bad things were for Blacks. As a result, discrimination, segregation, and unpunished violence toward Black Americans continued for many years. The court decision of *Plessy v. Fergusson* in 1896 showed that even a racist Supreme Court approved of *segregation*. Segregation was a policy that separated the races. Blacks could not go to school with Whites. They could not swim in public pools with Whites. They had separate drinking fountains and restrooms. They were treated as second-class citizens.

African Americans fought for civil rights. They saw some success. In 1910, W. E. B. Du Bois and others started the National Association for the Advancement of Colored People. They wanted to improve the sad conditions many Blacks faced. Thousands moved from the South to northern cities where life was better. In the 1920s, jazz musicians and Harlem Renaissance writers praised African American culture. They made African American music, art, poetry, and books more popular. Some White people felt sympathy toward African Americans. Other Whites opposed them even more.

In 1942, James Farmer Jr. and others started the Congress of Racial Equality (CORE). His group fought to end segregation. Six years later, President Truman ended racial segregation in the military. Civil rights leaders won a major victory when the Supreme Court ruled against the segregation of schools in 1954. Still, change was slow. Few southern states obeyed the court's ruling. Segregated neighborhoods in the North led to the segregation of

schools there, too. In spite of small successes like the Montgomery, Alabama, bus boycott in 1955, African Americans still faced big challenges.

Some civil rights laws were passed before the Civil Rights Act of 1964. In 1957, Congress passed a law that protected Blacks' right to vote. However, lawmakers who opposed the bill changed it so that it was hard to enforce. It did not do what reformers had hoped. In 1960, another Civil Rights Act was passed. It was meant to fix the problems with the earlier law. President Eisenhower insisted that schools integrate. He ordered that violence against African Americans be investigated. He demanded that job policies for firms with government contracts be fair. Though better than the 1957 law, the Civil Rights Act of 1960 still disappointed civil rights leaders.

In 1963, most civil rights reformers saw five big problems that minorities faced. First, many Blacks were still denied the right to vote. Second, Jim Crow laws still segregated the South. Laws kept Blacks from restaurants, hotels, swimming pools, and theaters enjoyed by Whites. Third, many schools were still segregated in spite of the Supreme Court's ruling against that. Fourth, Blacks were treated unfairly at work. Many were unemployed. Fifth, Blacks lived in poverty at much higher rates than Whites. Leaders of the civil rights movement hoped that President Kennedy would support a civil rights bill that fixed these five problems.

The Civil Rights Act of 1964

In November 1960, Kennedy was elected president. He promised to support civil rights. But after his election, civil rights became a lower priority for him. He did not do much to support civil rights for his first 2 years in office. He faced some challenges that made it hard for him to act. His Democratic Party was split. The liberal northern Democrats favored civil rights. But the southern Democrats energetically opposed civil rights. The Republican Party was also made up of people who supported some civil right reforms and people who opposed laws that affected businesses or state policies. If Kennedy were to propose a civil rights law, he would anger southern Democrats. Then they might block his other plans. If Kennedy did nothing, he would upset the liberal northern Democrats. The Republicans might take the lead and pass a weaker civil rights law.

Martin Luther King Jr. and other civil rights leaders were upset by the delay. They held a rally in Birmingham, Alabama, to protest Jim Crow laws there. The police attacked protesters, causing international outrage. Kennedy felt he should use federal troops to keep the peace. He was afraid that violence might happen across the South and in northern cities. Kennedy formed a team of advisors who wrote a civil rights plan that he shared with Americans in a speech on TV on June 11, 1963. Over the next weeks, Kennedy met with civil rights leaders. He and his advisors proposed a civil rights bill that would end segregated schools and discrimination in public places. It would also address voting concerns. But it did nothing to solve black poverty. Civil rights leaders were disappointed.

The bill went through many drafts. A subcommittee of the House Judiciary Committee strengthened the bill. Civil rights leaders praised the changes. Conservative Republicans and southern Democrats swore they would oppose it. After Kennedy's assassination, a "compromise bill," like Kennedy's original, passed through the House of Representatives and was sent to the Senate. Southern Democrats in the Senate organized a record-setting filibuster (a long speech made by many people) to slow down the bill. These tactics had weakened the earlier civil rights acts. The Senate had been unable to vote for *cloture* until the earlier bills had been weakened. Cloture meant ending the debate and voting on the bill. It required two-thirds of the Senate.

Many people who did not like the new bill worried about Title II, which outlawed discrimination in public places. They also opposed Title VII, which outlawed discrimination in jobs. They thought that business owners should be free to choose whether or not to discriminate. From March until June, a filibuster continued. Finally, on June 10, 1964, a changed bill had enough support that the vote for cloture passed. On July 2, the House approved the Senate's amended bill. President Lyndon B. Johnson signed it into law later that evening.

HISTORICAL THINKING SKILLS: CHANGE AND CONTINUITY

The investigation in this chapter highlights the ideas of *change* and *continuity*, important concepts in historical thinking (Seixas & Morton, 2013). Sometimes social structures, institutions, policies, practices, technologies, and attitudes endure for long periods of time. Historians study, describe, and explain these *continuities* as part of their interpretation of the past. Sometimes conditions undergo revolutionary or evolutionary modifications. Historians explore the long-range and immediate causes and effects of these *changes*. Some periods of history are marked by rapid changes, referred to as a *turning point*. At other times, changes occur slowly, as evolutionary processes—yet evolving conditions also constitute important and noteworthy change. In contrast, continuities are the primary feature of other periods of time. Most of history includes simultaneous continuities in some conditions and changes in others. Historians reflect on continuity and change either by comparing historical periods or by comparing a historical period with the present. And historians, as well as nonhistorians, often consider changes either *progress* or *decline*.

Historians judge the relative *significance* of change using several criteria. First, was there a dramatic difference between conditions before and after the change? Second, was the change relatively permanent? Third, were the effects of the change felt across a broad spectrum of people, locations, and institutions? Historians judge the significance of continuities using similar criteria. Did the continuities exist over long periods of time, within significant aspects of culture or society, and/or across a broad spectrum of groups? Significant changes and significant continuities are those worthy of attention, investigation, and discussion.

Many factors influence both changes and continuities, with historians debating the relative contribution of each. Sometimes, influential individuals promote changes. Other times, natural or geographic factors contribute to change. Often, change is a result of coincidence or chance. Changes in some features of society might be promoted by other changes. Continuities, too, are influenced by a number of factors. Sometimes, individuals, natural or geographic factors, or coincidence works to promote the status quo.

The civil rights era provides a unique opportunity to consider with students the themes of continuity and change. The civil rights movement represented a clash between forces for change and powerful institutions and people who were committed to continuities, such as a familiar way of life and traditional roles of government. The Civil Rights Act of 1964 represents a compromise between forces for change and forces for continuity. The documents provide evidence of the role of compromise in the process of passing the Civil Rights Act. In addition, conflicting evidence is provided about the degree of change and/or continuity associated with the act.

As students compare the conditions under which African Americans lived in the early 20th century with today's society, there can be little doubt that significant changes have occurred. Comparing the changes brought about by historic events, such as the passage of the Civil Rights Act of 1964, allows students to consider whether such acts should be considered turning points, or whether they were merely part of a more gradual, evolutionary process of change.

An understanding of the concepts of change and continuity can be useful in civic engagement. Students who are fluent with these concepts are more likely to recognize the need for change when abuses are observed. They will see change as a possibility. Further, they can fight for the continuities that they believe are vital to society. They can reflect on the role of individuals, special-interest groups, political parties, and the government in promoting changes and/or continuities.

LESSON IDEAS

Introduction

The following materials could be used during a unit on the civil rights movement. If a course is organized thematically, this lesson could instead be taught in connection with other lessons on the role of compromise as a tool for civic engagement.

Objectives

This lesson is designed to meet three objectives associated with knowledge, skills, and dispositions:

1. Students will analyze the compromises involved in the passage of the Civil Rights Act of 1964 and debate its place in the civil rights movement.
2. Students will describe the concepts of continuity and change as they apply to the civil rights movement in general and the Civil Rights Act of 1964 in particular.
3. Students will explain the role of compromise in a pluralistic democracy where individuals and groups possess different experiences, priorities, and values.

Build Background Knowledge

Begin the lesson by building students' background knowledge on the events leading up to the passage of the Civil Rights Act of 1964. The material provided in this chapter under the headings "Background of the Civil Rights Movement" and "The Civil Rights Act of 1964" provide a basic overview of what students will need to know in order to work with the documents that follow.

Ask Historical Questions

The background information provided above and the documents that follow were designed to help students ask and answer the following question: Should the Civil Rights Act of 1964 be considered a *turning point*, or is it part of a more evolutionary process as the conditions of African Americans gradually improved? Students might consider the following questions to help them arrive at a decision: How did the clash between forces for change and continuity result in the compromise referred to as the Civil Rights Act of 1964? What were the significant changes brought about by the Civil Rights Act of 1964 and what were the significant continuities it did not change?

Provide Strategy Instruction and Model an Analysis of Change and Continuity

The following documents provide many opportunities for students to think about the concepts of change and continuity. Teachers should take the time to model by analyzing one or more of the documents and by using the vocabulary associated with change and continuity—terms such as *turning point*, *progress*, *decline*, and *significance*. Students might

also be reminded to consider the role of individuals, groups, coincidence, and other features in the passage of the Civil Rights Act. Further, students could be reminded that continuities often involve as much intentional effort on the part of individuals as change does.

The teacher might model thinking about change and continuity using Document 1, President John F. Kennedy's speech, delivered on June 11, 1963, which marked the start of the legislative process that resulted in the Civil Rights Act of 1964. The teacher can use the graphic organizer at the end of the chapter to introduce important concepts of the activity. It provides a place for students to take notes on the source of each document and to record how the document serves as evidence of change, continuity, and compromise. To analyze Kennedy's speech, the teacher might first think about the source and context of the speech, modeling what might be written in the first column of the graphic organizer. (The teacher might even fill in the first cells for the students, before photocopying it for them, as shown on the graphic organizer at the end of the chapter.) The teacher might notice the date, recalling that the Birmingham demonstrations and violent police response occurred less than a month prior to this speech. While analyzing the source of the document, the teacher might remember that Kennedy was a Democrat in a divided Democratic Party. The teacher might realize that Kennedy's speech was a public document, which influenced what he said.

After thinking aloud about the source, the teacher could play the speech, listening for examples of continuity and change. The teacher could show the notes on Document 1 already provided on students' graphic organizers. After watching, the teacher might wonder why Kennedy did not mention the incidents in Birmingham, speculating that it might show his disapproval of activists' tactics of civil disobedience. The teacher might realize the continuities and changes Kennedy talked about. For example, the teacher might realize that the use of federal troops to escort two Black students, which Kennedy mentions, represents both a continuity (repeating what Eisenhower had done in Little Rock) and a change (by moving into the Deep South). After watching the speech, the teacher could replay the last part of the speech (7 minutes and 30 seconds in), with students reading a transcript and focusing on Kennedy's specific recommendations for a civil rights bill. The teacher could pause the recording when he/she hears something important, especially the three legal changes that Kennedy proposes: integrating public facilities, using federal lawsuits to end segregated schools, and greater protection of voters. After watching Kennedy, the teacher might wonder about which of the priorities of civil rights reformers Kennedy ignored, remembering that he said nothing about poverty or discrimination in employment in his proposed legislation.

The teacher could show students that the graphic organizer has a floating line that he/she needs to draw between the "change" column and the "continuities" column. That feature gives the reader flexibility in taking notes depending on the emphasis of the documents. The teacher might then realize for students how the speech represents a compromised proposal—Kennedy did not ask for all of the reforms that civil rights leaders hoped for because he knew such a bill would face significant opposition. Instead, he proposed more modest reforms that he thought might be supported by most lawmakers. The teacher might wonder whether this speech was a turning point—a significant change—thinking aloud about why it might or might not be.

The teacher might then have students turn to Document 9 and have them analyze it on their own. It is short and simple, with evidence that jumps off the page regarding the changes brought about by the Civil Rights Act of 1964. Students should be encouraged to fill out their graphic organizers on their own, and then the document could be discussed in class. The teacher might have to help students realize that the title of the book suggests the author's bias, but the story comes from a reliable source and makes the Civil Rights Act appear to be a turning point in history.

Students may experience some confusion thinking about change and continuity when working with Document 2. In it, President Johnson focuses on the need to "continue." Students might mistakenly conclude that this is a speech about continuity. However, Johnson is urging America to continue to work toward the changes that Kennedy promoted prior to his assassination. Ironically, this address, generally referred to as the "Let Us Continue" speech, promotes change rather than continuity. The teacher might model an analysis of Document 2 in order to clear up any confusion students might have. Or the teacher might allow students to work through the speech in groups, monitoring their comprehension and analysis of Johnson's ideas.

Group-Work

Once the teacher is confident that students understand the concepts of continuity, change, and compromise, and how to use the graphic organizer to gather evidence from the documents, he/she can have them analyze the remaining documents independently or in small groups. During group-work or independent work, the teacher should remind students about their objective: to use evidence from the documents to identify whether the Civil Rights Act of 1964 represented a turning point in history.

Debriefing

At the end of the lesson, during a debriefing, students can discuss the *knowledge* they have gained about the civil rights movement and the Civil Rights Act of 1964 using the following questions:

1. What were the major arguments made at the time in favor of and against the Civil Rights Act?
2. How could someone claim to be in favor of civil rights but oppose the Civil Rights Act of 1964?
3. How did the passage of the Civil Rights Act of 1964 fit in with the context of the civil rights movement? What other civil rights events were going on that might have influenced the legislative process?

A second phase of the debriefing can focus on the concepts of continuity and change with the following questions:

1. How does the Civil Rights Act of 1964 represent significant continuities and/or changes?
2. Would you consider the Civil Rights Act of 1964 a turning point in history? What evidence from the documents supports your interpretation?
3. Would you say that current conditions, in terms of minority rights, show more continuities or more changes from conditions in 1964? What would you say are the main areas of continuity and the main areas of change from 1964 to today?

The third phase of the debriefing focuses on the *disposition* to compromise with political opponents in order to accomplish some objectives:

1. On an issue as important as civil rights, should reformers have refused to compromise, even with the understanding that a stronger bill would have been unlikely to pass? Why or why not?
2. What lessons can be drawn about compromise from the passage of the Civil Rights Act of 1964?
3. What does the Civil Rights Act of 1964 have in common with the Great Compromise? How are they different?
4. How might compromise resolve some of the current issues in civil rights, such as voter access to polls, "stand your ground" laws, police violence, poverty, and underperforming inner-city schools?

INSTRUCTIONAL MATERIALS

Ten primary source documents are included in the pages that follow, some in a format that is modified for students. Links are shown to transcripts of recorded speeches and the original documents of those modified here. Documents 5 and 9, unavailable online, are provided below in their original form. Also included below is a graphic organizer for students to take notes about the sources of the documents and what the documents suggest about changes, continuities, and compromise.

Document Set

1. Video recording of a speech given by President Kennedy on June 11, 1963, outlining his civil rights goals with a link to the transcript (Kennedy, 1963)

2. An excerpt from a speech made by President Lyndon B. Johnson on November 27, 1963, after the death of President Kennedy to a joint session of Congress; source includes a link to a recording of the speech (Johnson, 1963)

3. A link to a political cartoon entitled "If They Don't Watch out They're Gonna Ruin It" created by Gib Crockett, published in the *Washington Star* on April 15, 1964 (Crockett, 1964)

4. A video recording of the opening statements of a recorded debate between Senators Hubert Humphrey (a Democrat from Minnesota) and Strom Thurmond (a Democrat from South Carolina) (CBS Reports, 1964)

5. An excerpt from a letter written by Democratic Senator Richard Brevard Russell to a constituent in Georgia on December 9, 1963 (Risen, 2014)

6. An excerpt from an opinion editorial in *The New York Times*, April 19, 1964 coauthored by Senator Hubert Humphrey (Democrat) and Senator Thomas Kuchel (Republican) (Humphrey & Kuchel, 1964)

7. An excerpt from an explanation given by Republican presidential candidate Barry Goldwater for his opposition to the Civil Rights Act on June 18, 1964 (Goldwater, 1964)

8. A video clip of the speech delivered by President Lyndon Johnson when he signed the Civil Rights Act of 1964 on July 2, 1964 (Johnson, 1964)

9. A story about the day after the passage of the Civil Rights Act of 1964, told in the book *The Bill of the Century: The Epic Battle for the Civil Rights Act* by journalist Clay Risen (Risen, 2014)

10. Results of an October 1964 Gallup Poll surveying the public's approval or disapproval of the recently passed Civil Rights Act and the enforcement of the law (Kohut, 2015)

Simplified Evidence

Document 1: Kennedy Speech

Source: Video recording of a speech given by President Kennedy on June 11, 1963, telling about his civil rights goals. Found at www.jfklibrary.org/learn/about-jfk/historic-speeches/televised-address-to-the-nation-on-civil-rights (Transcript can be found at the same site)

Document 2: Johnson Speech 1

We will serve the whole nation, not one section or one part, or one group, but all Americans. These are the United States—a united people with a united purpose. Our American unity does not depend upon being the same. We have differences. But now, as in the past, we can get from those differences strength, not weakness, wisdom, not despair. Both as a people and a government, we can unite on a plan, a plan which is wise and fair, smart and helpful....

On the 20th day of January, in 1961, John F. Kennedy told his countrymen that our national work would not be finished "in the first thousand days, nor in the life of this administration, nor even perhaps in our lifetime on this planet. "But," he said, "let us begin." Today, in this moment of new firmness, I would say to all my fellow Americans, let us continue.

This is our challenge. Not to wait. Not to pause. Not to turn around and stay at this evil moment. But to continue on our way so that we may fulfill the destiny that history has set for us. Our most immediate tasks are here on [Capitol] Hill [with lawmakers].

First, no memorial speech or praise could more powerfully honor President Kennedy's memory than the earliest possible passage of the civil rights bill for which he fought so long. We have talked long enough in this country about equal rights. We have talked for 100 years or more. It is time now to write the next chapter. It is time to write it in the books of law. I urge you again, as I did in 1957 and again in 1960, to pass a civil rights law. Then we can move forward to get rid from this nation every bit of discrimination and oppression that is based upon race or color. There could be no greater source of strength to this nation both at home and overseas.

Source: Part of a speech made by President Lyndon B. Johnson on November 27, 1963, after the death of President Kennedy to a joint session of Congress. [Changed for easier reading.] Transcript found at www.pbs.org/ladybird/epicenter/epicenter_doc_speech.html and video recording at www.vsotd.com/featured-speech/let-us-continue (starting at 8:35 and 13:47)

Document 3: Political Cartoon

Political cartoon available through the Library of Congress at www.loc.gov/exhibits/civil-rights-act/civil-rights-act-of-1964.html#obj281_01 showing Senators Hubert Humphrey as a baker and Frank Lausche in a business suit protecting a freshly baked loaf of bread, labeled Civil Rights Act, from demonstrators and extremists (freshly baked bread will "fall" or collapse if bumped or exposed to loud noises).

Source: Political cartoon created by Gib Crockett and published in the *Washington Star* on April 15, 1964, showing lawmakers Hubert Humphrey and Frank Lausche defending the Civil Rights

Act from extremists. Found at www.loc.gov/exhibits/civil-rights-act/civil-rights-act-of-1964.html#obj281_01

Document 4: Debate

Source: Opening statements of a recorded debate between Senators Hubert Humphrey (a Democrat from Minnesota) and Strom Thurmond (a Democrat from South Carolina) considering the Civil Rights Bill, hosted by Columbia Broadcasting System (CBS). Found at www.loc.gov/exhibits/civil-rights-act/multimedia/hubert-humphrey-and-strom-thurmond.html

Document 5: Russell Letter

I will oppose this misnamed civil rights bill with all the strength I have. I must say, however, that we are terribly disadvantaged in our opposition. The two major parties have combined in trying to get minority votes in a way that ignores states' rights. The opinion of Southern white people means nothing to them.

Source: Part of a letter written by Democratic Senator Richard Brevard Russell to a voter in Georgia on December 9, 1963. Cited in Clay Risen's (2014) book, *The Bill of the Century*, published by Bloomsbury Press. [Changed for easier reading.]

Document 6: Editorial Letter

Civil wrongs do not bring civil rights. Civil disobedience does not bring fair laws. Disorder does not bring law and order. . . . Unruly demonstrations and protests bring hardship and unnecessary problems to others. Even when led by those who have been treated unfairly for a long time, they are not helping the cause of civil rights. Indeed, they are hurting our efforts in Congress to pass an effective Civil Rights Bill—JOINT STATEMENT BY SENATOR HUBERT H. HUMPHREY, *majority whip*, AND SENATOR THOMAS H. KUCHEL, *minority whip*.

Source: Part of an opinion editorial in *The New York Times*, April 19, 1964, coauthored by Senator Hubert Humphrey (Democrat) and Senator Thomas Kuchel (Republican) in response to protesters' plans to sabotage the New York World's Fair. [Changed for easier reading.] Found at www.nytimes.com/1964/04/19/archives/opinion-of-the-week-at-home-and-abroad.html

Document 7: Goldwater Statement

I am absolutely opposed to discrimination or segregation based on race, color or creed, or for anything else. Not only my words, but more importantly my actions through the years have always shown how I feel about this.

I wish to make myself perfectly clear. There are two parts of this bill which I have always opposed. They are so important that they caused me to vote against the whole bill. I oppose those parts that would start to let the federal government control private businesses. These include the area of so called "public accommodations" and in the area of employment. To be more specific, I oppose Titles II and VII of the bill.

I do not find anything in the Constitution that lets the federal government control either of these areas. I believe that trying to take that power is a big danger to the very heart of our basic system of government. It goes against the idea of a constitutional republic in which 50 ruling states have kept for themselves and for the people those powers not specifically granted to the central or federal government.

To effectively enforce this bill will take the creation of a huge federal police force. It will also probably create an "informer" psychology in big areas of our national life. Neighbors will spy on neighbors. Workers will spy on workers. Businessmen will spy on businessmen. Those who want to bother their fellow citizens for selfish purposes will have enough reason to do so. These, the federal police force and an "informer" psychology, are the signs of the police state. They are signs of the destruction of a free society.

Source: Part of an explanation given by Republican Senator and presidential candidate Barry Goldwater for his opposition to the Civil Rights Bill on June 18, 1964. [Changed for easier reading.] Found on pages 14318–14319 of the *Congressional Record* at www.govinfo.gov/content/pkg/GPO-CRECB-1964-pt11/pdf/GPO-CRECB-1964-pt11-2-1.pdf

Document 8: Johnson Speech 2

Source: Video clip of the speech delivered by President Lyndon Johnson when he signed the Civil Rights Act of 1964 on July 2, 1964. Found at www.youtube.com/watch?v=FKfoJJA5xWM

Document 9: Story

At 8:00 A.M. on July 3, 1964, a thirteen-year-old boy in Kansas City, Missouri, named Eugene Young went into the barbershop at the historic Muehlebach Hotel to get a haircut. He hopped into the chair of Lloyd Soper, one of the barbers. He gave him two dollars. A few minutes later, Young left, another satisfied customer. Young's satisfaction went beyond the mere [haircut]. He was black, and the day before he had been refused service at the same shop.

Source: Story from the day after the passage of the Civil Rights Act of 1964, told in the book *The Bill of the Century* by journalist Clay Risen (2014), published by Bloomsbury Press. [Changed for easier reading.]

Document 10: Poll Results

Broad Support for New Civil Rights Laws in 1964

Percent . . . of the Civil Rights Act of 1964

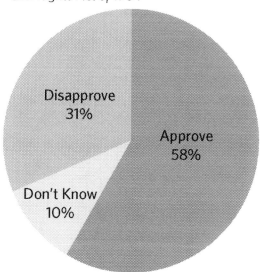

Source: Gallup, October 1964 Pew Research Center

Moderate Enforcement of 1964 Law Much Preferred

Percent who prefer . . . the new civil rights law

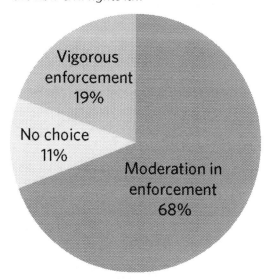

Source: Opinion Research Corporation, Nov 4–8, 1964

PEW RESEARCH CENTER

Source: Results of an October and a November 1964 Gallup Poll asking about the public's approval or disapproval of the recently passed Civil Rights Law and the public's views about the enforcement of the law. Found at www.pewresearch.org/fact-tank/2015/03/05/50-years-ago-mixed-views-about-civil-rights-but-support-for-selma-demonstrators/

Original Evidence

Document 5: Russell Letter

"I shall oppose this misnamed civil rights proposal with all the power at my command. I must say, however, that we are terribly handicapped in our opposition. The two major parties have combined in bidding for the minority bloc vote to such an extent that they disregard states' rights and the opinion of Southern white people amounted to nothing in their sight."

Source: Excerpt from a letter written by Democratic Senator Richard Brevard Russell to a constituent in Georgia on December 9, 1963. Cited in Clay Risen's (2014) book *The Bill of the Century*, published by Bloomsbury Press.

Document 9: Story

At 8:00 A.M. on July 3, 1964, a thirteen-year-old boy in Kansas City, Missouri, named Eugene Young went into the barbershop at the historic Muehlebach Hotel to get a haircut. He hopped into the chair of Lloyd Soper, one of the barbers, and gave him two dollars. A few minutes later, Young left, another satisfied customer. Young's satisfaction went beyond the mere [haircut]: he was black, and the day before he had been refused service at the same shop.

Source: Story from the day after the passage of the Civil Rights Act of 1964, told in the book *The Bill of the Century* by journalist Clay Risen (2014), published by Bloomsbury Press.

Graphic Organizer

Changes, Continuities, Compromises, and the Civil Rights Act of 1964

Complete the following graphic organizer as you consider how each of the documents related to the Civil Rights Act of 1964 demonstrates change, continuity, and compromise. Describe the source of the document in the first column. Tell how it gives evidence of change in the second column. Tell how it captures significant continuities in the third column. (You may adjust the line between the second and third column based on where you need more space, as in the example below.) Tell how the document gives evidence of compromise in the fourth column. Some cells of this matrix might be left blank if there is no evidence of change, continuity, or compromise in the document. After completing the matrix, answer the questions below, drawing from materials in the documents.

Source Information	Evidence of Change	Evidence of Continuity	Evidence of Compromise
1: President Kennedy's speech. Democrat, public, during Birmingham protests (but not mentioned), 2½ years after elected	Kennedy proposes legal changes—integrating public facilities, lawsuits to end segregated schools, greater protection of voters. Changes at University of Alabama.	Does not talk about poverty or employment issues, reformers' priorities	Doesn't mention extreme behavior of reformers in Birmingham or their most liberal requests
2			
3			
4			
5			
6			
7			
8			
9			
10			

1. How did the clash between forces for change and continuity result in the compromise referred to as the Civil Rights Act of 1964?
2. What were the significant changes brought about by the Civil Rights Act of 1964 and what were the significant continuities it did not alter?
3. Should the Civil Rights Act of 1964 be considered a turning point, or is it part of a more evolutionary process as the conditions of African Americans gradually improved? Defend your interpretation using evidence from the documents.

PART IV

GETTING ALONG WITH ADVERSARIES

In February 2017, vandals damaged 200 headstones on the sacred grounds of the Chesed Shel Emeth Jewish Cemetery near St. Louis, Missouri. Many people were outraged by the hate shown in this senseless destruction, but the local Muslim community sprang into action. Shortly after the vandalism, the St. Louis chapter of the Council on American-Islamic Relations condemned the hate crime and called on local Muslims to donate money to pay for headstone repairs. In faraway Philadelphia, New York City, and elsewhere, Islamic groups organized similar drives to raise money for repairs. Within weeks, over $130,000 had been raised. Multifaith groups worked together to clean up the cemetery. Historically, Jews and Muslims have not always seen eye to eye. However, this heartwarming story shows that people who sometimes disagree can cooperate when they determine to do so.

Because of different backgrounds, cultures, priorities, and perspectives, intelligent and moral people disagree with one another from time to time. Differences of opinion are generally not an indication of unreasonableness, stupidity, or evil intent, but more generally grow from different priorities, values, and experiences. How can a democratic republic survive and thrive in a multicultural and pluralistic nation where individuals carry a wide range of conflicting interests? Within such a society, the ability of individuals to collaborate and cooperate in spite of disagreements is an essential tool for civic engagement. Diplomacy is the art of working together without hostility even when priorities, objectives, and perspectives differ. Diversity becomes a strength as citizens develop the skills and dispositions needed to work together in spite of disagreements.

Perhaps no other period in U.S. history has required more collaboration between enemies than the reconstruction of the country following the Civil War. President Lincoln tried to bring together Confederates and Yankees, freedmen and former slave owners, former abolitionists and racists, and those who wanted radical changes and those who were committed to preserving their former way of life. In Lincoln's second inaugural address, he called for mercy toward the rebels as southern states were restored. Even as Confederate troops continued to wage war against the Union, Lincoln called for "malice toward none." Chapter 8 explores Lincoln's plan for Reconstruction, an evolving plan that was enacted throughout the war. Lincoln's assassination leaves historians to wonder how Reconstruction might have occurred had Lincoln directed it. Instead, Reconstruction is viewed nearly universally as a failure, resulting in a hundred years of racial violence and injustice, the effects of which are still felt in the 21st century.

Like Lincoln, President Ronald Reagan led the nation through a period of conflict, though Reagan's chief rival was foreign rather than domestic. Since the end of World War II, competing economic and political systems had created intense and lethal animosity between the United States and the Soviet Union. Within this context, Reagan forged an unlikely friendship with Mikhail Gorbachev, general secretary of the Soviet Union, which led to four summits and an easing of Cold War tensions. Chapter 9 investigates Reagan and Gorbachev's summits, and shows that even the bitterest of adversaries can work together to achieve the common good.

Lincoln and Reagan are two examples of people who have found ways to work together with former or present adversaries. Many others have done likewise. For example, following World War II, Secretary of State George C. Marshall promoted a plan of sending financial aid to the European nations devastated by the war. Through this Marshall Plan, hundreds of millions of dollars were spent assisting West Germany, a nation that only a few years earlier had been a bitter enemy of the United States. President Nixon broke down barriers between the United States and China, and later between the United States and the Soviet Union by meeting with the leaders of Cold War rivals. Supreme Court Justices Ruth Bader Ginsburg, a staunch liberal, and Antonin Scalia, a committed conservative, demonstrated that even bitter rivals could collaborate to improve one another's thinking. The warmness of their friendship in spite of their intense political disagreements serves as a modern model for students. History is full of examples, like the Muslims of St. Louis who helped their Jewish neighbors, of people working together with adversaries to achieve positive outcomes.

History also includes examples of the opposite, when political rivalries led to a lack of cooperation, usually with negative results. Aaron Burr's murder of Alexander Hamilton in a duel demonstrates the tragic effects of proud and hostile interaction. The impeachment of Andrew Johnson represents another such conflict, when disagreements between the president and Congress created a constitutional crisis that threatened the balance of power essential in the United States' democratic republic. Today's partisan gridlock serves as another example of the frustration that occurs when government officials attempt to overpower their political opponents, rather than forge collaborations and friendships. America's diversity is one of its greatest strengths. However, this diversity only becomes a strength when citizens respect their adversaries, give them the benefit of the doubt, seek the wisdom that comes from multiple perspectives, and collaboratively (rather than unilaterally) search for solutions to problems. A willingness to work with adversaries in spite of disagreements is an important tool for civic engagement.

In connection with the lessons included in Chapters 8 and 9, a teacher might discuss with students opportunities to practice diplomacy with the following questions:

- What advice would you give a friend who is assigned to complete a school project with someone he/she does not get along with?
- Is there a problem at a rival school that we might help them resolve?
- Are there opportunities for rival groups at this school to collaborate on some service project?
- If you emailed a political leader with whom you disagreed on most issues, how could you approach him/her in a way that could help him/her consider your perspective?

CHAPTER 8

Lincoln's Plan for Reconstruction

Binding a Nation's Wounds

No conflict in American history rivals the Civil War in terms of American deaths, destruction of American cities and farms, or political upheaval. Few Northerners avoided the personal loss of a loved one. Thousands of Union soldiers returned to their family farms missing an arm, a leg, or their eyesight, and carrying untold psychological harm. Southerners suffered even greater personal losses. In March 1865, as Lincoln delivered his second inaugural address, the South was running out of supplies and troops, but stubbornly fought on, adding to the casualties. Within this context, where hatred could prevail, Lincoln (1865) offered words of reconciliation: "Both [Northerners and Southerners] read the same Bible and pray to the same God," he reminded people, committing to "do all which may achieve a just and lasting peace among ourselves. . . ." Lincoln's plan for restoring the southern states to the Union is the subject of the investigation of this chapter. His willingness to lay aside past wrongs in an effort to solve pressing problems serves as a model of working together across disagreements. Further, his policies raise questions about the ethical judgment of historical figures' actions.

STUDENTS' BACKGROUND KNOWLEDGE

Abraham Lincoln is among the most beloved of American presidents, though students generally know little more about him than that he freed the slaves, a "fact" questioned by some historians (Harding, 1981). Students often associate Lincoln with the Civil War era, know that he was assassinated, and recall that he often wore a top hat. But students generally have little awareness of his policies for reconstructing the South during and following the Civil War. Nor do students think much about the process of Reconstruction, assuming that with Union victory, the war was over, the country reassembled, and the slaves freed. They generally fail to understand the complex issues facing policymakers who had no precedent to follow in restoring the southern governments. And students generally think of Reconstruction in physical and literal terms—the rebuilding of devastated cities and farms—rather than the readmission of southern states into the Union they had fought to destroy. Similarly, students generally fail to comprehend the challenges facing former slaves, assuming that when enslaved individuals received their freedom, the problems

facing them were resolved. They do not appreciate the ethical questions involved in reconstructing a socially segregated South. Mercy extended to former slave owners led to a restoration of pre–Civil War conditions, including the oppression of the formerly enslaved. Lincoln's choice was not whether to extend friendship to Southerners, but to whom friendship would be extended. Whose vision of the new South would Lincoln advance—those who wanted to preserve the traditional racist social structures or those who favored a more equitable society?

HISTORICAL BACKGROUND FOR TEACHERS AND STUDENTS

Background of Reconstruction

When Abraham Lincoln was elected president in 1860, seven southern states *seceded*, or left the United States. When Lincoln showed that he would use the army to fight to keep them in the Union, four more states seceded. For the next 4 years, the Civil War was fought. The northern states fought to keep the southern states in the Union. The southern states fought to create a new country, the Confederate States of America. As president, Lincoln had to figure out how to bring the rebellious states back. The process of readmitting states after they had left was called Reconstruction.

In March 1865, as the end of the war approached, Lincoln gave his second inaugural address. In it, he promised to treat former Confederates with mercy. By then, nearly everyone knew the Union would win the Civil War. Many southern towns and cities were already occupied by Union troops. Southerners in Louisiana, Tennessee, Arkansas, and other places were already trying to restore their states to the Union. The Confederate capital at Richmond, Virginia, would soon fall into Union hands. Within 5 weeks of Lincoln's second inauguration, the Civil War was over. Within 6 weeks, Lincoln was dead. But in March, the still-living Lincoln faced many questions—the same ones he had faced throughout the war. He wondered how to treat Southerners and southern states as the nation was reunified.

Two months before Lincoln's reelection, Congress passed the Thirteenth Amendment to the Constitution. It abolished slavery. But there were still many questions about what should happen to Southerners and *freedmen* (former slaves). For instance, what would Southerners have to do before a southern state could return to the Union? Should states that had waged war against the United States pay a penalty for their treason? How soon would Southerners be allowed to elect members of Congress to represent their states? How would the millions of freedmen be part of the new state governments? What would be done to help them? Would southern society have to change before southern states came back?

People had many different ideas about how the South should be readmitted. Many Northerners thought the Union victory was a win for right over wrong. They wanted Confederate political and military officers to be punished. Rebellion must not happen again! Some Northerners thought that anyone who helped the Confederacy should not be allowed to vote or hold political office. That would keep almost all White Southerners from voting. The most radical of Northerners thought that Blacks should be allowed to vote and hold office. Such an idea was shocking to many Southerners. Other Northerners believed that only rich Southerners had caused the war. They thought that average White Southerners had been tricked by the rich plantation owners. These Northerners thought that kindness would quickly win back the loyalty of most Southerners. After all, they argued, poor Whites had more in common with freedmen than they did with the rich plantation owners who dominated southern life. They thought that the poor Whites had never really hated the Union in the first place.

However, most White Southerners, rich and poor, thought that their reasons for fighting were good and right. They still thought so after losing the war. Many wondered how they could keep their old lifestyles. Most accepted that the time of slavery was over. But most White Southerners hoped to keep a segregated or separated society. They wanted to treat Blacks as second-class citizens. They hoped Reconstruction would bring back the "good old days" from before the war. Northerners' and Southerners' ideas about race and freedom affected Reconstruction. What they thought about opportunity and motivation was also important. Reconstruction created many ethical dilemmas.

The war had impacted many people, both Northerners and Southerners. Almost every American had been affected personally by the loss of a loved one. Thousands did not know what had happened to friends or family members who were missing after the war. Had they died? Stories of the cruelty of war were told across the North and the South, adding to hateful feelings. Most people on either side blamed the other for causing the war. If ever there was a period of history when bitter feelings threatened the ability to work together, it was at the end of the Civil War.

Lincoln's plan for Reconstruction did not matter very much. After he was killed, Andrew Johnson became president and more radical leaders took control of Reconstruction. They did not follow Lincoln's plans. Historians debate how things might have turned out if Lincoln had survived to lead Reconstruction.

Lincoln's Plan for Reconstruction

Lincoln had plans for Reconstruction long before his second inaugural address. As soon as the first southern state, South Carolina, seceded, Lincoln thought about how to bring the southern states back. At first, he did not demand much from the rebellious states. In his first inaugural address, before the war had even started, he said that the Union could be restored with few changes. Southerners could even keep their slaves. Once war broke out, however, Lincoln changed the rules for coming back. In 1863, after he issued the Emancipation Proclamation, which freed slaves in rebellious territory, Lincoln demanded that southern states make a plan for liberating slaves. Their plans might free the slaves gradually, over years. Or they could even pay slave owners for the loss of their slave property.

By the end of 1863, some Southerners who lived in states occupied by the Union Army wanted their state governments restored. Lincoln had two conditions to become a state again: Ten percent of voters had to take an oath of allegiance to the United States. And a plan had to be in place to free slaves. Lincoln's policy left the poor and uneducated freedmen on their own to work out their own survival. More radical Northerners thought that Lincoln's plan did not punish the South enough. They thought that plantation owners were responsible for the war. They argued that because of the brutality of the war and the centuries of Blacks living in slavery, the plantation owners should be punished. The most radical Northerners thought the government should take the lands of rich Southerners and give it to their former slaves. Lincoln thought such an idea violated a person's right to own property. Talking about such harsh punishment might make Southerners fight harder and prolong the war. And each day that the war continued, lives were lost. By the end of the war, Lincoln began to think that some Blacks should have the right to vote.

Lincoln and other leaders faced many ethical questions as they thought about Reconstruction. Before war broke out, they wondered whether slavery should be allowed to continue if it meant avoiding a war. After the war started, they wondered whether it was ethical to forgive those who had caused the war. Was it ethical to take the land of Confederate leaders to punish them for the war? Was it enough that former slaves had earned their freedom, or should they be given other rights? As southern states began to write new state constitutions, they faced these and other questions asked by federal leaders.

On March 4, 1865, Lincoln spoke more about his plan for Reconstruction in his second inaugural address. "With malice [hatred] towards none," he summarized (Lincoln, 1865). He did not live to carry out his plan. How Reconstruction should be done was a question that the nation considered during and long after the Civil War. Indeed, questions on ethical policies for Blacks, freedmen, and their descendants, were still being figured out during the 20th century and even into the 21st.

HISTORICAL THINKING SKILLS: ETHICAL JUDGMENT

Meaningful study of history often involves ethical judgments like those facing Lincoln. This book, for example, is full of ethical judgments. In Chapter 2, I praise John Adams's decision to defend the rights of political opponents and his role in the acquittal of the perpetrators of the Boston Massacre. With obvious ethical implications, I promote John Adams as a model of one who stood upon principles to defend civil rights. Students can identify ethical judgments when historians praise the actions of historical characters as right, good, or fair, or condemn actions as wrong or unjust. Historical periods sometimes include ethical dilemmas, the analysis of which can help students face today's ethical issues (Seixas & Morton, 2013).

Students' understanding of history carries two ethical dimensions in particular. First, how should people today respond to ethical issues that stem from historical events? The modern commemoration of Confederate leaders through monuments and memorials raises ethical questions surrounding race, treason, bravery, and duty that are grounded in historical events, both during the Civil War/ Reconstruction, the period when the monuments were erected, and today. Understanding the past influences modern interpretations involving ethical questions. Second, how should we make ethical judgments about historical figures, knowing that the social values that shaped historical actions were different from modern understandings of right and wrong? For instance, should slave owners, racist or sexist policymakers, or those who oppressed laborers be judged by the ethical standards of their time or by modern standards? How can we pass judgment while avoiding anachronistic thinking?

Numerous researchers suggest that civic engagement includes ethical judgments rooted in history. Barton and Levstik (2004) contend that visions of goodness and fairness, considered in history classrooms, might nurture ethical participatory democracy and shape current public policy decisions. Researchers argue that ethical dimensions of historical thinking give meaning to the discipline and provide insights for ethical action on current issues (Milligan, Gibson, & Peck, 2018; Seixas & Morton, 2013). Milligan and her colleagues (2018) summarize classrooms where students engage in ethical judgments: "students are asked to understand the historical context, distinguish between the values and climate of moral opinion in the past and present, and weigh individual agency against structural factors, including social contexts, environment, and social conditions" (p. 452). Thus, perspective taking, and understanding the context, values, priorities, and worldview of historical actors, is essential in making ethical judgments.

As much as any president in U.S. history, Lincoln faced numerous ethical dilemmas. On one hand, he perceived that slavery was morally indefensible as a social institution. On the other hand, he believed that a moderate stance toward slavery was more likely than radical measures to lead to its eventual abolition (Rodrigue, 2013). As an attorney, Lincoln respected property rights, even when those property rights were claimed by individuals who trafficked in slavery and waged war against the Union. (For a period of time, he favored compensated emancipation, with slave owners paid for their losses as slaves were freed.) As the leader of a warring nation, he understood that without military victory, there was little he could do to end slavery. And he believed that he needed the support of slaveholders in border states to win the war. Lincoln understood the social context during which he lived, rife with racism in both the North and South, and wondered how former slaves and former slave owners could ever live side by side in peace. (For a period, he favored voluntary *colonization*, the relocation of former slaves into colonies outside of the United States.) He understood the economic impact that could result from the abolition of slavery in communities where the majority of the population would suddenly find themselves free but unemployed. (He considered gradual emancipation over a period of years in order to reduce the impact of sudden, widespread unemployment.) He contemplated whether whole states should be punished for the actions of a rebellious majority, and whether it was just to mete out punishments upon individuals who had performed their duty as they understood it, even if their actions were treasonous. He understood the moral implications of the death and destruction associated with war (Rodrigue, 2013).

In the investigation included in this chapter, students consider the attitudes of those involved in Reconstruction, particularly Lincoln, about what was right, good, just, and fair. This investigation is intended to help students make more nuanced ethical judgments regarding current events impacted by Reconstruction, particularly current race relations in the United States. Rather than seeking a single "correct" answer to policy controversies, a study of past ethical judgments allows individuals with a diversity of opinions to collaboratively deliberate in an informed manner over what should be done today (Milligan et al., 2018). The documents provided in this investigation allow students to reflect on the ethical dilemmas Lincoln faced in reconstructing the South.

LESSON IDEAS

Introduction

The following materials could be used during a unit on the Civil War and Reconstruction. If a course is organized thematically, this lesson could instead be taught in connection with other lessons on the role of diplomacy and working with adversaries in civic engagement.

Objectives

This lesson is designed to meet three objectives associated with knowledge, skills, and dispositions:

1. Students will debate the issues Lincoln faced in reconstructing the Union, particularly questions involving emancipation, securing the blessings of liberty for former slaves, and the treatment of former Confederates.
2. Students will use evidence to pass ethical judgments on Lincoln and his contemporaries, recognizing the context in which Reconstruction occurred.
3. Students will recognize the need for diplomacy and compromise and for working together with opponents—even enemies—when solving problems.

Build Background Knowledge

Begin the lesson by building students' background knowledge on the conditions leading up to the reconstruction of southern states following the Civil War. The material provided in this chapter under the headings "Background of Reconstruction" and "Lincoln's Plan for Reconstruction" gives a basic overview of the things students will need to know about the broad and immediate context of Reconstruction in order to work with the documents that follow.

Ask Historical Questions

The background information provided above and the documents that follow were designed to help students ask and answer the following questions: Given Lincoln's context, were his proposed policies for restoring or reconstructing the Union good, right, just, and fair? How did the decisions he made reflect his priorities, values, and context? Who benefitted from his policies and who suffered from them? How should current policies concerning Confederate memorials be considered in light of Lincoln's ethical decisions?

Provide Strategy Instruction and Model Ethical Judgment

Teachers might begin this lesson by discussing with students explicitly the purpose of historical ethical judgments. When a modern person praises the actions of a historical figure as right, good, or fair, or condemns them as wrong or unfair, he/she is passing ethical judgment on that person. When the modern person describes what should or

should not have been done, he/she is judging the ethics of historical decisions. The teacher might outline three essential elements of historical thinking associated with ethical judgment:

(1) Consider whether judgments were reasonable in light of the interests of key groups involved. In the case of Reconstruction, these groups often had competing interests, such as conservative Northerners who supported slavery, northern abolitionists who opposed slavery, former Confederates who had waged war against the Union to retain slavery, and freedmen, the former slaves.

(2) Consider what other people knew and believed at the time. Think about whether conditions and social structures at the time constrained or influenced people's perspectives. For example, widespread racism made many people believe that White people and those formerly enslaved could not live peaceably side by side, competing for the same jobs, attending the same schools, or otherwise socializing.

(3) Consider whether current judgments of the past are plausible, given the historical evidence. As with other elements of historical thinking, a student's ethical judgments must be based upon historical evidence.

The sample classroom poster in this chapter has questions that could structure students' ethical evaluation of historical figures' actions.

The teacher could model ethical judgment using the graphic organizer with Document 1, Lincoln's first inaugural address. The historical context included in the source information can help students render an ethical judgment of Lincoln's words and proposed policies during his first inaugural address. The teacher might read the source information with the class, recalling that after Lincoln was elected in November 1860, seven states seceded from the Union before he took office. The teacher might reflect out loud, commenting, "I imagine that at the time of his inauguration Lincoln hoped to restore the Union and avoid war. That was probably his main purpose in speaking." With this background, the teacher might read out loud with the students the first document, pausing from time to time to consider the ethical decisions Lincoln made in this speech.

For example, in the first paragraph, Lincoln spoke in favor of retaining slavery in the states where it existed—of restoring the seceded states to the Union without requiring them to end slavery. The teacher might stop reading and consider out loud whether the statement "I have no intention, directly or indirectly, to end the institution of slavery in the states where it exists" was fair, proper, and good, or whether it was unfair, improper, and bad. Knowing that

Lincoln was generally opposed to slavery, the teacher might question out loud why he would promise to allow the enslavement of African Americans to continue. After reading the first paragraph out loud, the teacher might continue to model his/her thinking: "If I accept Lincoln's words at face value, it creates a challenging moral dilemma. On one hand, a strong stance against slavery would most certainly lead either to the destruction of the Union, or to civil war, with the loss of countless lives. And to end slavery without compensation would violate the property rights of those who claimed to own slaves, something Lincoln probably opposed. On the other hand, Lincoln's promise to allow slavery to continue, should the southern states be restored to the Union, held out the last hope to avoid war and/or the destruction of the Union, but with the guarantee that slavery, with all of its horrors, would continue." The teacher might wonder out loud, "Which was the more ethical course: to avoid war by restoring southern states with the promise that slavery would continue, or to wage a war that might potentially end slavery—an outcome still uncertain—at the cost of countless lives?"

The teacher might continue, "If I do not accept Lincoln's words at face value, his address poses a less challenging ethical dilemma. By the time of this speech, it was unlikely that the Union could be restored without war, a condition Lincoln probably understood. His words may have been intended not to restore the Union but to strengthen support for the Union among slaveholders in the border states of Maryland, Delaware, Kentucky, and Missouri. And it may have been intended to strengthen support among those who favored the preservation of the Union, both in the North and in the South—to increase their support for the war that seemed inevitable." The teacher might recall (out loud), "I have to remember that Lincoln did not know how things would turn out, nor did he fully understand whether he could keep the support of conservative Northerners who had no concerns about slavery, or whether he might win more support from the Southerners who might still hold out hope that the war could be avoided. These might have just been words to gain public support for the war."

The teacher might then read the second paragraph, pausing while reading to think out loud about the ethical issues associated with Lincoln's address. For instance, the teacher might pause and say, "It sounds like Lincoln was pleading for the South not to go to war and at the same time he was blaming the war, should it happen, on the Southerners. He warned that he would use power to hold U.S. positions in the South—I wonder whether this is an ethical decision. After all, Lincoln could also have avoided war by allowing the southern states to secede. He did not need to force them to return. In a way, it sounds like he was trying to remove himself from the ethical judgments he had to make, by promising how he would react as president if the South tried to seize federal positions, before it started to do so."

Continuing into the third paragraph, the teacher might point out that the same themes are repeated: The teacher might comment, "Lincoln claimed that keeping his oath to preserve the Union is worth waging a war. I wonder whether it would it be better for him to violate his oath in order to preserve lives. Which choice would be more ethical, given his understanding of the conditions of the time?" The teacher might leave these questions open, pointing out that a number of other documents will help clarify Lincoln's ethical dilemma, and will also make it more complex by introducing changing wartime conditions.

As the teacher considers the first document, he/she could record notes on the graphic organizer at the end of the chapter. Prior to passing out the worksheet, the teacher might complete the first row (as shown on the graphic organizer), modeling how to use the graphic organizer to gather information from the first document. Instead of using the graphic organizer, the teacher might model for students how to highlight and annotate the first document, writing notes in its margins.

Group-Work

Once the teacher is confident that students understand how to consider the ethical dimensions of Lincoln's Reconstruction policies and how to use the graphic organizer to consider the ethical questions raised by the content of the documents, he/she can have students analyze the remaining documents independently or in small groups. The teacher should remind students about their objective: to determine whether, given Lincoln's context (recalling that his context changed during the course of the war), his proposed policies for restoring or reconstructing the Union were good, right, just, and fair.

Debriefing

After students have had ample time to analyze the documents in small groups, the teacher can reassemble the whole class and conduct a debriefing discussion. During the debriefing, students can review what they have learned about Lincoln and the Reconstruction of the nation following the Civil War by discussing the following questions:

1. How did Lincoln's plan for reconstructing the Union compare with that of other leaders? How did his plan change over the course of the war?
2. How did Lincoln's plan for reconstructing the Union answer questions about who could participate in reconstructed governments, how freedmen would be treated, and how Confederate leaders would be punished?
3. How might Reconstruction have occurred differently if Lincoln had not been assassinated?

A second phase of the debriefing can focus on the ethical dimensions of Reconstruction with the following questions:

1. What were the ethical dilemmas Lincoln faced in reconstructing the Union?
2. How did the conditions, values, and priorities of the time period affect Lincoln's ethical decisions about Reconstruction?
3. How do policies during Reconstruction impact today's ethical choices about policies concerning African Americans and/or the memorializing of Confederate heroes?

The third phase of the debriefing focuses on the importance of diplomacy with enemies and former enemies in order to accomplish purposes:

1. How did Lincoln's policies of forgiveness toward White Southerners cause difficulties for freedmen?
2. What lessons can be learned from Lincoln about the need and/or wisdom of working together with adversaries in order to achieve shared interests?

INSTRUCTIONAL MATERIALS

Ten primary source documents are included in the pages that follow in a format that is modified for students, with links to the original documents. In addition, the graphic organizer included below can support students' analysis of the ethical questions Lincoln faced. A sample poster that could be displayed in the classroom also illustrates how a teacher might support students' ethical historical judgment during this lesson and others.

Document Set

1. An excerpt from Lincoln's first inaugural address given on March 4, 1861, pleading for the seceded states to be restored peacefully but warning that their secession would lead to war (Lincoln, 1861)
2. An excerpt from a letter Lincoln wrote to newspaper editor Horace Greely on August 22, 1862, suggesting his ambivalence about slavery and outlining the purposes of the war: to save the Union (Lincoln, 1862)
3. An excerpt from a letter written by Lincoln on August 26, 1863, to be read at a rally, justifying the Emancipation Proclamation as a tool for winning the war (Lincoln, 1863a)
4. An excerpt from Lincoln's Proclamation of Amnesty and Freedom, outlining his "10% plan" issued on December 8, 1863 (Lincoln, 1863b)
5. An excerpt from Lincoln's statement on the nature of loyalty oaths, taken from a letter he

wrote on February 5, 1864, to Secretary of War Edwin Stanton (Lincoln, 1864a)
6. An excerpt from a private letter written on March 13, 1864, by Lincoln to Michael Hahn, governor of Louisiana's reconstructed government, suggesting that some African Americans be allowed to vote (Lincoln, 1864b)
7. Part of Andrew Johnson's speech given in the summer of 1864, calling for the punishment of Confederates in Tennessee's plan for Reconstruction (Johnson, 1864)
8. An excerpt from a letter Lincoln wrote to Horace Greely on July 18, 1864, outlining Lincoln's conditions for a peace settlement (Lincoln, 1864c)
9. An excerpt from Lincoln's second inaugural address, given on March 4, 1865, near the end of the war, outlining Lincoln's hope of "malice toward none and charity for all" (Lincoln, 1865)
10. An excerpt from a speech given by Radical Republican Thaddeus Stevens on March 19, 1867, almost 2 years after Lincoln's assassination, calling for the punishment of former Confederates (Stevens, 1867)

Simplified Evidence

Document 1: Lincoln's First Inaugural Address

There seems to be fear among the people of the Southern States that by the rise of a Republican President their property and their peace and personal security will be endangered. There has never been any reason for such fear. Indeed, there is a lot of evidence against that idea that they can see. It is found in nearly all my published speeches. I quote from just one of those speeches when I say that— "I have no intention, directly or indirectly, to end slavery in the States where it exists. I believe I have no lawful right to do so, and I have no reason to do so." . . .

There does not need to be bloodshed or violence, and there will not be any unless it is forced on the national government. The power given to me will be used to hold, occupy, and possess the property and places that belong to the Government and to collect the taxes and fees. But beyond what is needed to do these things, there will be no invasion, no use of force against the people anywhere.

In *your* hands, my dissatisfied fellow-countrymen, and not in *mine*, is the important issue of civil war. The Government will not attack *you*. You will not have war unless you start it. *You* have not made an oath to destroy the Government, but I will make the most holy oath to "preserve, protect, and defend it."

I do not want to close. We are not enemies, but friends. We must not be enemies. Though feelings may have harmed, they must not break our bonds of love.

Source: After Lincoln's election in November 1860, seven states seceded from the Union before his inauguration, when he officially took office. This is part of Lincoln's first inaugural address, given when he took office on March 4, 1861. [Changed for easier reading.] Found at www.bartleby.com/124/pres31.html

Document 2: Lincoln's Letter to Greeley 1862

I want to save the Union. I want to save it the quickest way under the Constitution. The sooner the national authority can be restored; the nearer the Union will be "the Union as it was."... My main goal in this struggle is to save the Union, and is not either to save or to destroy slavery. If I could save the Union without freeing any slave I would do it. And if I could save it by freeing all the slaves I would do it. And if I could save it by freeing some and leaving others alone I would also do that. What I do about slavery, and African Americans, I do because I believe it helps to save the Union.

Source: Part of a letter written on August 22, 1862, by Abraham Lincoln to Horace Greeley, editor of the newspaper the *New-York Tribune*, in response to an angry letter written by Greeley calling on Lincoln to do more to free slaves. [Changed for easier reading and to remove language viewed as racist.] Found at housedivided.dickinson.edu/sites/lincoln/letter-to-horace-greeley-august-22-1862/

Document 3: Lincoln's Letter to Conkling

There are people who are dissatisfied with me. To those people I want to say: You desire peace and you blame me that we do not have it. But how can we get it? There are only three possible ways. First, to end the rebellion by force of arms [war]. I am trying to do this.... A second way is to give up the Union. I am against this.... [A third way is through] some form of *compromise*. I do not believe any compromise that saves the Union is now possible.

You say you will not fight to free blacks. Some of them seem willing to fight for you. But, it doesn't matter. You should fight, then, only to save the Union. I issued the [Emancipation] proclamation on purpose to help you save the Union. Whenever you have conquered all resistance to the Union, if I make you to keep fighting, then it will be a good time, for you to say you will not fight to free blacks....

Whatever blacks will do as soldiers, leaves less for white soldiers to do in saving the Union. . . . But blacks, like other people, do things for a reason. Why should they do anything for us, if we will do nothing for them? If they risk their lives for us, they must have the strongest reason—even the promise of freedom. And since the promise [of freedom] has been made, it must be kept.

Source: Part of a letter written on August 26, 1863, by Abraham Lincoln to be read by his friend, James C. Conkling, at a rally held in Lincoln's hometown of Springfield, Illinois. Lincoln spoke specifically to those people who opposed the Emancipation Proclamation. [Changed for easier reading and to remove language viewed as racist.] Found at www.abrahamlincolnonline.org/lincoln/speeches/conkling.htm

Document 4: Lincoln's 10% Plan

I, ABRAHAM LINCOLN, President of the United States, tell all people who have helped in the current rebellion, that a full pardon is given to them. It gives to them all of their property rights, except for slaves. They just need to take an oath [of loyalty to the United States], and keep that oath....

Some people will not be allowed to take the oath. They are the civil or diplomatic officers or agents of the so-called Confederate government [and some other officials]....

And I do further make known that the states of Arkansas [and eight other states] may create a government that will be recognized as the true government of the state. To do this they need to have a number of people take the oath. That number must be at least one tenth of the votes cast in the state in the presidential election of 1860. If they create a state government that is republican, and if they do not break the oath, the state will then have the benefits of the Constitution....

And I do further make known that state governments can make any plan for the freed people of the state. It should declare their permanent freedom. They might make plans for their education. It can be a temporary plan that remembers that they are currently a laboring, landless, and homeless group. The president will not object to such a plan.

Source: Parts of Lincoln's Proclamation of Amnesty and Reconstruction, issued on December 8, 1863, explaining Lincoln's "10% plan" for restoring southern states to the Union. [Changed for easier reading.] Found at www.freedmen.umd.edu/procamn.htm

Document 5: Lincoln's Letter to Stanton

On principle, I dislike an oath which requires a man to swear he has not done anything wrong. It rejects the Christian principle of forgiveness through repentance. I think it is enough if the man does not do wrong in the future.

Source: Part of a letter written on February 5, 1864, by Abraham Lincoln to Secretary of War Edwin Stanton, showing his views on the oath of loyalty required of Southerners who wanted to participate in reconstructed governments. His note was written in response to a former legislator in Tennessee who asked Lincoln for the chance to serve in the Union Army but would have been required to take an oath stating he had never been disloyal to the United States, something that was not true. [Changed for easier reading.] Found at quod.lib.umich.edu/cgi/t/text/text-idx?c=lincoln;rgn=div1;view=text;idno=lincoln7;node=lincoln7%3A358

Document 6: Lincoln's Letter to Hahn

Honorable Michael Hahn

My dear Sir:

I congratulate you for making history as the first free-state Governor of Louisiana. Now you are going to have a convention. Among other things, you will probably decide who will get to vote. I have a suggestion for you to think about privately. Some of the blacks might be allowed to vote. For example, the very intelligent, and especially those who have fought bravely in the Union army. They would probably help, in some difficult time in the future, to keep the jewel of liberty within the family of freedom. But this is only a suggestion, not to the public, but to you alone.

Yours truly,

A. LINCOLN

Source: Lincoln's private letter written on March 13, 1864, to Michael Hahn, governor of the reconstructed state of Louisiana prior to the convention that wrote Louisiana's new constitution. [Changed for easier reading and to remove language viewed as racist.] Found at teachingamericanhistory.org/library/document/letter-to-governor-michael-hahn/

Document 7: Johnson's Speech

I say that traitors should not lead in the work of restoration [Reconstruction]. If there are only five thousand men in Tennessee who are loyal to the Constitution, to freedom, and to justice, these true and faithful men should completely control the work of reorganization and reformation. I say that the traitor has stopped being a citizen. When he joined the rebellion, he became a public enemy. He gave away his right to vote with loyal men when he gave up his citizenship and tried to destroy our government. . . . I think that he should have to go through severe suffering before he is given back his citizenship. A man who takes the oath just to save his property, and breaks the oath, is a liar. He should not be trusted. Before these repenting rebels can be trusted, they should show the fruits of repentance. The men who helped to make all these widows and orphans, and who covered the streets of Nashville with sorrow, should suffer for their huge crime.

Treason must be made horrible. The traitors must be punished and made poor. Their great plantations must be taken and divided into small farms They should be sold to honest, hard working men. The day for protecting the lands and blacks of these leaders of the rebellion is over.

Source: Part of Andrew Johnson's speech calling for the harsh punishment of rebels, given during the summer of 1864 as Tennessee made plans to reenter the Union, cited by Thaddeus Stevens in a speech the following year. [Changed for easier reading and to remove language viewed as racist.] Found at history.furman.edu/benson/hst41/silver/stevens1.htm

Document 8: Lincoln's Letter to Greeley 1864

EXECUTIVE MANSION, WASHINGTON, July 18, 1864.

To whom it may concern:

The President of the United States will listen to any plan which includes restoring peace. It must restore the integrity of the whole Union, and give up slavery. It must come by an official who can control the armies now at war against the United States. It will be answered with generous terms on important and other points. And the people who bring the plans will have safe travel both ways.

ABRAHAM LINCOLN

Source: Letter written by Abraham Lincoln on July 18, 1864, to Horace Greeley, who had proposed a meeting between Confederate and Union officials to negotiate a peaceful settlement to the war. [Changed for easier reading.] Found at teachingamericanhistory.org/library/document/the-to-whom-it-may-concern-letter/

Document 9: Lincoln's Second Inaugural Address

During my inaugural address four years ago everyone thought nervously about the coming civil war. Everyone feared it. Everyone tried to avoid it. . . . Both parties [the North and the South] hated war. But one of them would make war rather than let the nation live, and the other would accept war rather than let it die. And the war came. . . .

We hope deeply, we pray truly, that this mighty curse of war will quickly pass away. Yet, if God wants it to keep going until all the wealth gained by the slaves' two hundred and fifty years of forced work shall be sunk, and until every drop of blood caused by a whip [slavery] will be paid by another drop of blood caused by the sword [war], as was said three thousand years ago, so still it must be said "the judgments of the Lord are true and righteous altogether."

With malice [hatred] toward none, with charity [love] for all, with confidence in what is right as God helps us to see the right, let us try to finish the work we are in. Let us bandage the nation's wounds. Let us care for him who has fought the battles and for his widow and his orphan. Let us do everything that will bring and love a fair and lasting peace among ourselves and with all nations.

Source: Parts of Lincoln's second inaugural address, given on March 4, 1865, as a northern victory in the war was almost sure, and Reconstruction would become Lincoln's top priority. [Changed for easier reading.] Found at avalon.law.yale.edu/19th_century/lincoln2.asp

Document 10: Stevens' Speech

Mr. SPEAKER: I am about to discuss the question of the punishment of rude traitors by taking some of their property. This would serve both as a punishment for their crimes and to pay the loyal men who were robbed by the rebels. It could increase the pay to our wounded soldiers. The punishment of traitors has been completely forgotten by a dishonest president [Johnson] and by a lazy Congress.

This bill is important to many groups of people.

It is important to our wounded and hurt soldiers. They cannot work for their living. The government payments are not enough to support them now. It is important to those sad wives and parents. Their funeral clothing is seen in every house. It shows the cruel losses which have been made for them because of the murderous hands of traitors.

It is important to the loyal men, North and South, who have been robbed and made poor by rebel raiders and rebel lawmakers.

It is important to four million injured, oppressed, and helpless men, whose ancestors for two hundred years have been held in slavery and forced to work on the land. We planned to return a small part of that land to them. They are now poor, helpless, hungry, and starving, because of the planned cruelty of their old masters.

It is also important to the criminals whose property we take as a fine. It punishes them for the great crime of making war to destroy this country. It punishes them for fighting the war against all the rules of civilized warfare. It is too small of a punishment for so deep of a crime. And it is too small of a warning to future ages.

Source: Part of a speech made by Representative Thaddeus Stevens on March 19, 1867, nearly 2 years after Lincoln's assassination, to the House of Representatives during a debate on a bill to provide greater relief to Civil War veterans. [Changed for easier reading.] Found at history.furman.edu/benson/hst41/silver/stevens1.htm

Graphic Organizer

Ethical Dimensions of Lincoln's Plans for Restoring/Reconstructing the Union

You will be given a number of documents associated with the ethical dilemmas and decisions Abraham Lincoln faced as he sought to restore or reconstruct the Union before, during, and after the Civil War. Use the following graphic organizer to record the ethical decisions associated with each document, and to record your ethical judgments—what you think about the proper thing to do, given the values, constraints, and realities of the time. After completing this graphic organizer, write a brief summary of your judgments about the ethics of Lincoln's words and policies and their current implications.

Document/Source Info	Summary of Contents	Ethical Decisions/ Dilemmas	Your Reaction/Judgment
1: Lincoln's first inaugural address given March 4, 1861, as he took oath of office after seven states had seceded	Lincoln promises to preserve slavery if states come back. Warns he will use his power to hold federal properties. Says he will keep his oath even if it takes war. Blames war on South.	Avoid war and keep slavery? Keep oath to preserve Union even if it causes war? Offers chance to come back without penalty. Must maintain support of proslavery people in border states and South.	The other documents will help, but understanding the many problems Lincoln was facing, this doesn't seem like the best time to take a strong position against slavery and there may have been hope to avoid war without sacrificing the Union.
2			
3			
4			
5			
6			
7			
8			
9			
10			

1. Given Lincoln's context, were his proposed policies for restoring or reconstructing the Union good, right, just, and fair?
2. How did the decisions he made reflect his priorities, values, and his context?
3. Who benefitted from his policies and who suffered from them?
4. How should current policies be judged in light of Lincoln's ethical decisions?

Sample Classroom Poster

QUESTIONS TO ENGAGE IN THE ETHICAL JUDGMENT OF HISTORICAL EVENTS

1. Were a person's actions right, good, and fair or wrong and unfair?
2. Were the person's actions reasonable given his/her understanding of right and wrong?
3. What did people know or think at the time that influenced the person's actions?
4. Were the person's choices limited because of laws, policies, or expectations?
5. Does evidence show that a person believed he/she acted ethically?
6. How does a person's actions reveal what he/she thought was ethical?
7. What are current ethical controversies that are related to historical events?
8. What ethical action can we take now to correct past mistakes?

CHAPTER 9

Reagan and Gorbachev
Adversaries and Friends

One of the most unexpected and world-changing friendships of the 20th century was that of U.S. President Ronald Reagan and Soviet Union General Secretary Mikhail Gorbachev. Their collaboration was instrumental in ending almost 50 years of animosity between their nations, a time referred to as the Cold War. Through collaboration, they halted the massive buildup of nuclear weapons and began a reduction in the arms race. To be sure, there were intense disagreements between them, though they did not let differences in ideologies or purposes obstruct their diplomacy. This chapter provides materials for an investigation of the interaction between Reagan and Gorbachev, with a focus on their four summits at Geneva, Reykjavik, Washington DC, and Moscow.

STUDENTS' BACKGROUND KNOWLEDGE

Unless U.S. history teachers are careful about following a comprehensive scope and sequence, they run out of time in the school year before considering the end of the 20th century. For this reason, it is likely that students may never have studied in school how the Cold War seemingly came to an end. Instead, their understanding of the Reagan era and other more recent historical topics is influenced to a great extent by their families' political leanings and/or cultural references. As Wineburg and his colleagues (2007) explained, students are not blank slates, but come into history classes with a plethora of historical ideas, some accurate and some not. This is particularly true of more recent history, events that are more likely to be topics of conversation at family functions or alluded to in movies or on the news (such as recent tensions caused by Russian expansion in the Crimean Peninsula.)

Thus, students enter the study of Reagan and Gorbachev and the end of the Cold War with a "rough-hewn" Cold War narrative (Wineburg, Mosborg, Porat, & Duncan, 2007). They may know that conflict between capitalism and communism played a role in Cold War tensions. Terminology such as *superpowers*, *arms race*, and *Berlin Wall* might have some meaning for some of the students. Some have undoubtedly seen popular movies that play on Cold War themes. And students may have heard of NATO and other Cold War–era alliances that remain in existence. When it comes to the end of the Cold War, students may know about the fall of the Berlin Wall, but most likely know little else about the easing of Cold War tensions. Most important, unlike the previous generation of Americans, students have little inkling of the animosity that existed between the United States and the Soviet Union in almost every aspect of life, from Olympic sports to proxy wars and the space race. They do not understand the fatalistic attitude that grew out of a constant threat of nuclear holocaust. Unlike their parents, who lived through it, students understand little about the impact of the Cold War on Americans' daily life. Without such an understanding, the collaboration of Reagan and Gorbachev cannot be fully appreciated.

HISTORICAL BACKGROUND FOR TEACHERS AND STUDENTS

Background of the Cold War

World War II was not yet over when conflict grew between the Soviet Union and its former allies, including the United States. After the war, Soviet General Secretary Joseph Stalin wanted to control Eastern Europe and other places around the world. He hoped that communism would spread. In 1946, British Prime Minister Winston Churchill warned that a symbolic Iron Curtain was being built across Europe. This Iron Curtain split the communist countries in the east from the capitalist countries of the west. Around the world, nations began to ally themselves with the United States or the Soviet Union (USSR). These two countries became the world's "superpowers" after World War II. In the 1950s and 1960s, European colonies in Africa and other places gained independence. As they did, many joined one or the other alliance network. The United States wanted to stop the spread of communism. Americans called their policy *containment*. Containment was tested when communists tried to take control of West Berlin and South Korea. Many Americans considered leaders of the USSR tough, iron-fisted, and uncompromising.

Competition between the United States and USSR spread into every part of life. A few years after the United States built the first atomic bomb, the Soviet Union tested its own. Soon, an arms race began. Both nations tried to build more destructive weapons. In time, both the United States and the USSR had enough nuclear bombs to completely destroy their enemies. This was called *mutually assured destruction*. The arms race spread into a space race. The Soviet Union launched the first satellite into space, as well as the first manned satellite. The United States responded by sending the first man to the moon. The Olympics were not only games between athletes but were tests between nations. American and Soviet equipment was used in *proxy wars*. In these wars, allies of each superpower fought using American and Russian weapons.

American and Soviet propaganda spread fear and hatred. The average citizen of each nation learned to fear the other. American schools held drills to prepare for nuclear attack. American families were told to build bomb shelters. Americans and Soviets faced the constant dread of nuclear war. During the 1950s, U.S. Senator Joseph McCarthy claimed that communists in Hollywood were putting propaganda in movies. He said that some communists had taken over American politics. Although some of his claims were true, he exaggerated the threat. The Cold War was still a major theme in American life in the 1980s. Popular movies used strong, uncaring, robotic, and dishonest Russians as villains. The Cold War affected every American.

At the start of the 1980s, it looked like the Cold War would continue. In 1980, the United States boycotted the Olympics, held in Moscow, in the Soviet Union. The Americans were protesting the USSR's invasion of Afghanistan. In 1983, Soviet pilots shot down a Korean passenger jet that flew into Soviet air space. All 269 passengers and crew, including 62 Americans, were killed. That same year, President Reagan ordered an invasion of the Caribbean island of Grenada. He hoped to stop communists from taking control of the island. In 1984, the USSR boycotted the Los Angeles Olympics. Leadership changes in the USSR made diplomacy hard. Between 1982 and 1985, four different men led that country. But after Mikhail Gorbachev came to power, it seemed like he might be more open to working with the United States.

Reagan and Gorbachev: Adversaries and Friends

USSR General Secretary Gorbachev seemed to be open to reform. He gave Soviets more freedom to buy and sell things. Soviets called this *perestroika*. He allowed some freedom of speech and the press. This was called *glasnost*. He also seemed willing to meet with Western leaders. Between November 1985 and May 1988, four summits, or meetings, were held between Reagan and Gorbachev. In November 1985, they met in Geneva, Switzerland. There, they debated human rights issues. They talked about getting rid of some nuclear weapons. But they could not agree on much. The summit prepared them for better talks that would follow. They met again in October 1986 in Reykjavik, Iceland. There, they worked on a treaty to ban some missiles. But they still could not reach an agreement. In October 1987, they met in Washington DC. They finally signed a ban

on intermediate range missiles. They talked about human rights issues and dangerous places in the world. Reagan traveled to Moscow in May 1988, just months before the end of his presidency. At that meeting, he and Gorbachev signed several small agreements. They talked more about issues from around the world and human rights.

One of the things they could not agree on was the U.S. Strategic Defense Initiative (SDI). This was a plan to build a system to defend against nuclear missile strikes. Reagan did not think the defensive system counted as "weapons." He did not feel that research on SDI broke any treaty. Gorbachev argued that defensive weapons would end the safety created by mutually assured destruction. If the United States could block a nuclear strike, it might not be afraid to attack first. Eventually, Reagan compromised on some SDI plans. Gorbachev agreed to change some Soviet policies.

From the start, Reagan thought that diplomacy should be built upon friendship. And during the summits, a friendship grew that allowed Reagan and Gorbachev to work together even though they still disagreed on many things. The friendship that developed out of their summits continued even after Reagan's presidency ended.

HISTORICAL THINKING SKILLS: ARGUMENTATIVE WRITING

Academic historians' success is contingent upon their ability to engage in argumentative writing. They do not receive tenure unless they produce cutting-edge research that presents new outlooks on historical topics. In argumentative writing, historians use historical evidence to substantiate fresh, debatable interpretations. Historical writing is a mix of description and narrative, to be sure, but the pinnacle of academic historical writing is always argumentative. Historians' writing often includes two arguments. The first outlines the flaws or gaps in other historians' research. Historians argue why their work is needed in terms of what others have done. Their second argument involves showing how historical evidence points to their new and unique interpretation. Embedded in the argument is a critical analysis of the relative strengths and weaknesses of the evidence they employ. Argumentative historical writing integrates all the critical reading strategies outlined in all of the chapters of this book, as well as historical imagination and general writing abilities.

How can teachers foster such complex and daunting writing? First, because argumentative writing springs out of the critical analysis of historical evidence, teachers must help students engage in critical historical reading (Monte-Sano, 2008). Strategies such as sourcing, corroboration, and contextualization, explained in Chapters 1, 2, 4, 10, 11, and 13, help historians distinguish solid from weak evidence. Yet research shows that even when students engage in some of these reading strategies, most still use poor evidence just as they do strong evidence in their construction and defense of an argument (if they use any evidence at all) (Nokes, 2017). The graphic organizers used throughout this book are designed to support students in their critical analysis of evidence and to prepare them to weed out weak evidence and use only strong evidence to develop and defend an argument. Further, the questions included on most of the graphic organizers in the chapters of this book require students to explain their interpretation of some historical question and to justify their response with the evidence they have reviewed. If completed as intended, many of these short responses constitute a simple historical argument.

How can teachers help students engage in longer, more complex historical writing? First, teachers could teach students the vocabulary of argumentation. Six concepts are essential for students to understand.

1. An *argument* is the author's entire attempt to defend his/her interpretation. The argument starts with the first word of the monograph's title and concludes with the last endnote.
2. An *interpretation* is an evidence-based opinion. I discourage students' use of the word *opinion* unless it involves a personal reaction for which there is no outside evidence—for example: "In my opinion, chocolate ice cream is better than vanilla."
3. A *claim* is a historical interpretation, stated in succinct and clear terms. Claims are debatable, evidence-based statements, such as a claim that "Reagan's charisma helped maintain the collaboration with Gorbachev in spite of disagreements over the Strategic Defense Initiative."
4. *Evidence* is the indisputable facts that support a claim. A photograph of Reagan smiling warmly and extending his hand to shake Gorbachev's might be used as evidence to substantiate the previous claim. In argumentative writing, written evidence is either paraphrased or it is quoted verbatim. Visual evidence might be described or included directly as an illustration in a text.
5. A *warrant* is a statement linking evidence with claims. Evidence does not speak for itself. Instead, an author must introduce evidence, and explain how it supports claims.
6. A *counterclaim* is an alternative way to explain the evidence. Because claims are always debatable, alternative claims are always possible. Strong arguments explain why the author's interpretation is better than counterclaims in light of all of the evidence, even evidence that seems to support counterclaims. For example, evidence might be flawed. Or, if the evidence were considered from a different perspective, it might support the author's interpretation rather than a counterclaim. Or a counterclaim may be partially correct, in which case it is up to the historian to explain why his/her claim is better or more complete.

Along with defining these concepts associated with argumentation, a teacher might provide writing samples that model simple arguments. Such samples are sometimes referred to in language arts instruction as *mentor texts*. Students might be asked to read a mentor text and identify claims, warrants, and evidence. They might diagram the author's logical flow, showing how evidence leads to claims as part of an overall argument, as in the graphic organizer. When engaged in writing, students can use the same format of graphic organizer to outline their argument.

Students can practice argumentation in a variety of ways. At times, a teacher might require students to write an argumentative essay to promote an independently developed interpretation. However, most teachers do not have the time to assign or provide feedback on such elaborate writing on a regular basis. Instead, teachers can have students practice argumentative writing by outlining an argument, engaging in argumentative speaking, writing simple arguments, giving argumentative class presentations, or in a number of other ways that can be assessed simply, with feedback given. Historians, too, produce arguments in a variety of genres, such as lectures, PowerPoint presentations, and testimony at public hearings. Because such argumentation represents the pinnacle of historical writing, students should have opportunities from time to time to engage in such reading, thinking, speaking, and writing.

Argumentation is one of the most important tools for civic engagement. Within a democracy people must work together to solve problems. Each individual brings insights, values, and biases—unique ways of looking at problems and solutions. As each citizen seeks to persuade others, the tools of argumentation enhance these interactions. Argumentation includes using evidence to back up claims and interpretations. But argumentation is more than an effort to convince others that they are wrong. It implies carefully weighing evidence, both as we see it and as others see it. Sound argumentation requires a person to seek out voices he/she may not agree with—just as historians' interpretations must account for all of the evidence. Argumentation includes a willingness to humbly listen to and consider another's interpretation of evidence. It is the process of sharing with others the reasons and evidence for our interpretation. It involves changing one's mind in the face of superior evidence or logic. Argumentation, when considered from a broader perspective, is a collaborative effort to work toward rational, evidence-based solutions. When viewed as a collaborative process, argumentation forms the foundation of civic engagement.

LESSON IDEAS

Introduction

The following materials could be used in a series of lessons during a unit on the Cold War, the Reagan administration, or the 1980s. If a course is organized thematically, this lesson could be taught in connection with other lessons on the importance of working with individuals who hold different perspectives. It is recommended that at least two class sessions be dedicated to this investigation, with the first on the critical analysis of the documents, formulating an interpretation, and gathering evidence, and the second on organizing the evidence into a brief argumentative essay.

Objectives

This lesson is designed to meet three objectives associated with knowledge, skills, and dispositions:

1. Students will describe the factors that contributed to an easing of Cold War tensions during the Reagan administration, including the summits between U.S. and Soviet leaders.
2. Students will engage in argumentative writing, developing an interpretation and defending it with historical evidence.
3. Students will explain the importance of diplomacy and cooperating with political adversaries. Students will be inclined to collaborate with individuals they disagree with.

Build Background Knowledge

Begin the lesson by building students' background knowledge of the Cold War and the events leading up the summits between Reagan and Gorbachev. The material provided in this chapter under the headings "Background of the Cold War" and "Reagan and Gorbachev: Adversaries and Friends" provides a basic overview of what students will need to know in order to work with the documents that follow.

Ask Historical Questions

The background information provided above and the documents that follow were designed to help students ask and answer the following question: How were Cold War disagreements between Gorbachev and Reagan overcome? Teachers could provide scaffolding to students by giving them possible hypotheses that they can then test with evidence. Rather than developing their own interpretation, students would then only have to choose between interpretations or combinations of interpretations such as those that follow, which is a much simpler task than developing an interpretation

independently. A label for each interpretation is included in brackets to facilitate class discussion about the ideas:

1. Reagan and Gorbachev, both horrified by the thought of the effects of nuclear war, were highly motivated by the high stakes involved to overcome differences. [high-stakes interpretation]
2. Reagan's powerful language before, during, and after the summits made Gorbachev negotiate and compromise. [Reagan's talk interpretation]
3. Reagan's and/or Gorbachev's charisma and optimism built a friendship that allowed for negotiation, leading to mutually beneficial agreements. [friendship interpretation]
4. Public support for disarmament within their nations and the world motivated Reagan and Gorbachev to negotiate. [public pressure interpretation]
5. Gorbachev and Reagan exercised patience and resilience as they worked through disagreements that were not resolved immediately. [patience interpretation]

Provide Strategy Instruction and Model Argumentative Historical Writing

The graphic organizer provided in this chapter is designed to help students identify the evidence found in the documents that supports each of the five interpretations listed above or an alternative interpretation. Instead of using the graphic organizer, a teacher could ask students to highlight and annotate the documents in a manner that allows them to identify evidence that supports or weakens the various interpretations. The teacher might explain that starting with possible interpretations and looking for evidence to support each is backwards to the way historians generally work. Instead, historians typically start with the evidence, which leads them to interpretations. The teacher provides possible interpretations from the start to simplify this complicated process of historical argumentation. Students might identify other interpretations, or might determine that a combination of interpretations best explains the success of Reagan and Gorbachev's diplomacy. When working with advanced students, the teacher might not suggest any plausible interpretations at all.

The teacher could model the process of drawing evidence from the documents, by analyzing with students Document 2, a letter written by Mikhail Gorbachev to Ronald Reagan in 1985. The teacher could project a copy of the document for the class to consider together. The teacher should think aloud while considering the source (General Secretary Gorbachev), the audience (President Reagan), and the context (shortly after Gorbachev's appointment and prior to the first summit at Geneva). After reading the source information and before reading the document, the teacher might say something like this: "I remember that this is early in their relationship, before they have met face-to-face. I imagine that Gorbachev was probably more guarded at this point than he might become later in their relationship, after they had built some trust. But I anticipate that this should be a very useful document in giving us some ideas about how they would get along."

After thinking about the source, the teacher could start to read out loud the document for the students, reminding them that he/she is looking for evidence that supports or weakens any of the five interpretations. After reading the first line, the teacher might pause and think aloud again, saying something like, "It sounds to me like an invitation, an important starting point in their relationship—the idea that there are certain differences between their countries that they are just going to have to accept and overlook. He also implies that patience will be needed to work through these differences." The teacher might read the next line and again pause and think about it: "It sounds like he thinks wisdom and accepting the facts will allow the leaders to cooperate. He refers to leaders in the past who have been able to accomplish some good through cooperation in spite of their differences. I wonder whether this is evidence that Gorbachev hoped that a friendship would develop between them—possibly evidence for the *friendship* interpretation. It shows Gorbachev's optimism and hints at his charisma. It lacks the feeling of an iron-fisted communist dictator. I remember what we learned in the background information and this shows that he was not the cold, heartless Russian dictator suggested in American propaganda."

After reading the next line, the teacher might pause again and think aloud: "He talks about doing useful things 'both for our peoples and for all other peoples.' This seems to start to get into the *high-stakes* interpretation. Their cooperation is vital for the good of the entire planet. I think I will list this as evidence of both the *high-stakes* interpretation and the *friendship* interpretation."

After reading the entire document, the teacher might model for students how to complete the graphic organizer, or, alternatively, how to annotate or highlight the document. If completing the graphic organizer, the teacher could point out that the document says nothing about Reagan's talk or public pressure, so those cells can be left blank. It provides some evidence of Gorbachev's charisma, his realization of the high stakes involved, and that patience will be needed in their diplomacy. In the cell for Document 1 under *friendship* interpretation, the teacher might write, "Gorbachev's style shows charisma and a willingness to be friendly." In the cell under *high-stakes* interpretation, the teacher might write, "Gorbachev realizes their diplomacy impacts all people on the planet." In the cell under patience interpretation the teacher might write "Gorbachev implies that they will need to patiently work through their differences."

If the teacher feels that students need more support, he/she might model with Document 3, a photograph of Reagan and Gorbachev. Alternatively, the teacher might allow students to work independently for a few minutes, then lead the class in a discussion of their analysis of the photograph. In using the photograph, the teacher and students should consider whether the photograph was spontaneous or staged, why the photographer snapped a photo at that moment, why the photographer made choices about the angle from which to take the photo, lighting, and so forth. Most students will see this photograph, taken at the Geneva summit, as evidence of an increasing warmness between Reagan and Gorbachev, supporting the *friendship* interpretation. Some might point out that their casual manner weakens the *high-stakes* interpretation—the two men do not look like they carry the weight of the world on their shoulders. Further, the photograph raises doubts that Reagan used confrontational rhetoric in their meetings, weakening the *Reagan's talk* interpretation. There is little evidence for or against the other interpretations in this photograph.

Group-Work

Once the teacher is confident that students understand how to draw evidence for the various interpretations from the documents and how to use the graphic organizer, he/she can have them analyze the remaining documents independently or in small groups. The teacher should remind students about their objective: to gather evidence from the documents that supports or weakens each interpretation. Students are preparing to craft an argument surrounding the motivation for Reagan and Gorbachev's collaboration.

Additional Instruction and Modeling

Once groups have analyzed each of the documents, students can write argumentative essays telling how the evidence supports an interpretation. The teacher might model how evidence might be used. First, a teacher might ask students to look over their graphic organizer and choose the interpretation that they think is most supported by the strongest evidence. Hopefully, students will disagree about the interpretation that they think is best. Such disagreements enrich class discussion, place a greater demand on students to defend their claims, and allow the teacher to show that claims should be disputable. Next, the teacher might ask a student to explain how one piece of evidence led him/her to the interpretation that he/she reached. The teacher might then model how to write in a manner that uses the evidence to support the claim. One way to do so would be to explain that evidence should be packed in ICE. The *I* reminds the writer to *introduce* the evidence. For example, if using Document 1, the teacher might write the following sentence to introduce the evidence: "In June 1985, shortly after coming to power in the Soviet Union, General Secretary Gorbachev wrote a letter to President Reagan." The *C* in ICE reminds students to *cite* the evidence. This can be done by a direct quote or through paraphrasing. The teacher might write, "In the letter Gorbachev calls for wisdom and cooperation, promising that 'confident, peaceful views' could be the result of their diplomacy." The *E* in ICE reminds the writer to *explain* how the evidence supports the claim. The teacher could continue modeling by writing, "Gorbachev's plea for cooperation, wisdom, and realism shows his charisma and desire for warming relations."

Depending on a teacher's objectives, he/she could also model how to address a counterclaim in writing. For example, a writer who claims that high stakes led to the successful diplomacy would have to explain the casualness of Reagan and Gorbachev in Document 3, the photograph. The teacher might do this by writing, "This photograph was included in the document set, in place of other photos that may have shown a more serious relationship. This is a result of picking out the evidence that is wanted rather than considering all of the evidence, which may or may not show a growing friendship." The teacher should remind students that all evidence must be accounted for—that which supports a claim as well as that which weakens it.

Debriefing

At the conclusion of the lesson students should discuss what they have learned about Reagan and Gorbachev's diplomacy and the easing of Cold War tensions and nuclear disarmament by considering the following questions:

1. What were the most important effects of the four summits?
2. What were some of the fundamental disagreements between Gorbachev and Reagan and what did they agree on?
3. What were some of the roadblocks to diplomacy and how were they overcome?

A second phase of the debriefing can focus on the process of argumentative writing with the following questions:

1. What were some of the most challenging parts of constructing an argument?
2. How did you deal with evidence that weakened your claims?
3. How important was the careful analysis of the documents in your writing? For example, how did you use sourcing and other strategies to strengthen your writing?

The third phase of the debriefing focuses on the importance of diplomacy to reach the common good. The teacher might use questions such as the following:

1. How might the interaction between Reagan and Gorbachev serve as a model of cooperation and diplomacy for opposing politicians in the United States today?
2. How might their interaction serve as a model for warring parties in the world today?
3. What are some risks involved in diplomacy? How did Reagan and Gorbachev work through the risks and other challenges?
4. Where do needs for diplomacy exist within your school, family, or community?

INSTRUCTIONAL MATERIALS

Ten primary source documents are included in the pages that follow. They have been modified to a format that is easier to read, with links to the original documents. The originals of those texts that are not easily available online are included. Further, Document 6, Reagan's "Tear Down This Wall" speech, was not modified so that teachers might have students read along as they watch a video recording of the speech. A generic argumentative writing graphic organizer is included that teachers might use when students read and diagram the argumentative writing of others or to outline an argumentative essay they will write. A second graphic organizer is included for students to use to collect evidence supporting or weakening possible interpretations during this investigation. In addition, a sample poster is provided that a teacher might display in his/her classroom to remind students of the elements of argumentative writing.

Document Set

1. An excerpt from a diary entry written by Reagan on October 10, 1983, after watching a tape of the television movie *The Day After*, which depicted a Soviet nuclear strike (Reagan, 1983)
2. An excerpt from a letter written by Gorbachev to Reagan on June 10, 1985, in response to a letter from Reagan (Gorbachev, 1985)
3. A photograph taken on November 19, 1985, of Reagan and Gorbachev during the Geneva summit (Reagan & Gorbachev, 1985)
4. An excerpt from a letter written by Reagan to Gorbachev on May 23, 1986, after a Soviet nuclear power plant accident at Chernobyl (Reagan, 1990)
5. Excerpts from notes taken by Gorbachev's advisor Anatoly Chernyaev during his return flight after the Reykjavik summit, October 12, 1986 (Savranskya & Blanton, 2016)
6. A clip from a video recording of a speech given by Reagan on June 12, 1987, in front of the Brandenburg Gate at the Berlin Wall in West Berlin (Reagan, 1987)

7. An excerpt from a report of a newspaper article published in the USSR on September 10, 1987 (Reagan Speeches Suggest Lack of Strength, 1987)

8. An excerpt from a luncheon toast made by Secretary of State George Shultz to Gorbachev during the Washington summit, December 9, 1987 (Shultz, 1987)

9. An excerpt from a memorandum of conversation from a working lunch held at the conclusion of the Washington summit, December 10, 1987 (Savranskya & Blanton, 2016)

10. Excerpts from a joint speech delivered on June 1, 1988, by Gorbachev and Reagan at the end of the Moscow summit (Gorbachev & Reagan, 1988)

Simplified Evidence

Document 1: Reagan Diary Entry

Columbus Day. In the morning at Camp David. I ran the tape of the movie ABC [a television station] is showing on the air November 20. It's called "The Day After." It has Lawrence Kansas wiped out in a nuclear war with Russia. It is powerfully done—all $7 million worth. It's very effective & left me greatly depressed. So far, they haven't sold any of the 25 spot advertisements scheduled & I can see why. Whether it will be of help to the "anti-nukes" or not, I can't say. My own reaction was one of our having to do all we can to have a deterrent & to see there is never a nuclear war. Back to the White House.

Source: Part of a diary entry written by Ronald Reagan on October 10, 1983, after watching a tape of the television movie *The Day After*, which shows a Soviet nuclear missile strike in Kansas. [Changed for easier reading.] Found at www.reaganfoundation.org/ronald-reagan/white-house-diaries/diary-entry-10101983/

Document 2: Gorbachev Letter

Of course, our countries are different. This fact cannot be changed. There is also another fact, however that experience of the past shows. When the leaders of both countries had enough wisdom and realism to overcome bias caused by the difference in societies and in ideas, we cooperated successfully. We did quite a few useful things both for our peoples and for all other peoples. Of course, we still had differences and different views. But it was our working together that was the biggest reason. And it opened up confident, peaceful views.

Source: Part of a letter written by Mikhail Gorbachev to Ronald Reagan on June 10, 1985, 3 months after Gorbachev's appointment as general secretary, written in response to a letter from Reagan. [Changed for easier reading.] Found at www.margaret-thatcher.org/document/110656

Document 3: Geneva Photograph

Source: Photograph taken by an unknown press photographer on November 19, 1985, of Reagan and Gorbachev in the Boat House at Fleur d'Eau, during their summit at Geneva. Found at commons.wikimedia.org/wiki/File:Reagan_and_Gorbachev_hold_discussions.jpg

Document 4: Reagan Letter

Mr. General Secretary, our recent history gives us a lot of evidence that, if you wait for a perfect time to try to resolve our differences, we are unlikely to resolve anything. This is the time which has been given us. We should take advantage of it. It is a time of historic and possibly unique potential. Let us not lose it because we don't try.

Source: Part of a letter written by Reagan to Gorbachev on May 23, 1986, after a Soviet nuclear power plant accident at Chernobyl. [Changed for easier reading.] Found in the book *Ronald Reagan: An American Life*, an autobiography by Ronald Reagan (2011, pp. 664–665).

Document 5: Gorbachev Reflections

I often read foreign newspapers, and I can get a feel for the common reaction caused by reports about the Reykjavik summit. And the guesses started right away—who won and who lost there. But winning was not our goal going to Reykjavik. We had quite an important reason for our plan. The fact is that Geneva had reached a deadlock. We felt that a major step forward was needed, for time is working against the good of humankind.

And now Reykjavik has gone by. As it turned out, it was quite easy to agree on the first and second parts of our plan—the strategic weapons and the intermediate range missiles. That alone has given us much experience. We understood the President's problems. We understood that he was not free in making his decisions. We did not make a big deal out of the fact that the Strategic Defense Initiative problem stopped Reykjavik from being a total success. We thought, "let the President think everything over, let him seek counsel from the Congress." Maybe we will need one more try to step over [the barrier], which still divides us. We can wait. We can still think about the proposals we brought to Reykjavik.

We don't need to be sad. Reykjavik led us to the most important part of the understanding of where we stand. Everybody saw that agreement is possible. From Reykjavik, we learned that the need for talks has grown even more. That is why I am even more of an optimist after Reykjavik.

Source: Part of the notes taken by Gorbachev's advisor, Anatoly Chernyaev, during his return flight after the Reykjavik summit, October 12, 1986. [Changed for easier reading.] Found in the book *The Last Superpower Summits: Gorbachev, Reagan, and Bush* by Svetlana Savranskaya and Thomas S. Blanton (2016, p. 238).

Document 6: Reagan Speech

In the 1950s, Khrushchev predicted: "We will bury you." But in the West today, we see a free world that has achieved a level of prosperity and well-being unprecedented in all human history. In the Communist world, we see failure, technological backwardness, declining standards of health, even want of the most basic kind—too little food. Even today, the Soviet Union still cannot feed itself. After these four decades, then, there stands before the entire world one great and inescapable conclusion: Freedom leads to prosperity. Freedom replaces the ancient hatreds among the nations with comity [friendly association] and peace. Freedom is the victor.

And now the Soviets themselves may, in a limited way, be coming to understand the importance of freedom. We hear much from Moscow about a new policy of reform and openness. Some political prisoners have been released. Certain foreign news broadcasts are no longer being jammed [blocked]. Some economic enterprises have been permitted to operate with greater freedom from state control.

Are these the beginnings of profound changes in the Soviet state? Or are they token gestures, intended to raise false hopes in the West, or to strengthen the Soviet system without changing it? We welcome change and openness; for we believe that freedom and security go together, that the advance of human liberty can only strengthen the cause of world peace. There is one sign the Soviets can make that would be unmistakable, that would advance dramatically the cause of freedom and peace.

General Secretary Gorbachev, if you seek peace, if you seek prosperity for the Soviet Union and Eastern Europe, if you seek liberalization: Come here to this gate! Mr. Gorbachev, open this gate! Mr. Gorbachev, tear down this wall!

I understand the fear of war and the pain of division that afflict this continent—and I pledge to you my country's efforts to help overcome these burdens. To be sure, we in the West must resist Soviet expansion. So we must maintain defenses of unassailable strength. Yet we seek peace; so we must strive to reduce arms on both sides.

Source: Part of a speech given by Reagan on June 12, 1987, in front of the Brandenburg Gate at the Berlin Wall in West Berlin. Speech transcript found at www.historyplace.com/speeches/reagan-tear-down.htm. Videotape of the speech found at www.youtube.com/watch?v=5MDFX-dNtsM (excerpt starts about 9:25)

Document 7: Report of Soviet Article

A Soviet expert on the U.S. said on Thursday President Reagan's recent comments on superpower relations suggested he lacked strength and self-assurance. "Despite all the rudeness, even the disrespect of these statements, they do not show strength and confidence in himself," Georgy Arbatov, who heads the Soviet Union's USA and Canada Institute said. "The opposite is more likely: these are the speeches of a leader who has been forced to go on the defensive by events themselves," Arbatov wrote in the Communist Party daily newspaper *Pravda*. Arbatov's article followed Soviet media attacks on a speech about East-West affairs that Reagan gave in Los Angeles on August 26 and in a later presidential radio speech. Press commentaries made fun of Reagan's request for Moscow to share details of its military budget, and criticized him for saying that the Soviet Union should tear down the Berlin Wall and encourage Western-style elections in Eastern Europe. Arbatov said the feeling of Reagan's speeches did not hide his desire for an agreement on medium- and short-range nuclear missiles that would permit a summit with Soviet leader Mikhail Gorbachev.

Source: Part of a report of a newspaper article published in the USSR on September 10, 1987. [Changed for easier reading.] Found at archive.org/details/GorbachevVisitWashingtonSummit

Document 8: Shultz Toast

Your visit here, Mr. General Secretary, and the plan for a visit by President Reagan to Moscow, should make us think about rules for controlling our relations. What should we both remember? First, ours is a relationship as important as it is unique. It is important because we each carry a huge burden of leadership in the world. It is unique because the nuclear era demands that we talk to each other even though we have our big differences. . . . Second, our relationship will continue to be a difficult one to manage. We have different beliefs, political systems and national goals. Our basic values, systems and interests will stay the same, even as the need to work together increases. Third, we must be realistic. We must avoid extremes either of anger or joy through the ups and downs of our relations. . . . Fourth, we must speak clearly and with honesty to one another about our differences. . . . You have not hesitated to speak your mind to us. And we have made some progress. As President Reagan has said, we owe each other the gift of honesty. Honesty will help get results. We must seek steady progress toward a freer, more predictable, more stable and helpful relationship. In this time of change, a complicated mix of international relationships makes working with each other more difficult. But new patterns of talks also offer new opportunities for cooperation and progress. Let us grab those opportunities. Mr. General Secretary, Mrs. Gorbachev, to your health. To the health of the President and Mrs. Reagan. And to the Soviet and American peoples!

Source: Part of a luncheon toast made by Secretary of State George Shultz to Mikhail Gorbachev during the Washington summit on December 9, 1987. [Changed for easier reading.] Found at www.reaganlibrary.gov/sites/default/files/digitallibrary/smof/cos/bakerhoward/box-002/40-27-6912132-002-015-2017.pdf

Document 9: Luncheon Notes

Gorbachev said that soon he would be saying goodbye to the President and the President's friends. Gorbachev said he had decided that the third summit had been a success. It had seen important agreements and other questions had been talked about seriously. Most importantly the atmosphere had been good. There had been more shared understanding. Gorbachev said that he would like to thank the work of the President toward making this a successful summit, as well as to the work of other Americans who were there. Gorbachev added that he would like the momentum of this summit to continue. He then said that on his way to the White House lunch he had ridden with Vice President Bush. He had looked out the car window and seen Americans responding warmly to what had happened in the negotiations. When the car had stopped at a red light, he jumped out of the car and had talked freely with some random person. When it was time to go, he did not want to end their talk.

Source: Part of the notes kept during a working lunch held at the conclusion of the Washington summit on December 10, 1987, in the family dining room of the White House. [Changed for easier reading.] Found on in the book *The Last Superpower Summits: Gorbachev, Reagan, and Bush* by Svetlana Savranskaya and Thomas S. Blanton (2016, p. 353).

Document 10: Joint Speech

Gorbachev: Judging the work done over these past few days, we can be happy. We can say that what has been happening these days in Moscow is big politics. It is politics that influence millions and millions of people. Each such meeting weakened the foundations of the Cold War. Each of them weakened the Cold War fortress and opened up a way to modern, civilized, world politics good enough for the truly new times. . . . The feeling in our relations is getting better. We're working to keep better feelings all the time. We do this not only in our official contacts but also in the

day-to-day work of Soviet-U.S. relations. In this, too, we are guided by a demand from our people. . . .

Reagan: Mr. General Secretary, we've agreed many times that there remain differences—important basic differences—between us. Yet as we work over the long run to narrow these differences, as we work for what I hope will be a new time of peace and greater human freedom, we must also take on our important duty to take steps now to reduce the chances of conflict and to prevent war. This we have done today. It is a first step toward a brighter future, and a safer world.

Source: Parts of a speech delivered by Gorbachev and Reagan together on June 1, 1988, at the end of the Moscow summit. [Changed for easier reading.] Found at www.reaganlibrary.gov/research/speeches/060188a

Original Evidence

The documents above appear in a modified format. In most cases the source information includes links to the original documents. Three documents are not easily accessed online so the originals are included below.

Document 4: Reagan Letter

Mr. General Secretary, our recent history provides ample evidence that if you wait for an ideal moment to try to resolve our differences, we are unlikely to resolve anything. This is the moment which has been given us. We should take advantage of it since it is a time of historic and possibly unique potential. Let us not lose it for lack of effort.

Source: Part of a letter written by President Ronald Reagan to Mikhail Gorbachev on May 23, 1986, after a Soviet nuclear power plant accident at Chernobyl. Found in the book *Ronald Reagan: An American Life*, an autobiography by Ronald Reagan (2011, pp. 664–665).

Document 5: Gorbachev Reflections

I regularly read foreign press, and I can feel a sense of the broad resonance that information about the Reykjavik summit has triggered. And the speculations started right away—who won over whom there. But that was not our goal going to Reykjavik. We had quite a significant reason for our initiative. The fact is that Geneva had reached a deadlock. We felt that a major breakthrough was needed, for time is working against the interests of humankind. And now Reykjavik has gone by. As it turned out, it was quite easy to reach an understanding over the first and second points of our platform—the strategic weapons and the intermediate range missiles. That alone has given us enormous experience. We understood the President's problems, understood, that he was not free in making his decisions. We did not make a tragedy out of the fact that the SDI problem prevented Reykjavik from becoming a total success. We thought, let the President think everything over, let him seek counsel from the Congress. Perhaps we will need one more try to step over [the barrier], that still divides us. We can wait. We do not take back the proposals we brought to Reykjavik. We need not fall into despair. Reykjavik led us to the most important stage of understanding of where we stand. Everybody saw that agreement is possible. From Reykjavik, we drew the conclusion that the necessity for dialogue has increased even more. That is why I am even more of an optimist after Reykjavik.

Source: Part of the notes taken by Gorbachev's advisor Anatoly Chernyaev during his return flight after the Reykjavik summit on October 12, 1986. Found in the book *The Last Superpower Summits: Gorbachev, Reagan, and Bush* by Svetlana Savranskaya and Thomas S. Blanton (2016, p. 238).

Document 9: Luncheon Notes

Gorbachev said that soon he would be saying goodbye to the President and the President's colleagues. Gorbachev said he had arrived at the conclusion that the third summit had been a landmark. It had witnessed important agreements and other questions had been discussed intensively. Most importantly the atmosphere had been good. There had been more elements of mutual understanding. Gorbachev said that he would like to pay tribute to the contribution of the President toward making this a successful summit, as well as to the contributions of other American participants. Gorbachev added that he would like the momentum achieved at the summit to continue. He then said that on his way to the White House lunch he had ridden with Vice President Bush. He had looked out the car window and seen Americans responding warmly to what had happened in the negotiations. When the car had stopped at a red light, he jumped out of the car and had had a spontaneous conversation with some passerby. When it was time to go, he did not want to leave the conversation.

Source: Part of the notes kept during a working lunch held at the conclusion of the Washington summit on December 10, 1987, in the family dining room of the White House. Found in the book *The Last Superpower Summits: Gorbachev, Reagan, and Bush* by Svetlana Savranskaya and Thomas S. Blanton (2016, p. 353).

Argumentative Writing Graphic Organizer

Evidence		Evidence		Evidence

Evidence		Evidence		Evidence

Evidence		Evidence		Evidence

Claim 1:		Claim 2:		Claim 3:

Graphic Organizer

Use the following chart to record evidence from the documents that supports or weakens each of the possible interpretations listed below. If there is nothing in the documents to support or weaken an interpretation, leave the cell empty.

Document	High-Stakes	Reagan's Talk	Friendship
1	*Gorbachev realizes their diplomacy impacts all people on the planet*		*Gorbachev's style shows charisma and a willingness to be friendly*
2			
3			
4			
5			
6			
7			
8			
9			
10			
Document	**Public Pressure**	**Patience**	**Other:**
1		*Gorbachev implies that patience is needed to overcome differences*	
2			
3			
4			
5			
6			
7			
8			
9			
10			

Use the evidence compiled on this form to write a persuasive essay supporting your interpretation of the reason or reasons Reagan and Gorbachev's diplomacy was successful. Explain in your essay why other interpretations are less compelling than yours.

Sample Classroom Poster

PARTS OF ARGUMENTATIVE WRITING

- **Argument**—the author's entire attempt to support his/her interpretation
- **Interpretation**—an evidence-supported but disputable way of thinking
- **Opinion**—a way of thinking that is unsupported by evidence
- **Claim**—a short, clear statement that expresses a disputable interpretation
- **Warrant**—an explanation of how evidence supports a claim
- **Evidence**—indisputable facts that are used to support a claim
- **Counterclaim**—an alternative way to explain evidence

The purpose of argumentation is to work together toward a rational, evidence-based understanding.

PART V

DEMONSTRATING DISAPPROVAL:
Courageously Taking a Stand

On September 30, 2018, Senator Jeff Flake of Arizona entered an elevator shortly after announcing that he would vote in support of the controversial Supreme Court justice nominee Brett Kavanaugh. Kavanaugh had been accused of sexually assaulting a teenage girl when he was a 17-year-old boy. With television cameras recording the incident, two women approached Flake and began to berate him for his decision to support the nomination. "You have children in your family. Think about them. I have two children. I cannot imagine that for the next 50 years they will have to have someone in the Supreme Court who has been accused of violating a young girl," one of the women shouted. "What are you doing, sir?" (Shabad, 2018). The small protest continued for several minutes. Eventually, Flake thanked the women as they allowed him to leave the elevator. A short time afterward, he announced that he would not vote to confirm Kavanaugh until after an FBI investigation.

Government involves numerous power relationships. The Constitution outlines many of these. The ultimate authority of government, however, is captured in the Constitution's first three words: *We, the people*. Normally, people influence government by collectively selecting those who represent them and by individually asking for their support on issues of interest. At times, matters of great concern to people do not draw requisite attention from government representatives. When such is the case, when those who are in positions of power will not pay attention to those who have little power, what recourse is available? How can relatively powerless people gain the attention and the action of those in power? One way is through public demonstrations.

The most effective demonstrations have a stage, an audience, a moment, and a message. Demonstrators have chosen a wide variety of *stages* throughout American history. The two protesters described above chose an elevator for their stage. Protests have taken place on merchant ships, in parks, on buses, in the streets, and, in the case of the demonstrations described in this section, on the sidewalks surrounding the White House and on the Olympic medal podium. Demonstrators hope to have a large and/or powerful *audience*—large enough to pressure policymakers and/or powerful enough to cause change. The two protesters mentioned above had both—an influential senator, and the cameras of a respected news agency—to capture their

protest. The Silent Sentinels described in Chapter 11 targeted President Woodrow Wilson and his legislative colleagues who could propose a constitutional amendment granting women the right to vote. The victorious athletes who demonstrated at the 1968 Olympics had a stadium full of observers and a global television audience. Sometimes, a demonstration produces its own audience, such as the 2017 Women's March that mobilized millions of people from across the United States.

The most effective demonstrations also have a *moment*. The Kavanaugh confirmation hearing provided a moment when the spotlight was on the activists mentioned above. Some moments are truly only a moment, such as the 1968 Olympic protest, which occurred only during the 90-second National Anthem. Other moments have lasted for weeks, months, or longer, as in the case of the Silent Sentinels, who picketed the Wilson White House for almost 2½ years. Moments are sometimes spontaneous, an unplanned reaction to a perceived injustice. Other moments are well orchestrated and timed to coincide with events that increase the audience—major sporting events, political gatherings, or other news-making occurrences, when media coverage is present. Although moments are often fleeting, and timing is often critical, some demonstrations, such as the Women's March, have become annual events.

Further, all demonstrations have a *message*. The Silent Sentinels featured in Chapter 11 demanded women's suffrage. Their message was captured on banners with biting slogans, as well as in their silence, a symbol of their silenced political voice. In contrast, the message of the raised, black-gloved fists at the 1968 Olympics was the poverty, history of abuse, and resurgence of pride experienced by African Americans during the civil rights movement. Booed off the podium, their act was as controversial as protests by modern athletes, also occurring during the National Anthem.

Not all demonstrations share the nonviolent or relatively harmless nature of those described in this section. On occasion, demonstration organizers lose control and violence results. When such happens, demonstrators can do more harm than good to their cause. The New York City "Hard Hat Riot" on May 8, 1970; the Los Angeles race riot on April 29, 1992; as well as numerous other violent demonstrations contrast sharply with the peaceful demonstrations described in this book. The irony of violating the rights of others in an effort to draw attention to the violations of one's own rights runs counter to the dispositions of civic engagement promoted throughout this book. Protesting in order to silence a controversial speaker, for instance, smacks of hypocrisy. Effective demonstrations do not include bullying, and are not orchestrated by people who hold political power. (Their rallies serve different purposes.) Nor are social media petitions that never reach the desks of policymakers "demonstrations." Demonstrations must have a large and/or powerful audience to be successful.

History is full of examples of demonstrations, some of which have achieved the goals of the protesters, and others of which have been less successful. The Occupy Wall Street demonstrations that began in September 2011 included thousands of people in major cities across the United States. The civil rights movement was propelled by nonviolent demonstrations, some within the bounds of the law

and others involving illegal activities, the topic of the next section of this book. From the Boston Tea Party to the ongoing protests made by individuals who raise their voices as part of the Me Too Movement, demonstrations have done much to shape American history.

The teacher might help students apply the concepts related to demonstrations by discussing with them the following questions in connection with the lessons included in Chapters 10 and 11:

- When are demonstrations most productive? When are other forms of civic engagement more effective?
- Do problems exist in our school or community that are ignored by those in power? Would a peaceful demonstration draw attention to the problem?
- What would be the best stage, audience, moment, and message of such a demonstration?

CHAPTER 10

Alice Paul and the Silent Sentinels

How can people who have no political power, and to whom government officials will not respond, gain the attention and action of those who have power? The First Amendment guarantees the right of citizens to peaceably assemble. So, some people who are civically engaged turn to public demonstrations when other attempts to promote reform are unsuccessful. This chapter provides materials for an investigation of the Silent Sentinels, women who demonstrated at entrances to the White House for over 2 years, from 1917 until 1919, seeking the right to vote.

STUDENTS' BACKGROUND KNOWLEDGE

A handful of people and events related to women's suffrage may be familiar to students, but few students are familiar with the demonstrations described in this chapter. Students have likely heard of Susan B. Anthony and one or two other women's rights advocates. They may know about the Seneca Falls Convention of 1848. Students undoubtedly know that women can vote today, but may fail to realize that there was a long period before the 19th Amendment was passed when most women could not vote. Most students have never heard of Alice Paul, the National Woman's Party or the Silent Sentinels who picketed the White House from 1917 to 1919, only ending their protests when Congress passed the 19th Amendment.

Not only are students unaware of many of the facts associated with the women's suffrage movement, but they lack background knowledge about the context of the demonstrations, familiarity that is essential for engaging with the documents and images included in this investigation. For instance, students may have difficulty imagining a context when the general view of women as "the fairer sex" created expectations for their behavior that were different from today's norms. Most Americans, both men and women, thought that women should be mild, soft-spoken, calm, nonconfrontational, and gentle. Students may fail to understand that many people opposed women's suffrage because they feared it would lead women to violate these norms. Politically active women, like those who picketed the White House, were viewed as unnatural, uncivil, and disorderly, even when they protested peacefully. The actions of Alice Paul and the other Silent Sentinels were shocking, drawing criticism from many groups, including other suffragists. It is important for students to understand this context. The

women studied in this investigation crossed the line of what respectable women did in 1917.

HISTORICAL BACKGROUND FOR TEACHERS AND STUDENTS

Background of the Women's Suffrage Movement

For most of the 1800s, women in the United States could not vote. They had few other civil rights. Girls had to obey their fathers. Married women were expected to obey their husbands. Laws allowed men to beat their wives. Married women did not have the right to sign contracts or own property. Women had few chances for an education. They had few job options. Any money a woman earned at work belonged to her husband. Women could not hold office, serve on juries, or testify in court. They had to have a man with them when traveling. They were expected to remain quiet in public. Some people, usually men, said that such standards placed women above men. It freed them from the worries and nastiness of politics, business, and the world outside of their home. And some women were satisfied caring for a family and home. However, many women and men thought that the legal system, social rules, educational policies, and religious traditions that gave women few rights were unfair. They argued that a nation that kept half of its citizens from voting was not a democracy. *Suffrage*, the right to vote, was seen as a key to changing other unfair laws and policies.

In 1848, a convention was held in Seneca Falls, New York. There, the drive for women's suffrage began. Elizabeth Cady Stanton and Lucretia Mott presented the Declaration of Sentiments, which demanded changes in the way women were treated. They asked for changes in education, employment, property rights, and religious practices. And they asked for the right to vote for women. Many people became angry by the women's demands. But over the next few years, conventions like it were held all over the country.

Over time, more women joined the fight for women's suffrage. Susan B. Anthony and others brought more attention to the problems that women faced. Debate over women's rights went on until the Civil War started. Most reformers, people who wanted change, thought it was more important to win the war and end slavery. They planned to renew their fight for women's suffrage after the war. But when the war ended, reformers who fought for African Americans' rights did not help women. These reformers did not include women's suffrage in the changes they demanded. Women began again their fight for the right to vote.

Because states set the rules for voting, and western states were quicker to give women the vote, some suffragists moved their fight to western states. In 1869, Wyoming gave women the vote. In 1870, Utah followed. However, in 1872, when Susan B. Anthony voted in New York, she was arrested and convicted of breaking New York's election laws. But people were changing. Within a few years, an amendment was proposed that would give women suffrage. It failed. The amendment was introduced again the next year and every year, but could not get the support it needed to pass. Women's rights activists had more success in other ways. By 1900, most states allowed married women to own property and keep their own paychecks. Women could attend most public universities and could speak in public. But they still did not have the right to vote.

From 1900 to 1910, the first generation of suffragists grew older and began to pass away. The new generation of leaders had little success. American women who were peaceful in their struggle for the right to vote were called *suffragists*. They did not want to use the more extreme tactics of the *suffragettes* in England. There, suffragettes destroyed property, fought with police, chained themselves to railings, staged hunger strikes, and bombed churches. But the American suffragists began to try new strategies. Harriot Stanton Blatch and others held a suffrage parade in New York City. The parade appealed to younger activists. Some of the leaders in the fight for women's suffrage were becoming more willing to violate society's rules for women.

Alice Paul and the Silent Sentinels

Alice Paul grew up in a Quaker family near Philadelphia. She went to college and earned a bachelor's degree and a master's degree. She traveled to England to continue her education. There, she joined with the suffragettes in their violent protests. She was arrested several times. After returning to the United States, Paul earned a PhD in sociology. She became a popular speaker at women's suffrage meetings. Soon, Paul and Lucy Burns, a woman she had met in jail in England, began to work together on a constitutional amendment. Using the New York suffrage parade as a model, Paul organized a parade in Washington DC. It took place the day after President Woodrow Wilson's inauguration and followed the same route. The suffragist paraders were confronted by angry spectators. The observers taunted them, spat upon them, and blocked their path. At first, Alice Paul was frustrated. But then she found that the newspaper articles about the parade brought attention and sympathy to their cause. The hecklers had helped them.

Paul thought that President Wilson could help women gain the right to vote. She wanted him to take the lead on women's suffrage. In October 1916, he spoke in favor of the vote for women. But he would not be the strong supporter that Paul hoped for. On January 9, 1917, Paul met with Wilson. He would not promise to help the way she wanted him to. So, Paul and a group of women decided to picket the White House until an amendment passed. The next day, they arrived at the east and west entrances of the White House. They carried banners that read "How long must women wait for liberty?" and "Mr. President, what will you do for woman suffrage?" Two shifts of demonstrators stayed in place from 9:00 in the morning until 5:00 that afternoon. They returned the next day and the next, determined to stay until an amendment passed. The women kept silent during their demonstration to symbolize their silenced political voice. In 1917, picketing the White House like this had not happened before. It was considered unwomanly. Newspaper reporters noticed and wrote about the Silent Sentinels and women's suffrage.

The suffragists returned almost every day for the next 29 months. They marched as Congress voted to enter World War I. They sometimes changed their banners with new, carefully worded messages. Many criticized Wilson. Some called him a hypocrite, someone who says one thing but does something else. How could Wilson say the United States was fighting a war for democracy when American women could not vote? The messages on the women's banners became more provocative. One compared Wilson to the German kaiser whom America was fighting. It called him Kaiser Wilson.

Some people thought that the Silent Sentinels' banner during a visit by Russian officials went too far. The banner told the Russians not to support the United States in World War I as long as American women could not vote. The police issued a warning. If the Silent Sentinels returned to the White House the next day, they would be arrested. They ignored the warning and some were arrested. The picketing continued, with several arrests over the next days. When spectators began to attack the suffragists, the police arrested the women. Some of the women were put in jail. But the picketing continued. President Wilson began to fear that the women who had been arrested would become heroes and inspire more protests. He pardoned them and stopped the arrests.

In August and September 1917, the police started arresting demonstrators again. They said that the women blocked traffic or broke other laws. When Paul was arrested and sentenced to a long jail term, she and others began a hunger strike. They refused to eat until freed. Jail officials were afraid they might die, so they roughly force-fed them.

Some suffragists disagreed with the tactics of the Silent Sentinels. They worked in different ways to gain the right to vote. They sent letters to government officials and gave speeches. More Americans began to support the suffragists. Many thought the Silent Sentinels acted within their rights of assembly and free speech. They thought the arrests were wrong. Under pressure, Wilson became a stronger supporter of an amendment giving women the right to vote. On January 10, 1918, the House of Representatives passed the amendment. But the Senate would not follow. The Silent Sentinels' pickets continued. They attracted even greater attention by burning Wilson's speeches in bonfires on the sidewalks near the White House. On June 4, 1919, over a year later, the Senate finally passed the amendment. Only then did the Silent Sentinels end their picketing. President Wilson wrote to some suffrage leaders, congratulating them for their work. But he did not write to Alice Paul or the other leaders of the Silent Sentinels.

HISTORICAL THINKING SKILLS: PHOTOGRAPH ANALYSIS

One of the most useful genres of historical evidence that has become increasingly available since the mid-19th century is the photograph. Photographic images include portraits of famous and everyday people, landscapes and cityscapes, snapshots from historical events, and pictures of everyday life. Photographs can not only enhance the historical narrative, but can serve as pieces of evidence, useful in constructing historical interpretations. This investigation uses images of the Silent Sentinels to support inferences about the public and official reaction to their demonstration.

Historians use many of the same strategies when working with photographs that they use with other genres of evidence; however, they also employ some unique photoanalysis strategies. Historians engage in sourcing, considering the photographer, his/her background, and his/her purpose. They think about the photographers' decisions involving perspective, content, and cropping. Historians understand that photographs, like other accounts, both reveal and conceal—photographers make decisions about what to include and exclude from their images. Historians consider if and how the photograph was originally published or shared—its audience. For example, was it published in a newspaper, as part of an artistic collection, or included in a family scrapbook? Did the photographer take a picture for personal use, or was he/she commissioned by a business, newspaper, or government agency? Even when such information is lacking, historians can engage in a critical analysis of photographs. They use clues within the photograph to identify whether it was staged or spontaneous. Using their background knowledge, they make inferences about events immediately before and after the photograph was taken (Foster, Hoge, & Rosch, 1999).

Though useful, photographs can present a challenge for students, who often view photos as true and objective snapshots of reality (Callahan, 2013). History teachers and textbooks often use photographs as illustrations rather than evidence. Captions generally explain to students the correct information to be gathered from the image, leaving little room for critical analysis or interpretation (Callahan, 2013).

As a result of this training, when given images as historical evidence, young students fail to think about why a photograph might have been taken. Based upon their own experiences, they often falsely assume that the photographer was intimately associated with the subjects of his/her photo (Foster et al., 1999). High school students have a more nuanced understanding of a photographer's purpose and, when prompted, make inferences about the potential audience of a photo (Foster et al., 1999). Perhaps the greatest barrier to students' ability to construct meaning with photographs is that they lack the needed background knowledge to make inferences. Lacking background knowledge, students sometimes make wild speculations that are unwarranted by the photographs' subject (Foster et al., 1999). A key to helping students make plausible, defensible inferences using photographs is to provide appropriate scaffolding (Callow, 2006), to teach explicitly strategies for making sound inferences, to nurture background knowledge, to correct misconceptions (Callow, 2006), and to demand that students justify their inferences with evidence in the image.

One instructional tool that supports students as they use visual historical evidence like photographs is the Observation/Inference (O/I) Chart (Nokes, 2008). This chart breaks down students' analysis of an image into two phases: observing and inferring. An O/I Chart is a simple T-chart, with observations recorded in the left column and inferences recorded in the right. To prepare students to work with the O/I Chart, the teacher might instruct them explicitly about observations. Observations include the information gathered from the five senses—sight, in particular, when working with photographs. Observations are enhanced when students focus their attention on the details of one section of an image, as well as when they make connections across the entire photograph. Additionally, collaborating with peers increases the number and quality of observations. Students can also be taught explicitly about inferences. Defensible inferences are based upon accurate background knowledge and careful observations. Simple explanations of things observed are generally preferred to more complex explanations. Using the O/I Chart, students might draw arrows linking specific observations (written on the left) to the inferences they lead to (written on the right). The O/I Chart can help students base inferences on the photograph, avoiding the wild speculations that result when they make unsupported claims (Nokes, 2008).

The O/I Chart can be used to gather information that can help students consider the photographer. Central to the entire analysis of the photograph is a consideration of the photographer's purpose, even when he/she may be unknown. Skilled students approach photographs as they do any other account, acknowledging that there is a person with a purpose, biases, motives, and insights who took the picture. An image reveals to some degree the author's intention as it captures one moment and one place in time. The students must consider the physical context of the photograph and make inferences about why the photographer positioned the camera as he/she did. Finally, teachers can help students analyze photographs by asking authentic historical questions that can be answered with evidence gleaned from the photo.

LESSON IDEAS

Introduction

The following materials could be used in a lesson during a unit on the Progressive Era, 20th-century reforms, the women's rights movement, or the civil rights movement. If a course is organized thematically, this lesson could instead be taught with other lessons on the use of demonstrations to draw attention to a problem. All photographs used in this investigation can be found at the Library of Congress website at www.loc.gov/photos/?q=women+suffrage+pictures. This lesson could be extended by analyzing any of the hundreds of images of the Silent Sentinels found there.

Objectives

This lesson is designed to meet three objectives associated with knowledge, skills, and dispositions:

1. Students will evaluate the significance of the Silent Sentinels in the struggle for women's suffrage.
2. Students will analyze primary source photographs, using observations to make defensible inferences about the photographer, the context, and the content of the photograph.
3. Students will debate the effectiveness or ineffectiveness of political demonstrations in promoting reform, evaluating the stage, audience, moment, and message of the Silent Sentinels' demonstration.

Build Background Knowledge

Begin the lesson by building students' background knowledge on the events leading up to the Silent Sentinels' protest. The essays provided in this chapter under the headings "Background of the Women's Suffrage Movement" and "Alice Paul and the Silent Sentinels" provide a basic overview of what students will need to know to work with the photographs and documents that follow.

Ask Historical Questions

The background information provided above and the photographs and documents that follow were designed to help students ask and answer the following question: To what

extent, if any, did the demonstrations of the Silent Sentinels build public support for the 19th Amendment? In order to address this question, students could also consider the following questions: How do photographs taken at the time of the demonstrations reveal the tactics used by the Silent Sentinels? How do photographs show public and/or official support of, or opposition to, their picketing? How did the messages on the banners of the Silent Sentinels as well as the other content of the photographs reflect the context of the time period?

Provide Strategy Instruction on Photograph Analysis

After providing students with background knowledge related to the women's suffrage movement, Alice Paul, and the Silent Sentinels, the teacher can introduce students to the photographic evidence at the heart of this investigation. Before showing the first image, the teacher could show students a blank O/I Chart and explain to them the processes of observing and inferring, as well as ways of judging inferences. Specifically, the teacher can tell students that observations include what a person can see, hear, smell, taste, and feel, but for purposes of this lesson, observations will come exclusively through sight. The teacher might point out that observant people are unusually skilled at observing. Some of the strategies that observant people use are taking sufficient time to focus on details, moving from quadrant to quadrant to study parts of an image, and seeing connections between details within an image. The teacher might then project Document 1 and lead the class in a discussion of the things that they observe.

For example, students might observe that there are three women holding banners. Two banners have three stripes that appear to be different colors. The banner in the middle has some writing. Students might even be able to make out some of the words on the banner, which faces away from the photographer and toward the White House. The woman on the left is smiling. She and the woman next to her are looking at the camera while the woman on the right looks to the side of the camera. The women are wearing heavy coats, hats, and have muffs (students may not know what these are called). They are wearing a sash that has three stripes, perhaps the same colors as their banners. The women are standing in front of a wrought-iron fence. There are trees in the background. There is a thermos between two of the women. The woman on the right is standing on a folded blanket. They are all wearing dark, ankle-length dresses or skirts. Their mouths are all closed. The teacher might sketch an O/I Chart on the board and jot down the students' observations as they make them.

At some point in the discussion, a student might make an inference, such as "It looks cold" or "The women seem happy." When this happens, the teacher might point out that the student's comment is an example of an inference rather than an observation. The teacher can help students understand what an inference is and can talk about the process of making inferences. He/she might explain that good inferences come from background knowledge combined with observations. For example, if a student has commented that it looks cold, the teacher might ask what background knowledge and observations led to that inference. Stated simply, students know from experience that when it is cold, they wear coats and they observe women wearing coats, hats, and muffs. If the teacher has listed observations on the board, he/she can draw an arrow from the observation that "Women are wearing coats" to an inference (listed on the right side of the diagram) that "It is cold." The teacher might then ask students to list and justify inferences based upon their background knowledge and evidence found in the picture. They might list: These are suffragists, they are at the White House, they are planning to stay for a long time (suggested by the thermos), they are happy, and their feet are cold. It is possible that students will make important observations as they are making inferences, in which case the teacher might add these observations to the left column of the O/I Chart.

Eventually, the students can begin to consider how the photograph provides evidence that might answer the historical questions listed above. As part of this analysis, the students should consider the photographer, his/her purposes and biases. Using the source information on the photograph, students can be shown that little is known about the photographer. The teacher might use the Internet to do a reverse image search to see if any additional information can be found about the source of the photo. The teacher might ask whether students believe the photographer was sympathetic to the suffragists' cause or whether he/she opposed them (suggesting that this, too, is an inference). A related question associated with all photographs is whether the picture was staged or spontaneous. The teacher might suggest that it appears that the women were aware that the picture was being taken and smiled for it, though their positions look fairly spontaneous, with the woman on the right still standing on the blanket as she may have done throughout the demonstration. Students might also consider what the women were doing right before this picture was taken and what they did right after. The teacher might suggest that there was probably little change in their activities before, during, or after the picture except to look and smile at the photographer. There is nothing in the picture to suggest that the photographer opposed the suffragists, but nothing that suggests he/she was a strong advocate either.

Finally, students might consider what this image suggests about the suffragists' tactics and how those tactics might have impacted others. Demonstrating in the cold shows that suffragists were willing to picket in all weather. It suggests their determination. Their closed mouths might be coincidental or might reflect their silence during the protests—a symbol of their silenced political voice. Their pleasant faces indicate that they were not hostile or belligerent with passersby. Their banners show that they wanted to be noticed—that they wanted an audience. They were probably pleased to be photographed because that would spread their message. This image suggests little about how others might have reacted. However, understanding society's views of women at the time might help students infer that these women were pretty radical and that more conservative people might not have approved of their protest. The teacher might inform students that some of the photographs they will analyze are a series of connected photographs giving multiple glimpses of the same event as it occurred.

Group-Work

Once the teacher is confident that students understand how to make observations and inferences with the images, and how to use them to try to answer the historical questions of the lesson, he/she can have students analyze the remaining photographs and documents independently or in small groups. The teacher should remind students about their objective: to consider to what extent, if any, the demonstrations of the Silent Sentinels built public support for the 19th Amendment.

Debriefing

After students have had time to analyze the photographs and other documents, they can discuss what they learned about Alice Paul and the Silent Sentinels, responding to questions such as the following:

1. What tactics were used by the Silent Sentinels during their demonstrations?
2. How did people react to the Silent Sentinels' picketing?
3. To what extent did the Silent Sentinels' protests contribute to the passage of the 19th Amendment?

A second phase of the debriefing can focus on the skills associated with analyzing historical photographs, particularly observing and inferring, using these questions:

1. What strategies did you use to make observations? Was anyone in your group particularly observant? What did he or she do that was different?
2. What were some of the most important or insightful inferences that you made during the analysis of the photographs?
3. Did disagreements ever develop within your group about the inferences that could be made about a photographer or a photograph? If so, how did you settle those disagreements?

The third phase of the debriefing can focus on demonstrations as a tool for achieving reform. Consider using the following questions:

1. What was the stage, audience, moment, and message of the Silent Sentinels? In what ways were their decisions about these features of the demonstration wise or unwise?
2. Why were some suffragists hesitant to demonstrate?
3. What strategies or slogans used by the Silent Sentinels during their demonstrations were most effective and least effective?
4. What lessons can we learn about effective demonstrations from the Silent Sentinels?

INSTRUCTIONAL MATERIALS

Nine primary source documents with photographs are included in the pages that follow, along with an example of a simple Observation/Inference (O/I) Chart. Rather than producing hard copies of these images, students might access them on the Library of Congress website. There, students can zoom in to facilitate more detailed observations. The online location for each image is provided in the source information below. Photographs, all taken by unknown photographers, many of whom worked for the Bain News Agency, were donated to the Library of Congress in 1955 by the Harris & Ewing Collection. Documents 2 and 9 are included both in a modified format and in their original format below.

Document Set

1. An image of three women picketing the White House in 1917. Found at www.loc.gov/resource/hec.07292/
2. A quote by a journalist, Gilson Gardner, reporting his impression of the Silent Sentinels. (Conkling, 2018, p. 221)
3. An image of women picketing the White House in the rain in 1917. Found at www.loc.gov/resource/hec.10339/
4. Photograph taken in 1917 entitled "Women Suffrage Banner." Found at www.loc.gov/resource/hec.09043/
5. A two-photograph series taken in 1917 entitled "Women Suffrage." Found at www.loc.gov/resource/hec.09404/ and www.loc.gov/resource/hec.09403/
6. Three photographs taken in 1918 entitled "Suffrage Fire," "Women Suffrage," and "Bonfire on Sidewalk before White House." Found at www.loc.gov/resource/npcc.00931/ and www.loc.gov/resource/hec.11588/ and www.loc.gov/item/2016869624/

7. Photograph taken in 1917 entitled "Woman Suffrage Banners." Found at www.loc.gov/resource/hec.09835/
8. Two-photograph series taken in 1917 entitled "Women Suffrage. Arrests." Found at www.loc.gov/resource/hec.11448/ and www.loc.gov/resource/hec.11450/
9. Statement made by a *New York Sun* reporter, Eleanor Booth Simmons, on March 7, 1917 (Adams & Keene, 2008, p. 163)

Simplified Evidence

Document 1: Three Protesters

Source: Photograph entitled "Women Suffrage Pickets" taken in 1917 by an unknown photographer, donated to the Library of Congress in 1955 by the Harris & Ewing Collection. Found at www.loc.gov/resource/hec.07292/

Document 2: Gardner Account

During the eighteen years I have been a newspaper reporter in Washington, I have not seen a more impressive sight than the show of the pickets surrounding the White House on the afternoon on March fourth. The weather gave this event its feel. If there had been fifteen hundred women carrying banners on a sunny day the sight would not have been a pretty one. But to see a thousand women marching in a rain that almost froze as it fell was impressive. They included young women, middle-aged women, and old women. There were women in the line who were over 70. To see them standing and marching and holding their heavy banners, growing heavier every moment, was impressive. They held them against a wind that was half a hurricane for hour after hour. They held them until their gloves were wet and their clothes soaked.... This was a sight that impressed even people who are worn out from seeing so much.

Source: Statement made by Gilson Gardner, newspaper reporter for Scripps and a husband of a suffragist, on March 17, 1917, quoted in the book *Alice Paul and the American Suffrage Campaign* by Katherine H. Adams and Michael L. Keene (pp. 166–167). [Changed for easier reading.]

Document 3: Picket Parade

Source: Photograph entitled "Women Suffrage Picket Parade" taken in 1917 by an unknown photographer, donated to the Library of Congress in 1955 by the Harris & Ewing Collection. Found at www.loc.gov/resource/hec.10339/

Document 4: Banner to Russian Envoy

Source: Photograph entitled "Women Suffrage Banner" taken in 1917 by an unknown photographer, donated to the Library of Congress in 1955 by the Harris & Ewing Collection. Found at www.loc.gov/resource/hec.09043/

Document 5: Protester Arrests

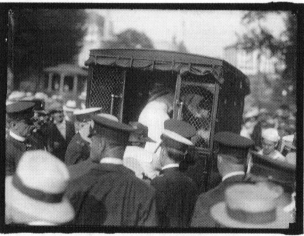

Source: Two-photograph series entitled "Women Suffrage" taken in 1917 by an unknown photographer, donated to the Library of Congress in 1955 by the Harris & Ewing Collection. Found at www.loc.gov/resource/hec.09404/ and www.loc.gov/resource/hec.09403/

Document 6: Protest Bonfire

Banner reads: President Wilson is deceiving the world when he appears as the prophet of democracy. President Wilson has opposed those who demand democracy for this country. He is responsible for the disfranchisement of millions of Americans. We in America know this. The world will find him out.

Source: Three photographs taken in 1918 by unknown photographers. Photos are entitled "Suffrage Fire," "Woman Suffrage Demonstrators at White House," and "Women Suffrage. Bonfire on Sidewalk before White House," donated to the Library of Congress in 1955 by the Harris & Ewing Collection. Found at www.loc.gov/resource/npcc.00931/ and www.loc.gov/resource/hec.11588/ and www.loc.gov/item/2016869624/

Document 7: Kaiser Wilson Banner

Source: Photograph entitled "Woman Suffrage Banner," taken in 1917 by an unknown photographer, donated to the Library of Congress in 1955 by the Harris & Ewing Collection. Found at www.loc.gov/resource/hec.09835/

Document 8: Protest Confrontation

Source: Two-photograph series entitled "Women Suffrage. Arrests" taken in 1917 by an unknown photographer, donated to the Library of Congress in 1955 by the Harris & Ewing Collection. Found at www.loc.gov/resource/hec.11448/ and www.loc.gov/resource/hec.11450/

Document 9: Simmons Account

I supposed no one event got quite so much advertising as did the picketing of the White House by the National Woman's Party. Their press agent [person over publicity] told me that one day's picketing—it was the Sunday of Woodrow Wilson's inauguration, the day that 1,000 pickets marched round and round the White House in the pouring rain, calling on the walls of Jericho to fall—well, 1,000 newspapers told about that trick in their pages.... And groups of photographers also gave them much attention.... Before Alice Paul and the pickets came, days would pass when the word suffrage didn't appear in the news. Since their activities, no word is written more frequently than this.

Source: Statement made by Eleanor Booth Simmons, newspaper reporter for the *New York Sun*, on March 7, 1917, quoted in the book *Alice Paul and the American Suffrage Campaign* by Katherine H. Adams and Michael L. Keene (p. 163). [Changed for easier reading.]

Original Evidence

Documents from the previous set have been modified and appear here in their original language.

Document 2: Gardner Account

During the eighteen years I have been a newspaper correspondent in Washington I have seen no more impressive sight than the spectacle of the pickets surrounding the White House on the afternoon on March fourth. The weather gave this affair its character. Had there been fifteen hundred women carrying banners on a fair day the sight would not have been a pretty one. But to see a thousand women—young women, middle-aged women, and old women—and there were women in the line who had passed their three score years and ten—marching in a rain that almost froze as it fell; to see them standing and marching and holding their heavy banners, momentarily growing heavier—holding them against a wind that was half a gale—hour after hour, until their gloves were wet and their clothes soaked through . . . was a sight to impress even the jaded sense of one who has seen much.

Source: Statement made by Gilson Gardner, newspaper reporter for Scripps and husband of a suffragist, on March 17, 1917, quoted in the book *Alice Paul and the American Suffrage Campaign* by Katherine H. Adams and Michael L. Keene (pp. 166–167).

Document 9: Simmons Account

I supposed no one undertaking captured quite so much advertising as did the picketing of the White House by the National Woman's Party. Their press agent told me that one day's picketing—it was the Sunday of Woodrow Wilson's inauguration, the day that 1,000 pickets March round and round the White House in the pouring rain, calling on the walls of Jericho to fall—well 1,000 dailies opened their pages to that stunt to the amount of an average of half a column in a paper. At least 500 tri-weeklies and semi-weeklies gave a column each, and the picture syndicates gave much space. . . . Before Alice Paul and the pickets came, days would pass when the word suffrage didn't appear in the dispatches. Since their activities, no word occurs more frequently than this.

Source: Statement made by Eleanor Booth Simmons, newspaper reporter for the *New York Sun*, on March 7, 1917, quoted in the book *Alice Paul and the American Suffrage Campaign* by Katherine H. Adams and Michael L. Keene (pp. 166–167).

Graphic Organizer

Observations	Inferences

CHAPTER 11

Tommie Smith, John Carlos, and the 1968 Olympic Protests

The Silent Sentinels picketed the White House for almost 2½ years. In contrast, the reformers featured in this chapter demonstrated for about 90 seconds. Yet, the image of Tommie Smith and John Carlos with their black-gloved fists raised in the Black Power salute during the playing of the "Star-Spangled Banner" during a medal ceremony at the 1968 Olympic Games in Mexico City has become an icon of the civil rights movement. In this chapter, I provide information on the context and lesson materials for conducting a document-based investigation of their protest.

STUDENTS' BACKGROUND KNOWLEDGE

Students' limited background knowledge of the civil rights movement is reviewed in Chapter 7. Students are even less likely to know about the people and events associated with the struggle for civil rights in the late 1960s and 1970s than they are with earlier civil rights leaders and events. Some may never have seen or been taught about the iconic image of Smith and Carlos on the medal podium. Students' unfamiliarity with Smith and Carlos does not mean they are unaware of athletes protesting during the national anthem. In August 2016, Colin Kaepernick, a quarterback in the National Football League (NFL), gained attention by sitting during the National Anthem as a way to protest police brutality and the ongoing oppression of African Americans. Some students are probably familiar with the protests that his act sparked, which President Donald Trump and some National Football League team owners have criticized. These recent events provide students with insight into the historical context of Smith and Carlos's protest.

Today, Smith and Carlos are viewed by most Americans, including most students who learn about their protest, as civil rights heroes. However, 50 years ago, the demonstration took place when the majority of White Americans were scandalized by their disrespect, even more than some Americans in recent years have reacted to the protests of Kaepernick and other athletes. This chapter focuses on the strategy of contextualization, placing oneself in the physical and social context of historical events. It is only through contextualization that students can more fully appreciate the courage required of Smith and Carlos to protest under those circumstances. Chapter 7 outlines the context of the civil rights movement, particularly the legislative battles in the fight for equality, and might provide a useful review before the following investigation.

HISTORICAL BACKGROUND FOR TEACHERS AND STUDENTS

Background of Athletes and Civil Rights

Civil rights activists have used athletic fields to fight for equality. During the first half of the 20th century, Black and White children did not play sports together. This was especially true in organized leagues. But as colleges started to admit Black students, their sports teams also integrated. Jesse Owens was one of the first Black athletes to become famous. He was a sprinter at Ohio State University. Owens won four gold medals in the 1936 Olympics. He was successful even though he was often treated unfairly. Owens fought for civil rights until his death in 1977. In 1947, Jackie Robinson became the first Black player in Major League Baseball. Larry Doby soon followed. Robinson and Doby's success showed that Black baseball players could compete with White athletes. And they could get along with one another too. The success of Black athletes grew as they were given the chance to play with White athletes at the highest levels of sports.

By the late 1960s, some Americans thought that integrated sports, new civil rights laws, and court victories had brought equality to Blacks. They thought Black athletes' success in sports showed that discrimination had ended. Some Americans thought that the civil rights movement had reached its goals. It was over. However, African Americans still faced many problems. Many were treated unfairly at work. Millions lived in poverty. Many had no chance to get a good education. And in spite of some success, many were still treated unfairly by the courts. Some Black people saw professional sports as another place where rich, White team owners and fans took advantage of them. Black athletes worked for White people's profit and entertainment. And some Black athletes, such as boxer Cassius Clay and basketball star Lew Alcindor, used their fame to draw attention to the problems Black people still faced.

Racism and other problems made 1968 a hard year for many Americans. In 1968, news reporter Walter Cronkite suggested that the United States might not win the Vietnam

War. Most Americans believed him. In April, Martin Luther King Jr. was assassinated. His death showed that racism still existed. Riots broke out in Chicago after King's murder. In June, presidential candidate Robert Kennedy was killed. In August, 10,000 protesters fought with 26,000 police and soldiers at the Democratic National Convention in Chicago. The Black Panther Party grew. It became more militant. The Black Power salute—a raised fist—became their symbol. It represented violent Black resistance to unfairness. By October, many Americans looked forward to the Olympics in Mexico City. They thought it might heal the nation after a divisive and chaotic year. But as the Olympics approached, some Black athletes saw the Olympics as another chance to draw attention to the problems Black Americans faced.

Tommie Smith, John Carlos, and the Olympic Project for Human Rights

In 1968, Tommie Smith and John Carlos were sprinters at San Jose State University, a leading center of the civil rights movement. Faculty members there, including Dr. Harry Edwards, influenced Tommie Smith and other Black students on campus. They demanded equal housing and scholarships. They wanted more Black faculty members. In 1967, a movement began among African American athletes there and at other schools to boycott the upcoming Olympics. They formed an organization. It was called the Olympic Project for Human Rights (OPHR). The OPHR spoke to the International Olympic Committee (IOC). They demanded that Muhammad Ali (Cassius Clay) be allowed to compete. They wanted the IOC to ban racist South Africa from the Olympics. They ordered that the IOC fire its leader, who had connections with the former Nazi Party in Germany. The OPHR also spoke with the United States Olympic Committee (USOC). They demanded that the USOC include at least one African American. They also asked for other changes. Soon, Jesse Owens was placed on the committee. But the OPHR's other demands were ignored. Rumors of a Black boycott of the 1968 Olympics spread.

But athletes who had trained their whole lives to go to the Olympics did not want a boycott. So, the leaders of the OPHR changed its plan. Instead, it encouraged Black athletes to find their own way to draw attention to the social injustices faced by African Americans. As the Olympics approached, officials from the IOC feared that Black athletes might protest during the games. The IOC warned officials from the United States that no demonstrating would be allowed. The Olympics must stay nonpolitical. But Tommie Smith and John Carlos wondered what, if anything, they could do to draw attention to social injustice. They knew that first they had to win the 200-meter race. Then they would gain access to the medal stand, the perfect stage for a protest.

On October 16, 1968, Smith and Carlos came in first place and third place in the 200-meter race. Australian Peter Norman finished between them. As they awaited the award ceremony, Smith found a pair of black gloves but was not sure what to do with them. As his plan became clearer, he offered the left glove to Carlos. Peter Norman, the Australian runner, found an OPHR button. He pinned it to his jacket to show his support of the American runners. Smith and Carlos climbed onto the awards podium in their socks and laid their shoes beside them. As the National Anthem was played, Smith and Carlos defied the IOC and the USOC and raised their black-gloved fists in the Black Power salute. Boos rang out from the stadium as the "Star-Spangled Banner" played and their protest continued.

The IOC and USOC responded quickly. Smith and Carlos were suspended from the Olympics. They were removed from the Olympic Village and sent home. Smith and Carlos's act was cheered by civil rights activists in the United States, even though some thought they did not do enough. Many White Americans opposed their actions. But some observers who had been bugged by their demonstration became more sympathetic as they watched the athletes' mistreatment by Olympic officials. Time has changed most Americans' attitudes. Today, a statue depicting the 1968 Olympic protest stands at San Jose State, the two athletes' university.

HISTORICAL THINKING SKILLS: CONTEXTUALIZATION

One of the most basic, yet most difficult, historical thinking strategies is contextualization, discussed in Chapter 4. As historians analyze evidence and construct interpretations of the past, they keep in mind the context of the event they study. Sometimes, the *physical context* plays a role in an event—factors such as the distance between locations; the topography of a place; the weather conditions during an event; whether land was forested, cleared, or swampy; and whether it was day or night at the time. Often, the *social context* influences an event: How did different races interact at the time? How did different classes of people view one another? What social norms were expected for men and women? How did adults communicate with one another and with children? How did people with different religious affiliations see one another? Sometimes, the *technological context* is important, factors such as how people communicated over long distances, how they traveled, how things were made, how they dressed, or how widespread the use of certain gadgets was.

Numerous other contextual factors come into play. The *linguistic context* includes the meanings of words and phrases at the time they were written—words that may have changed meanings through the years. The *biographic context* involves the people who influenced an event. Knowing a little about their personalities might help explain how an event transpired. The *historiographic context* is how people at the time a document was written perceived the past that they studied. Confederate war memorials, controversial today, shed light on the way history was interpreted at the time and within the setting where the monuments were erected. The modern removal of some statues reveals that citizens today live within a different historiographic context—a time when the past is understood differently.

One fundamental concept underlies the entire process of contextualization—that conditions in the past were different from current conditions, and that people and events of the past cannot be fully understood if viewed from a modern perspective. Some researchers have criticized the practice of *presentism*—using modern values, norms, and conditions as the lens through which to understand and evaluate people of the past. Historians, studying within their field of expertise, possess such rich background knowledge that contextualization occurs nearly automatically (without conscious effort). Historians studying outside of their area of expertise use clues from texts to make inferences about the context (Wineburg, 1998). However, students, who rarely possess rich background knowledge and often fail to sense the need to imagine historic contexts, tend to impose familiar, modern conditions on the people of the past. Numerous studies have documented the difficulties that students experience in re-creating contexts (Nokes et al., 2007; Reisman, 2012; Wineburg, 1991).

One strategy that historians use to imagine historical contexts is to consider modern or historic analogies. A modern event that might be familiar to students, that of the protests of NFL quarterback Colin Kaepernick, might help students better understand the social context of the 1968 Olympic protest of Smith and Carlos. Both protests occurred during the playing of the National Anthem in association with athletic events. Both involved Black athletes protesting the living conditions of Black Americans. Both protests divided the nation, to some degree, along racial lines. Both carried costs to the athletes. Observing the reaction to Kaepernick's protests might help students understand the widespread animosity to Smith and Carlos at the time of their protest.

Although historians use analogous events to understand the past, they are careful to avoid overstating the similarities between the events. The detailed contexts of the 1968 protests and the ongoing NFL protests, including the social and political contexts, are different enough that the analogy must not be taken too far. For instance, Colin Kaepernick received a lucrative sponsorship from Nike after his protests, while corporate America shunned Smith and Carlos after their demonstration. The investigation in this chapter compares and contrasts the 1968 protest with the modern NFL protests in order to better understand the nuanced context of each.

LESSON IDEAS

Introduction

The following materials could be used during a unit on the civil rights movement or the 1960s. If a course is organized thematically, this lesson could instead be taught in connection with other lessons considering the place of demonstrations in promoting reform.

Objectives

This lesson is designed to meet three objectives associated with knowledge, skills, and dispositions:

1. Students will compare the struggle to end poverty and to promote racial equality in the 1960s with the 21st-century struggle to end poverty and police brutality.
2. Students will use analogous events to engage in contextualization, understanding both the affordances and limitations of contextual analogies.
3. Students will debate the risks and benefits associated with political demonstrations, considering the stage, audience, moment, and message of Smith and Carlos's 1968 Olympic protest.

Build Background Knowledge

Begin the lesson by building students' background knowledge on the events leading up to Smith and Carlos's Olympic protest. The essays provided in this chapter under the headings "Background of Athletes and Civil Rights" and "Tommie Smith, John Carlos, and the Olympic Project for Human Rights" provide a basic overview of what students will need to know in order to work with the documents that follow.

Ask Historical Questions

The background information provided above and the documents that follow were designed to help students ask and answer the following questions: How do protests by National Football League players after 2016 compare and contrast with the protest of Smith and Carlos in the 1968 Olympics? How can the modern protests help a historian interpret the protests of the 1960s? How does the reaction to the protests of the two eras compare? To what degree have these demonstrations produced their desired effects?

Provide Strategy Instruction and Model Contextualization

Historians often use current or historic events that are familiar to them to imagine the context of historical events that are unfamiliar (Nokes & Kesler-Lund, 2019). A teacher might help students understand that recent protests by NFL players might help them understand of the context for Smith and Carlos's 1968 Olympic demonstration. The documents for this investigation allow students to make direct comparisons between the events of 1968 and 2016, noting similarities and differences. Historians understand that any comparison across time periods, though useful to reconstruct a context, also includes many distinctions unique to each period. The teacher can think through two of the documents to model for students the process of comparing and contrasting the contexts of two events.

After providing background information and asking the historical question that is the focus of the lesson, the teacher might explain the structure of the graphic organizer at the end of the chapter. Down the center of the graphic organizer is a series of questions about the context of the protests. On the left side of each question there is a place to record an interpretation of the NFL protests and a place to note the evidence that led to that interpretation. On the right side of the graphic organizer there is a place to record an interpretation of the same question as it relates to the 1968 Olympic protest. The teacher might read through all the questions and explain that these are the elements of the context that this investigation will compare.

Next, the teacher might consider the first question on the graphic organizer: "What were the specific problems Black people faced at the time of the protests?" The teacher might model the process of comparing across events by looking at the sources of each document in the document set. Doing so, the teacher would discover that Document 1 and Document 7 are both interviews with the athletes who organized the demonstrations, recorded a few days after each demonstration. The teacher might model the process of analyzing the source of each, thinking out loud as he/she explores each document. For instance, he/she might start by noticing the similarities between the sources of Document 1 and Document 7. Both are primary source accounts revealing the motivation of the demonstrators. By looking at the sources, the teacher figures out that they provide evidence of the conditions that led to the protests, from the perspective of the protesters themselves. After modeling the process of thinking about the source, the teacher might read Document 1. As he/she reads, he/she might pause after each claim made by Smith—the protest was for power, unity, pride, and to address poverty. The teacher might project the graphic organizer and write on it that Smith claimed to symbolically address the problem of poverty and a racist America in his demonstration by walking in his socks to the medal podium. In the cell under the heading of Evidence, the teacher might show that the evidence comes from a reliable source—the protester himself shortly after the protest. The teacher can write that on the projected graphic organizer.

The teacher might then read Document 7, noticing that Kaepernick listed police brutality as the primary motive for his demonstration. Again, the teacher might write under the heading of Evidence that this comes from the protester himself a few days after his first protest. The teacher might

then explain that each of the other documents in the collection is intended to help students imagine the contexts of the protests and to answer the questions posed on the graphic organizer about the social context of each.

Group-Work

Once the teacher is confident that students understand how to make comparisons across the two events using the documents and the graphic organizer, he/she can have them analyze the remaining documents independently or in small groups. The teacher should remind students about their objective: to use evidence from the documents to identify how protests by NFL players after 2016 compare and contrast with those of the athletes in 1968. Questions appear at the bottom of the graphic organizer for students to answer after they have sifted through the evidence.

Debriefing

At the end of the lesson students can review what they have learned about the 1968 Olympic protest and the NFL demonstrations that began in 2016 by discussing the following questions:

1. What were the main similarities and differences between the 1968 Olympic protests and those started by Kaepernick in 2016?
2. How is the social context of the NFL demonstrations similar to and different from the social context of the Olympic demonstration?
3. How did the public reaction to the two demonstrations compare?

A second phase of the debriefing can focus on the use of analogies to understand context with the following questions:

1. How did the analysis of the modern demonstration help you understand the social context of the 1968 Olympic demonstration?
2. How might the understanding of the modern demonstration interfere with you developing an accurate understanding of the 1968 Olympic demonstration?
3. How were the demonstrations of the Silent Sentinels different from or similar to these two protests?
4. What other similar events might enhance your understanding of both/either demonstration(s)?

The third phase of the debriefing can focus on demonstrations as a tool for citizens to gain attention for their cause:

1. What was the stage, the audience, the moment, and the message of the 1968 Olympic demonstration and the NFL demonstrations?
2. Which demonstration do you think was most effective? What factors made it better?
3. Do you think that the demonstrators chose these elements of the demonstrations wisely, or could they have chosen a better time, place, or manner to protest?
4. Do you think these demonstrations achieved their desired outcomes? In other words, to what degree have the problems highlighted by these demonstrations been resolved?

INSTRUCTIONAL MATERIALS

Ten primary source documents are included in the pages that follow. Some documents have been modified for students with links to the original documents. A graphic organizer that supports students in making comparisons across periods is also included. The teacher could also display the sample poster in Chapter 4 to remind students of the different elements of the context that they should remember.

Document Set

1. An excerpt from an interview of Tommie Smith, conducted by sportscaster Howard Cosell, on October 17, 1968 (Edwards, 1969, p. 104)
2. A photograph of Tommie Smith and John Carlos during the Olympic 200-meter awards ceremony on October 16, 1968, (Associated Press Photo File, 1968)
3. An excerpt from an article in *Ebony* magazine, published primarily for an African American audience, written in October 1968 (Hartmann, 2003, p. 12)
4. An excerpt from a formal apology and official statement issued by the United States Olympic Committee on October 18, 1968 (Sheehan, 1968)
5. Part of an interview of John Carlos by *Time* Magazine reporter Madison Gray on October 16, 2012 (Gray, 2012)
6. An excerpt from an article written by sportscaster Brent Musburger from Mexico City for the *Chicago American* newspaper on October 19, 1968 (Hartmann, 2003, p. 11), and a Tweet sent by Musburger on October 17, 2018 (CBC News, 2017)
7. An excerpt from an interview with National Football League quarterback Colin Kaepernick, explaining why he chose to sit during the National Anthem starting in August 2016, conducted by a group of newspaper reporters from the San Francisco area on August 28, 2016 (Biderman, 2016)

8. An advertisement that was part of the ad campaign "Believe in Something, Even if it Means Sacrificing Everything," produced by Nike with Colin Kaepernick as the spokesperson (Nike, 2018)
9. A photograph of a modern protest by NFL players on the Philadelphia Eagles taken on October 1, 2017 by Kevin Terrell (Terrell, 2017)
10. Part of a speech by President Donald Trump, given in Louisville, Kentucky, on March 20, 2017 (Trump, 2017)

Simplified Evidence

Document 1: Smith Explanation

My raised right hand stood for the power in black America. Carlos' raised left hand stood for the unity of black America. Together they formed an arch of unity and power. The black scarf around my neck stood for black pride. The black socks with no shoes stood for black poverty in racist America. The totality of our effort was the regaining of black dignity.

Source: Part of an interview of Tommie Smith, conducted by sportscaster Howard Cosell, on October 17, 1968, cited in *The Revolt of the Black Athlete* by Harry Edwards (p. 104). Found at archive.org/details/TheRevoltOfTheBlackAthlete/page/n123

Document 2: Photograph of Olympic Demonstration

Source: Photograph of Tommie Smith and John Carlos during the Olympic 200-meter awards ceremony on October 16, 1968 taken by an unidentified Associated Press photographer. Courtesy of Associated Press.

Document 3: *Ebony* Magazine Criticism

In this nation, black protest has reached such heights as ghetto riots, school boycotts, and heated requests for a separate state. In comparison, the Smith/Carlos demonstration should look like child's play. In this nation, white Vietnam protesters have flown Viet Cong flags. They have burned or torn American flags. They have burned draft cards. In comparison, the Smith/Carlos demonstration was as quiet as a church service.

Source: Part of an article in *Ebony* magazine, a magazine published primarily for an African American audience, written in October 1968. Found in Douglas Hartmann's book *Race Culture and the Revolt of the Black Athlete* (2003, p. 12). [Changed for easier reading.]

Document 4: USOC Apology

The United States Olympic Committee expresses how sorry it is to the International Olympic Committee. It apologizes to the Mexican Organizing Committee. It apologizes to the people of Mexico for the rudeness shown by two members of its team. They did not follow tradition during a victory ceremony at the Olympic Stadium on October 16. The unusual show of these athletes breaks the rules of good manners and sportsmanship. These values are important in the United States. So, the two men involved have been suspended from the team. They have been ordered to leave the Olympic Village.... If other members of the United States team do these kinds of things it will be viewed as breaking Olympic principles. It would lead to the worst punishment that can be used by the United States Olympic Committee.

Source: Part of a formal apology and official statement issued by the United States Olympic Committee on October 18, 1968. [Changed for easier reading.] Found at archive.nytimes.com/www. nytimes.com/learning/general/onthisday/big/1018.html

Document 5: Carlos Interview

TIME: After the '68 Olympics, your life took a very negative turn. Looking back were there things you think you could have done to avoid any of it?

JC: I wouldn't add nor take anything away because anything that happened to me was secondary to the need to make that demonstration. We wished people would have taken a more serious look as to why it would have been necessary to attempt an Olympic boycott. People would ask us why we would sacrifice our day in the sun to bring these issues to the table. I wish people would have been more clear minded.

TIME: In your book, you seem to still be steadfast in your resolve that what you did in Mexico was right. If you had it to do over again, what more would you have done?

JC: There was nothing more that I could do. There's nothing I could add or take away. The demonstration said what it needed to say. If you're still interviewing about it 44 years later, it must have hit the nail on the head.

Source: Part of an interview of John Carlos by *Time* Magazine reporter Madison Gray on October 16, 2012. Found at keeping-score.blogs.time.com/2012/10/16/john-carlos-looking-back-at-a-raised-fist-and-at-a-raised-consciousness/

Document 6: Musburger Criticism

1968 Newspaper:

One gets a little tired of having the United States run down by athletes who are having fun at the expense of their country. Protesting and working hard against racism in the United States is one thing. But airing one's dirty clothing before the entire world during a fun-and-games tournament was just a childish act. It was done by two athletes who should have known better.

2017 Tweet:

Yo #49ers. Since you instigated protest, 2 wins and 19 losses. How about taking your next knee in the other team's end zone?

Source: Part of an article written by American sportscaster Brent Musburger from Mexico City for the *Chicago American* newspaper on October 19, 1968. [Changed for easier reading.] Found in Douglas Hartmann's book *Race Culture and the Revolt of the Black Athlete* (2003, p. 11). And a tweet Brent Musburger sent on October 8, 2017. Found at www.cbc.ca/news/world/pence-leaves-nfl-game-players-take-a-knee-protest-1.4346076

Document 7: Kaepernick Explanation

I'm going to continue to stand with the people that are being oppressed. To me, this is something that has to change. When there's significant change, and I feel that flag represents what it's supposed to represent, and this country is representing people the way that it's supposed to, I'll stand.

There's a lot of things that need to change. One specifically? Police brutality. There's people being murdered unjustly and not being held accountable. People [police officers] are being given paid leave for killing people. That's not right. That's not right by anyone's standards.

This stand wasn't for me. This is because I'm seeing things happen to people that don't have a voice, people that don't have a platform to talk and have their voices heard, and effect change. So I'm in the position where I can do that and I'm going to do that for people that can't.

It's something that can unify this team. It's something that can unify this country. If we have these real conversations that are uncomfortable for a lot of people. If we have these conversations, there's a better understanding of where both sides are coming from.

Source: Parts of an interview of National Football League quarterback Colin Kaepernick, explaining why he chose to sit during the National Anthem starting in August 2016, conducted by a group of newspaper reporters from the San Francisco area on August 28, 2016. Found at ninerswire.usatoday.com/2016/08/28/transcript-colin-kaepernick-addresses-sitting-during-national-anthem/

Document 8: Nike Advertisement

Source: Controversial advertisement, part of the ad campaign "Believe in Something, Even if It Means Sacrificing Everything," produced by Nike with Colin Kaepernick as the spokesperson, after he was cut from National Football League teams following his injury-plagued protest season. Found at globalnews.ca/video/4428833/believe-in-something-even-if-it-means-sacrificing-everything-colin-kaepernick-in-nike-commercial

Document 9: Photograph of NFL Demonstration

Source: Photograph of Philadelphia Eagles defensive end Chris Long (56), safety Malcolm Jenkins (27), and safety Rodney McLeod (23), taken by Kevin Terrell on October 1, 2017 during the National Anthem prior to a football game. Used courtesy of Associated Press.

Document 10: Trump Criticism

And you know, your San Francisco quarterback, I'm sure nobody ever heard of him [crowd boos], I'm just reporting the news.... There was an article today reported that NFL owners don't wanna pick him [Kaepernick] up [cheers] because they don't wanna get a nasty tweet from Donald Trump. Do you believe that? [cheers] I just saw that. I just saw that. I said, "if I remember that one I'm gonna report it to the people of Kentucky. 'Cause they like it when people actually stand for the American flag, right?" [applause]

Source: Part of a speech by President Donald Trump, given in Louisville, Kentucky, on March 20, 2017, referring to the fact that no National Football League team signed Colin Kaepernick to a contract. Found at www.youtube.com/watch?v=xiAtN1ziQ9o (starting at 39:32)

Original Evidence

Most of the previous documents are unedited or can be found online at the links provided. The following documents are not easily available online so I provide them in their original format.

Document 3: *Ebony* Magazine Criticism

In a nation where black protest has reached such heights as ghetto riots, school boycotts, and impassioned requests for a separate state, the Smith/Carlos demonstration should look like child's play. In a nation where white Vietnam protesters have flaunted Viet Cong flags, burned or torn American flags and burned draft cards, the Smith/Carlos demonstration appeared as solemn as a church service."

Source: Part of an article in *Ebony* magazine, a magazine published primarily for an African American audience, written in October 1968. Found in Douglas Hartmann's book *Race Culture and the Revolt of the Black Athlete* (2003, p. 12)

Document 6: Musburger Criticism

One gets a little tired of having the United States run down by athletes who are enjoying themselves at the expense of their country. Protesting and working constructively against racism in the United States is one thing, but airing one's dirty clothing before the entire world during a fun-and-games tournament was no more than a juvenile gesture by a couple of athletes who should have known better.

Source: Part of an article written by sportscaster Brent Musburger from Mexico City for the *Chicago American* newspaper on October 19, 1968. Found in Douglas Hartmann's book *Race Culture and the Revolt of the Black Athlete* (2003, p. 11)

Graphic Organizer

Athletes' Protests Then and Now

You will be given a number of primary sources and photographs related to the 1968 Olympic protest of sprinters Tommie Smith and John Carlos and of the 2016 protests of National Football League players. Use evidence from these documents and your background knowledge to make interpretations about the following questions comparing the social context of the protests in 1968 and more recently. Cite the evidence that led you to your interpretations. After completing the chart, answer the questions below.

Modern NFL Protests		Questions About the Context	1968 Olympic Protests	
Evidence	**Answer**		**Answer**	**Evidence**
		What specific problems did Black Americans face at the time of the protests?		
		How did most African Americans react to the protests?		
		How did most White Americans react to the protests?		
		How did those in positions of power react to the protests?		
		How do (or will) most people look at the protests 50 years later?		

1. How do protests by National Football League players after 2016 compare and contrast with those of the athletes in 1968?
2. How has the reaction to the protests of the two eras compared?
3. How can the modern protests help a historian interpret the protest of 1968?
4. To what degree have these demonstrations, then and now, produced their desired effects?

PART VI

CIVIL DISOBEDIENCE:
When All Else Fails

When the Silent Sentinels began their protests, they did not act in violation of any laws and they were allowed to continue without interference from police. As their banners became more provocative, some of them were eventually arrested for "blocking traffic" or for other similar violations. When their peaceful demonstrations ran counter to the orders they received from the police, they engaged in civil disobedience. Civil disobedience is the topic of the two investigations described in the following two chapters.

Civil disobedience has two primary characteristics. First, it involves *disobedience* to laws, police orders, business policies, or other established practices. Those who engage in civil disobedience are often confronted by law enforcement officers, which is, interestingly, an intent of the protesters. Confrontations often draw media attention and increase the public awareness of the problem for which the protesters demonstrate. Second, civil disobedience involves *civility* on the part of those who break the laws. Demonstrators do not damage or steal property, engage in violence, or even speak uncivilly to the spectators who may threaten them or to police officers who arrest them. The force behind civil disobedience comes from the wider public's reaction when people observe protesters engaged in harmless acts (such as riding a bus or voting) being accosted by vicious bystanders or police. Protesters count on the media coverage of such incidents to sway public opinion in their favor. They often pay heavy penalties, such as expensive fines, jail terms, unpopularity, violence, and police records, in return for modest, almost imperceptible, gains in public support. At its best, civil disobedience generally accomplishes only gradual, subtle reform. For this reason, civil disobedience is often seen as a last resort as a tool for civic engagement.

The concept of civil disobedience has both a national and international history. The transcendentalist thinker Henry David Thoreau defined it as disobedience to civil authority, in contrast to the definition above. He refused to pay taxes to a U.S. government that defended slavery and waged an unjust war against Mexico. He argued that it was the responsibility of citizens to do what was morally right whether or not such actions were legal. Susan B. Anthony followed this principle when she voted in the 1872 election, claiming moral and constitutional support for her act. Chapter 12 includes an investigation of Anthony's civil disobedience.

Decades later, Mahatma Gandhi was influenced by Thoreau's argument as he organized resistance to oppressive British policies in India. Gandhi, however, placed greater emphasis on nonviolence and civility than Thoreau had. James Farmer Jr. and other civil rights leaders of the 1960s studied Gandhi's tactics and adopted his position on civil disobedience. The Freedom Riders, who are the focus of the investigation in Chapter 13, were trained by James Farmer Jr. and the Congress of Racial Equality with strategies for facing, with civility, the life-threatening violence of those who opposed reform.

U.S. history includes other examples of civil disobedience, equally worthy of study. Students are most likely familiar with Rosa Parks. Many others who engaged in civil disobedience are less well known but have no less interesting stories. During the Vietnam War, tens of thousands of draftees, including Cassius Clay (later called Muhammad Ali), illegally refused to report for military service in a war they viewed as unjust. In 1969, scores of Native Americans occupied the island of Alcatraz in San Francisco Bay in order to draw attention to the unfairness of federal land policies toward aboriginal peoples. Their protest continued for 19 months until the U.S. government forcibly ended it.

In recent years, civil disobedience has become a favorite tactic of environmentalists who feel ignored by policymakers. In 1997, Julia "Butterfly" Hill, lived on a small platform 180 feet off the ground in a giant redwood tree for 738 days in order to prevent a logging company from cutting it down. In 2008, environmentalist Timothy DeChristopher illegally disrupted the leasing of land to gas and oil companies by fraudulently bidding during an auction. He served 21 months in prison for his crime. Between 2011 and 2014, many groups used legal and illegal tactics to protest the construction of the Keystone Pipeline, a conduit for transporting oil from Canadian oilfields to Texas refineries. Native American groups used similar tactics to protest the construction of the Dakota Access Pipeline in 2016. Those desiring less federal regulation of the environment have also used civil disobedience. In 2014, residents near Blanding, Utah, protested the closure of all-terrain-vehicle (ATV) trails in Recapture Canyon by illegally riding their ATVs on the closed paths. Protest organizers were jailed and fined.

The flurry of civil disobedience in recent years raises a number of concerns about its effectiveness. First, sanctioning civil disobedience as a legitimate tool for civic engagement encourages individuals of all political persuasions to ignore laws. With the wide range of opinions in society, the advocacy of civil disobedience is a call for anarchy. Second, civil disobedience rarely brings quick results. Susan B. Anthony did not live to see women vote across the nation. Finally, the severe punishments—legal and extralegal—faced by those who engage in civil disobedience might discourage would-be protesters. The harassment, safety risks, incarceration, fines, public disgrace, and unpopularity faced by the disobedient make civil disobedience a questionable strategy in all but the most desperate of circumstances. An essential question to consider when viewing brave acts of civil disobedience in the past is whether better tools for civic engagement exist in the 21st century.

In connection with the lessons included in Chapters 12 and 13, a teacher might discuss with students the applications of civil disobedience with the following questions:

- If a problem existed at this school or in your community, why would civil disobedience be a last resort in seeking a resolution? What other steps could be taken first?
- When do the benefits of civil disobedience outweigh the negative consequences associated with it?
- What are current examples of civil disobedience? Do you view the individuals involved in these acts of civil disobedience as heroes or villains?
- Do conditions exist in society today that might warrant civil disobedience?
- Do you view those who engage in civil disobedience as heroes, whether or not you agree with their cause? How does considering the civil disobedience of someone with whom you disagree help you understand historical contexts when civil disobedience was used?

CHAPTER 12

Susan B. Anthony and the Election of 1872

One of the great ironies of civil disobedience is that, at the time it occurs, it is often viewed with disgust by the majority of contemporaries. Yet, decades or centuries later, many individuals who engaged in civil disobedience are viewed as heroic. Such is the case for Susan B. Anthony, who voted illegally in 1872 and was arrested, convicted, and fined for her act—a fine she refused to pay. Of course, today Anthony is viewed as a hero, having had a coin minted with her image and receiving countless tributes every election day. Her act of illegally voting has gained great historical significance. However, her disregard for the law was scorned by many of her contemporaries. This chapter includes an investigation of Anthony's civil disobedience and the public reaction to it, then and now, considering what makes a historical event significant.

STUDENTS' BACKGROUND KNOWLEDGE

Students' background knowledge of the women's rights movement is addressed in Chapter 10. Unlike Alice Paul, the subject of that chapter, Susan B. Anthony is likely to be a name familiar to students. They probably associate her with the struggle for women's suffrage and may connect her, incorrectly, with the 1848 Seneca Falls Convention. (She actually joined the movement a few years later.) The incident of her voting in 1872, and her subsequent arrest and trial, is something students may or may not have heard of, though her story attracted national attention at the time. A substantial challenge in this investigation is that most students fail to comprehend the context of the struggle for women's suffrage and other basic civil rights for women. In the absence of background knowledge, students project present conditions, values, norms, and laws onto landscapes of the past. As a result, Anthony's actions seem natural today—almost expected. When viewing this investigation through a modern lens, it is surprising that more women did not behave like Anthony. However, when viewed from a historical perspective, her actions were so outrageous that they have gained historical significance. Chapter 10 outlines the legal and social discrimination faced by women in the middle of the 19th century, and might provide a useful review before the following investigation.

HISTORICAL BACKGROUND FOR TEACHERS AND STUDENTS

Background of Women's Roles in Politics

Historians disagree about the historical significance of Susan B. Anthony's illegal vote in 1872. But there are a number of things about the status of women at the time that almost all historians agree on. During most of the 1800s, women were treated as second-class citizens in the United States. Many people thought that women were emotional rather than rational by nature. This made them unfit for politics, business, or other "manly" work that took thinking rather than feeling. People thought that women were only good for domestic roles. They were meant to raise children and care for a husband and a home. Most women who worked outside of the home had jobs related to their domestic nature. They worked as teachers, cooks, nurses, and in child care. Women who did not marry were looked down on as social misfits. To die an unmarried "old maid" was among the greatest fears of many young women. To attract a man, a woman had to follow the social rules of the time. Women were expected to stay away from things like politics.

Within this setting, women began to demand more freedom and better treatment. They wanted economic freedom. They asked for the right to own property and to keep their own paychecks. They wanted fair divorce laws and protection from abusive husbands. The most radical demand they made was for the right to vote. This right is also called the *franchise* or *suffrage*. When the 15th Amendment was passed in 1870, African American men received the right to vote. Many women were disappointed that they had not been included when suffrage was given to Black men. Some asked why the 14th Amendment, which said that all people born in the United States were citizens, did not give women all the rights of citizenship. They said that this amendment should have given them the right to vote, to serve on juries, and even to hold political office. However, for many Americans at that time, the reasons the 14th Amendment did not give women such rights were clear. They wrongly believed that women were not smart enough to vote or to serve thoughtfully. Susan B. Anthony faced opposition from men who believed these things in her quest to obtain the vote for women.

Susan B. Anthony and the Election of 1872

Susan B. Anthony was born in 1820 into a Quaker family. From a young age, she was active in the social reform movements of her time. She shared in her family's fight against slavery until that institution ended. She worked in the temperance movement, speaking about the problems that came from drinking alcohol. It is not surprising that over time she became more aware of her second-class status as a woman. She began to fight to solve this problem. She thought that the right to vote was the key to equality for women. So, she became a powerful leader for women's suffrage.

In 1872, Susan B. Anthony convinced election workers in her home town of Rochester, New York, to let her vote. About 2 weeks later, she was arrested for breaking New York's voting laws. At the time of her arrest, it was said that she told the gentle policeman to "arrest me properly" as he would a man. Anthony was ordered to stand trial. During the 7 months before her trial, Anthony traveled through the region giving speeches. She argued that the 14th Amendment, passed 14 years earlier, made her a citizen. She should have all the rights of any other citizen, including the right to vote. Her message was published in local newspapers. A judge found out that Anthony was speaking to possible jurors for her trial. He decided to move the trial to a neighboring county. Anthony began a speaking tour there. She hoped to influence the possible jurors there, too.

Many people were very interested in Susan B. Anthony's trial. Newspapers reported what happened. After the closing arguments, Judge Ward Hunt told the jurors that they had to return with a guilty verdict. They did. As was common at the time, Anthony was not allowed to speak until after the guilty sentence had been given. But during the sentencing, Anthony was finally allowed to talk. She gave a powerful speech in support of women's suffrage. Anthony was ordered to pay a fine of $100. She refused to pay it. In order to avoid more publicity and a legal appeal to the Supreme Court, Anthony was set free and her $100 fine was never collected.

After her trial, Anthony continued to fight for women's suffrage until her death in 1906. She gave speeches, published a newspaper called *The Revolution*, and led national organizations. She trained the next generation of suffragists. Because she helped write the amendment and because of her work for women's suffrage, many people called the 19th Amendment, which gave women the right to vote, the Anthony Amendment. But she died before it was passed.

HISTORICAL THINKING SKILLS: IDENTIFYING HISTORICAL SIGNIFICANCE

Open any high school survey U.S. history textbook and browse its index. Odds are that Susan B. Anthony is included somewhere in that text. The Seneca Falls Convention undoubtedly appears in its pages. You will probably find Elizabeth Cady Stanton and Lucretia Mott. You may or may not find a reference to Alice Paul or to the Silent Sentinels, though there might be an image of them picketing the White House. Why is it that certain things get included in the textbook and other things are left out? The answer has to do with *historical significance*, the metaconcept or second-order concept in historical thinking that is highlighted in this chapter.

The past includes an infinite number of events and occurrences, a small fraction of which are noticed, and an even smaller number of which are recorded or shared. Most happenings attract little attention and are quickly forgotten. What a child ate for breakfast on a certain date, or the fact that a driver sneezed during his commute to work, soon becomes part of the unremembered past. However, there are some events that are deemed important enough to be remembered, documented, and studied. These events become *history* because they carry some significance that distinguishes them from more commonplace occurrences of the past. This notion of historical significance is an important element of historical thinking, and includes a critical consideration of why some things become a part of history while other things are forgotten.

Historical significance is something that is determined during the present about things that occurred in the past. It involves subjective judgments and evaluations, but it also includes evolving criteria. For instance, the individuals who appear on currency in the United States have been identified as significant. In 2015, Secretary of the Treasury Jack Lew announced that the image of an undetermined woman would replace Alexander Hamilton on the $10 bill. In spite of the protests of some historians, who argued that Alexander Hamilton was the visionary who established the economic foundation of the United States as its first secretary of the treasury, Lew's plan moved forward. He reassured them that Hamilton would maintain a place on some form of currency. Less than a year later, however, Lew changed his mind. Hamilton would remain on the $10 bill and Harriet Tubman would replace Andrew Jackson on the $20 bill. What had caused this change of plans? The answer has nothing to do with Tubman, Hamilton, the past, or historians' protests. Instead, Lin-Manuel Miranda had produced an immensely popular Broadway play *Hamilton*, which had created a popular interest in that founding father, and widespread public outrage arose over the idea that he might be removed from the nation's currency (Imbert, 2016). Thus, Hamilton's historical significance is determined not only by what he accomplished during his lifetime, but by modern interests spurred on by the Broadway play. Lew concluded that a number of women's rights activists, including, perhaps, Susan B. Anthony, would be pictured on the back of the $10. Who these women would be is another matter of historical significance.

Historian Lis Cercadillo (2006) proposed that historical significance is shaped by a number of factors. *Contemporary significance* is evaluated by considering the degree to which the importance of an individual or an event was recognized at the time, by his/her contemporaries. In contrast, *present significance* is a judgment based upon the current impact of or interest in an event. Hamilton's present significance is an example. Present significance is not as highly esteemed by historians as other types of significance, but it is valued within popular culture. *Causal significance* is judged by the changes caused by a historical figure or event. *Revelatory significance* is evaluated by the way an individual or event tells us something important about the past. For instance, Martha Ballard lived a relatively common life from 1735 to 1812. However, the journal she kept for 3 decades reveals a great deal about the life of a midwife during that time—a rare resource treasured by historians. Ballard may not have changed society or achieved contemporary significance, but her life and record is important for what it reveals about women in her society (Ulrich, 1991). Events might be considered important enough to be remembered when they have *symbolic significance*, representing a time period or a milestone. Though not included in Cercadillo's description, an event or individual might have *personal significance* or *familial significance*, such as when the life of a deceased grandfather is studied by a grandchild and shared with interested family members. When reading about a historical event or person, the reader can judge significance based upon these criteria, understanding that even with these standards, a great deal of disagreement about significance occurs based upon the perspective, priorities, and values of those studying the past.

LESSON IDEAS

Introduction

The following materials could be used during a unit on progressive reforms and/or the women's suffrage movement. If a course is organized thematically, this lesson could instead be taught with other lessons on the role of civil disobedience in promoting reform.

Objectives

This lesson is designed to meet three objectives associated with knowledge, skills, and dispositions:

1. Students will analyze the public reaction to Susan B. Anthony's act of civil disobedience when she voted during the election of 1872.
2. Students will use criteria to evaluate historical significance.
3. Students will debate the role of civil disobedience as a tool for civic engagement, focusing on its advantages, disadvantages, and alternative methods.

Build Background Knowledge

Begin the lesson by building students' background knowledge on the events leading up to the Susan B. Anthony's voting in the 1872 election. The essays provided in this chapter under the headings "Background of Women's Roles in Politics" and "Susan B. Anthony and the Election of 1872" provide a basic overview of what students will need to know in order to work with the documents that follow.

Ask Historical Questions

The background information provided above and the documents that follow were designed to help students ask and answer the following question: To what degree, and in what ways, was Susan B. Anthony's 1872 vote historically significant? In order to answer that question, students should also consider the following questions: How did her contemporaries react to her voting? To what degree has her voting impacted current events? Did it initiate important changes in her time? Was her voting symbolic of her time period or does it reveal important characteristics of her time? Why are other women who also voted illegally in 1872, or the male election officials who illegally allowed Anthony to vote, not remembered the same way Anthony is? Each of these questions helps students evaluate the historical significance of her act of civil disobedience.

Provide Strategy Instruction and Model Evaluating Historical Significance

Along with providing background information, the teacher should teach students about the metaconcept of historical significance. A teacher might consider using the example of Alexander Hamilton, the $10 bill, and Lin-Manuel Miranda's Broadway play given earlier in this chapter to illustrate the concept. A teacher might take some class time to introduce the different ways to evaluate historical significance, and may consider using simplified language, such as *significance then* or *significance now* instead of *contemporary* or *present significance*, respectively. The teacher might display a poster in the classroom reminding students of the criteria for judging significance, such as the sample classroom poster at the end of this chapter. After explaining the different ways of evaluating historical significance, the teacher might model the analysis of the first document, either using the graphic organizer to record ideas or by highlighting and annotating the document.

For example, the teacher might project the first document and show students how he/she would analyze it. The teacher might start by saying, "I first need to think about the source." As the teacher reads, he/she might pause to say, "I see that this is the opening statement of Susan B. Anthony's trial. I notice that this is from the prosecution, so I know that he is trying to have Anthony found guilty. I also see that the trial took place in June, and I remember that elections are usually in November, so the trial was about 7 months after she voted. I remember from the background information that she traveled throughout the region for those 7 months talking about the injustice of her upcoming trial. I also know a little bit about opening statements—this is when the lawyers tell the jurors the basic story of the crime, from their perspective. So, before I start to read the opening statements, I already have some expectations—this will be the basic story of Susan B. Anthony voting, told by someone who wants to prove her guilty and who knows that she has been trying to sway public opinion for the past 7 months." As the teacher reads and thinks aloud, he/she might project the graphic organizer and model how to take notes in the first column. Alternatively, the teacher might model how to highlight and annotate the document itself.

The teacher might continue modeling by looking at the text of the document, and saying something like this: "Now that I know a little about who is talking, I am ready to see what he says." After reading the first two sentences, the teacher might pause and explain his/her thinking: "This sounds like he is just sharing indisputable facts." Then the teacher might read the next two sentences, then think out loud about what he/she has read: "This sounds a little funny for him to say that Susan B. Anthony was a woman at the time she voted. But I know that this is pretty typical of an attorney's opening statement. He is showing that there is no dispute about her breaking the law just as there is no dispute about her being a woman. There is no question she is guilty." The teacher might read the remainder of the statement, pausing to make comments after every sentence or two. Additionally, the teacher might model the completion of the second column of the graphic organizer while reading and thinking aloud, or he/she might continue to highlight and annotate the document.

After reading the entire document, the teacher could demonstrate how to use the graphic organizer to record ideas about the significance of Susan B. Anthony's 1872 vote. Looking at the graphic organizer, the teacher might think aloud about how the prosecuting attorney's statement demonstrates Anthony's historical significance: "I don't think it says much about the present significance, but it certainly shows the contemporary significance of her act—the significance then." Continuing through each criterion on the graphic organizer (or on the sample classroom poster at the end of this chapter), the teacher might then think about the causal significance: "I'm not sure what to think about the causal significance. On one hand, the attorney seems to have some fear that jurors will side with Anthony because they feel empathy for her. If such is the case, her act might have caused greater support for women's suffrage. On the other hand, it was still almost 50 years before women achieved the right to vote. So, her act did not seem to cause any immediate changes. I'm going to judge her act to have little causal significance. Or at least this document

gives only weak evidence of any direct link between her act and important changes."

The teacher could then consider the other criteria for judging significance: "Her arrest and prosecution, and the matter-of-fact way this attorney addresses the law does reveal a great deal about how women were viewed at the time, and how this action was viewed. This document provides some evidence of revelatory significance. However, there might be better evidence in the other documents of the symbolic significance of her act—we can't really tell from this opening statement whether the action was symbolic of the time period. Finally, I have no personal connection with Anthony, even though I am very deeply interested in the story of her civil disobedience." As the teacher talks through each criterion for judging historical significance, he/she might circle those criteria on the graphic organizer, or might annotate the document with his/her ideas. If the teacher feels that the students are still uncertain about how to evaluate historical significance, he/she could model with a second document.

Group-Work

Once the teacher is confident that students understand how to evaluate significance and how to use the graphic organizer to gather evidence from the documents, students can analyze the remaining documents independently or in small groups. It can be helpful during group-work or independent work to remind students about their objective: to use evidence from the documents to evaluate the degree to which Susan B. Anthony's civil disobedience was historically significant.

Debriefing

Teachers are more likely to achieve the objectives of this lesson if they conclude it with a debriefing—a discussion of the students' work, thinking, and interpretations. First, students can discuss what they have learned about the civil disobedience of Susan B. Anthony, discussing questions such as the following:

1. What do you think are the most important parts of Susan B. Anthony's story?
2. How did Susan B. Anthony attract attention to the women's suffrage movement?
3. How did people react to her civil disobedience? How would you have reacted if you would have been reading the newspaper about Susan B. Anthony in 1872 (thinking of yourself as a product of that time period with the values common then)?

A second phase of the debriefing can focus on the skills associated with evaluating historical significance with students discussing the following questions:

1. To what degree was Susan B. Anthony's illegal vote historically significant? What made and makes Susan B. Anthony's illegal vote historically significant?
2. Why do you think other women who also voted illegally in 1872 or the male election officials who illegally allowed Anthony to vote are not remembered the same way Anthony is? Is their act less historically significant than hers, when they did a similar thing?
3. What did you learn about evaluating historical significance from this investigation?

The third phase of the debriefing can focus on civil disobedience as a tool for civic engagement:

1. Did Susan B. Anthony's act of civil disobedience produce the desired effects?
2. What strategies might have been more productive for her to use? Would a more provocative or less provocative act have been more effective?
3. What lessons can we draw about civil disobedience from Anthony's story?

INSTRUCTIONAL MATERIALS

Seven primary source documents are included in the pages that follow in a format that is simplified for students. In addition, a graphic organizer is included that provides a place for students to gather evidence of the significance of Anthony's illegal vote. Further, the sample classroom poster at the end of this chapter might be displayed to remind students about the criteria for judging historical significance.

Document Set

1. An excerpt from the opening statement of the prosecution at the trial of Susan B. Anthony, given on June 17, 1873 (Crowley, 1873)
2. An excerpt from the transcript of the testimony of Susan B. Anthony during the sentencing phase of the trial (Anthony, 1873)
3. An excerpt from an anonymous editorial letter published in the *Rutland* [Vermont] *Herald* on June 26, 1873 (*Rutland Herald*, 1873)
4. An excerpt from a letter from Susan B. Anthony to Elizabeth Cady Stanton on November 5, 1872 (Anthony, 1872)
5. An excerpt from a eulogy delivered by Reverend Anna Howard Shaw at Susan B. Anthony's funeral in Rochester, New York, on March 15, 1906. (Shaw, 2016)
6. A photograph of a "Susan B. Anthony dollar," a coin minted in the United States from 1979 to 1981 and again in 1999 (U.S. Mint, 1981)

7. A video posted by Cable News Network (CNN), "I voted stickers put on Susan B. Anthony's grave" (CNN, n.d.)

Simplified Evidence

Document 1: Prosecution Opening Statement

May it please the Court and Gentlemen of the Jury:

On the 5th of November, 1872, there was held an election for different officers. Among those, were elections for Congress of the United States. The defendant, Miss Susan B. Anthony, lived in the city of Rochester. On November 5, 1872, she voted for a representative in the Congress of the United States. At that time, she was a woman. I do not think there will be any question about that. We think that there is no question about either the facts or the law. Whatever Miss Anthony's intentions may have been—whether they were good or otherwise—she did not have a right to vote. And if she did vote without having a lawful right to vote, then there is no question but what she is guilty of violating a law of the United States.

Source: Part of the opening statement of the prosecution at the trial of Susan B. Anthony, given on June 17, 1873, by Richard Crowley, an attorney for the United States. [Changed for easier reading.] Found at score.rims.k12.ca.us/score_lessons/womens_suffrage/pdf/susan_b_anthony_trial.pdf

Document 2: Anthony Speech

Judge Hunt: (Ordering the defendant to stand up). Has the prisoner anything to say why sentence shall not be given?

Miss Anthony: Yes, your honor. I have many things to say. For in your ordered verdict of guilty, you have trampled underfoot every vital principle of our government. My natural rights, my civil rights, my political rights, my judicial rights, have all been ignored. Robbed of the basic privilege of citizenship, I am lowered from being a citizen to being a subject. And not only myself but all women. We are, by your verdict, doomed to be the political slaves of this so-called government.

Judge Hunt: The court cannot listen to you repeat your lawyer's arguments which already took three hours.

Miss Anthony: May it please your honor. I am not arguing the question, but simply stating the reasons why the sentence cannot fairly be given against me. When you deny my right to vote, you deny my right to representation as someone who is taxed. You deny my right to a trial by a jury of my peers. Therefore, you deny my sacred rights to life, liberty, property and . . .

Judge Hunt: The court cannot allow the prisoner to keep talking.

Miss Anthony: But your honor should not deny me this one and only small chance to protest against this outrageous violation of my rights. May it please the Court to remember that since the day I was arrested last November, this is the first time that either myself or any other oppressed woman has been allowed to say anything in their defense before a judge or jury.

Judge Hunt: The Court orders the prisoner to sit down. It will not allow another word.

Miss Anthony: When I was brought before your honor for trial, I hoped for a fair interpretation of the Constitution and its recent amendments. I hoped to have the . . . equal rights of everyone born or given citizenship in the United States. But I did not get this justice—or even a trial by a jury *not* of my peers. I don't ask for mercy, but for the full punishment of the law.

Judge Hunt: The Court must insist . . . (Here the prisoner sat down.) The prisoner will stand up. (Here Miss Anthony arose again.) The sentence of the Court is that you pay a fine of $100 and the court costs.

Miss Anthony: May it please your honor. I shall never pay a dollar of your unfair penalty. . . . And I shall strongly and stubbornly continue to urge all women to follow the old revolutionary saying, that "Resistance to tyranny is obedience to God."

Source: Part of the transcript of the testimony of Susan B. Anthony during the sentencing phase of the trial *United States of America v. Susan B. Anthony*. [Changed for easier reading.] Found at www.rit.edu/cla/statesmanship/media/ap-friday/AnthonyStanton/SBA%20speech%20before%20the%20Court.pdf

Document 3: Editorial Letter

The question of the right of women to vote, under the 14th Amendment to the Constitution, has finally been decided by judges. The U.S. Court in New York has found Susan B. Anthony and her "fellows" guilty of breaking the election laws. It does not matter what opinion people have about women suffrage. The result of this trial should be celebrated as a win for the law over popular opinion. Miss Anthony and her supporters' actions were unlike any that have been seen before in trials. We hope, for the honor of the country, they never will be again. She and they knew that the Fourteenth Amendment did not give women the right to vote. . . . Could she have done anything more shameful or bolder to corrupt the courts and jurors [than attempting to bias them through her speeches]?. . . Before the trial she spoke to the citizens of every town, city, and school district, about her trial. She had pled for their sympathy. She did this so much that the district attorney thought it would be best to ask for the trial to be delayed. The trial was moved to a new place. . . . The verdict of the jury, and the judgment of the court has shown that she is a trouble-maker.

Source: Editorial letter by an anonymous author that was published in the *Rutland* [Vermont] *Herald*, June 26, 1873. [Changed for easier reading.] Found at chroniclingamerica.loc.gov/lccn/sn84022367/1873-06-26/ed-1/seq-1/#date1=1873&index=6&rows=20&words=ANTHONY+Anthony&searchType=basic&sequence=0&state=Vermont&date2=1873&proxtext=Anthony&y=15&x=16&dateFilterType=yearRange&page=1

Document 4: Anthony Letter to Stanton

Rochester November 5, 1872

Dear Mrs. Stanton,

Well I have been and gone and done it!! I voted for the Republicans this morning at 7:00. . . . I registered to vote on Friday and 15 other women followed me—then on Sunday about 20 or 30 other women tried to register, but all of them except for two were refused—all my three sisters voted—Roda De Garmo too—Amy Post was rejected and she will immediately file a law suit like that done at Washington—and Honorable Henry R. Selden will be our lawyer. He has studied the law and all of our arguments and thinks that we are right. So does the Old Judge Selden, his older brother. So we are going to have excitement in Rochester on the question [of women voting]—I hope the morning's telegrams will talk about many women all over the country trying to vote. It is splendid that without any organized planning so many women have done this spontaneously. . . . Haven't we forced ourselves into this cause pretty fairly & fully? . . . When the Democrat said my vote should not go into the ballot box, one Republican said to the other, "What do you say Marshall? I say put it in!" "So do I," said Jones, "and we'll fight this out if it takes all winter." . . . If only now all the women suffrage women would work with the goal of enforcing the Constitution and national law over state law—what progress we might make this winter. But I'm awful tired. For five days I have been on the constant run, but for a great purpose. So all right. I hope you voted too.

Affectionately,
Susan B. Anthony

Source: Part of a letter from Susan B. Anthony to Elizabeth Cady Stanton, November 5, 1872, after Anthony voted illegally in a New York election. [Changed for easier reading.] Found at law2.umkc.edu/faculty/projects/ftrials/anthony/voteletters.html

Document 5: Shaw Eulogy

Susan B. Anthony was truly a reformer, who was not stopped in her service by the rules and negative power which often, so sadly, slows down the work of true reform. . . .

In our last conversation, when her prophetic soul knew that she was going to die, she said: "I leave my work to you and to the others who have been so faithful—promise that you will never let it go down or lessen our demands. There is so much to be done. Think of it! I have struggled for sixty years for a little bit of justice and die without getting it."

Oh, the terrible cruelty of it! The time will come when at these words every American heart will feel the awful shame and wrong of such a martyrdom [death of a hero].

She did not gain the little bit of freedom for herself, but there is not a civilized land, not even our own, where she has not helped women gain rights that she did not gain for herself. She did not reach the goal, but all through the tiring years what great successes, how many victories! The whole progress has been a successful march, with sadness and hard times, but never with despair. The heart sometimes wanted sympathy and the way was long, and oh! so lonely. But every step we could see little signs of progress, some mistakes corrected, some rights gained.

Source: Part of the eulogy [speech] given by Reverend Anna Howard Shaw at Susan B. Anthony's funeral in Rochester, New York, on March 15, 1906. [Changed for easier reading.] Found in *Great Eulogies throughout History*, edited by James Daley.

Document 6: Anthony Dollar

Source: Photograph of a "Susan B. Anthony dollar," a coin minted in the United States from 1979 to 1981 and again in 1999, discontinued because its smaller size caused some confusion. Found at en.wikipedia.org/wiki/Susan_B._Anthony_dollar#/media/File:1981-S_SBA$_Type_Two_Deep_Cameo.jpg

Document 7: Anthony Tribute

Source: Video posted by Cable News Network (CNN), "I voted stickers put on Susan B. Anthony's grave." Uploaded November 22, 2016. Found at www.cnn.com/videos/us/2016/11/04/people-are-leaving-i-voted-stickers-on-susan-b-anthonys-grave-orig-tc.cnn

Original Evidence

This document is not easily accessible online and is provided in its original format below.

Document 5: Shaw Eulogy

She was in the truest sense a reformer, unhindered in her service by the narrowness and negative destructiveness which often so sadly hampers the work of true reform....

In our last conversation, when her prophetic soul saw what we dare not even think, she said: "I leave my work to you and to the others who have been so faithful—promise that you will never let it go down or lessen our demands. There is so much to be done. Think of it! I have struggled for sixty years for a little bit of justice and die without securing it."

Oh, the unutterable cruelty of it! The time will come when at these words every American heart will feel the unspeakable shame and wrong of such a martyrdom.

She did not gain the little bit of freedom for herself, but there is scarcely a civilized land, not even our own, in which she has not been instrumental in securing for some woman that to which our leader did not attain. She did not reach the goal, but all along the weary years what marvelous achievements, what countless victories! The whole progress has been a triumphal march, marked by sorrow and hardship, but never by despair. The heart sometimes longed for sympathy and the way was long, and oh! so lonely; but every step was marked by some evidence of progress, some wrong righted, some right established.

Source: Part of the eulogy [speech] given by Reverend Anna Howard Shaw at Susan B. Anthony's funeral in Rochester, New York, on March 15, 1906. Found in a book called *Great Eulogies throughout History*, edited by James Daley.

Graphic Organizer

The Significance of Susan B. Anthony

Use this graphic organizer and the evidence in the documents to identify criteria to make a case for the significance of Susan B. Anthony's illegal 1872 vote. After collecting evidence from the documents, use that evidence to answer the questions that follow.

Doc	Source information (genre, author, purpose, audience, etc.)	Summary (what are the main ideas from this source?)	Criteria for significance	Reasons that the document suggests these criteria for significance
1			contemporary (then) present (now) causal revelatory symbolic personal	
2			contemporary (then) present (now) causal revelatory symbolic personal	
3			contemporary (then) present (now) causal revelatory symbolic personal	
4			contemporary (then) present (now) causal revelatory symbolic personal	
5			contemporary (then) present (now) causal revelatory symbolic personal	
6			contemporary (then) present (now) causal revelatory symbolic personal	
7			contemporary (then) present (now) causal revelatory symbolic personal	

1. To what degree, and in what ways, was Susan B. Anthony's 1872 vote historically significant?
2. How did people react to her voting during her time?
3. To what degree has her voting impacted current events? Did it create important changes in her time?
4. Was her voting symbolic of her time period or does it reveal important characteristics of her time?

Sample Classroom Poster

WAYS OF JUDGING HISTORICAL SIGNIFICANCE
1. Did people at the time think the person or event was important (significance then)?
2. Do people today think the person or event was important (significance now)?
3. Did the person or event cause important changes (causing significance)?
4. Is the person or event important for helping us understand the time (revealing significance)?
5. Is the person or event an important symbol of the time (symbolic significance)?
6. Is the person or event important to me or my family (personal or family significance)?

CHAPTER 13

James Farmer Jr. and the Freedom Riders

Eighty-nine years after Susan B. Anthony challenged New York's election laws, a handful of civil rights activists took on segregated busing in the South. Led by James Farmer Jr. and the Congress of Racial Equality, these Freedom Riders, Black and White, sat together on buses as they traveled into the Deep South. This simple act was met with violent opposition, arrests, and a great deal of national and international attention. This chapter provides materials for an investigation of James Farmer Jr. and the Freedom Riders as models of civil disobedience.

STUDENTS' BACKGROUND KNOWLEDGE

Chapters 7 and 11 provide insights into what students commonly know and do not know about the civil rights movement. With reference to the current chapter, the average student is unlikely to know much about James Farmer Jr. or the Congress of Racial Equality (CORE). If they have heard of the Freedom Riders, they may not know how they fit in with the larger context of the civil rights movement. They are unlikely to understand very clearly the tactic of civil disobedience employed by the Freedom Riders, or the training and policies that were put in place by CORE to make it work. Nor do students know much about the price paid by those who used and continue to use this dangerous strategy for promoting reform.

HISTORICAL BACKGROUND FOR TEACHERS AND STUDENTS

Background of Segregation

Most African Americans in the United States had ancestors who were taken from their homes in Africa. They were brought to the United States under terrible conditions. When they got here, they were forced into slavery. Some people in America taught that Blacks were not as good as White people. They taught that slavery was natural. Some even said it was good for the slaves because it helped them be more civilized. They taught that Whites were meant to be the leaders and Blacks were meant to be the workers. This racist idea was learned in homes, in school, and in churches, especially in the South. Over time, many people in America began to believe that White people were better than Black people. After the Civil War, slaves were freed by the Thirteenth Amendment. Even though African

Americans had gained their freedom, many people held on to their racist ideas.

Because of this racism, many places had laws that were unfair to Blacks and kept them separated from Whites. African Americans went to schools that were not as good as the schools that White children attended. African Americans could not drink from the same drinking fountains or swim in public swimming pools. If they went to movies, they had to sit in the balcony, away from White people. Some restaurants, hotels, and even hospitals would not serve African Americans. Black and White children were not allowed to play together. This separation of the races was called *segregation*. Sometimes, a Black person did something that White people thought broke the rules of segregation. When he/she did, the person might be arrested or sometimes even killed. White people were determined to keep things the way they were. In 1896, in a case called *Plessy v. Fergusson*, the Supreme Court ruled that segregated train cars were legal. Many of the Supreme Court justices had been raised in a racist society and believed that Whites were better than Blacks.

Racist ideas began to change during the civil rights movement. In 1954, the Supreme Court decided that segregated schools were not allowed by the Constitution. But White people who had grown up being taught racist ideas did not want African American children to attend school with their children. Traditions were hard to change, even when those traditions were unfair and wrong. Many White people had been raised in a racist society. They still thought Blacks were not as good as Whites. They did not think any changes were needed. In fact, they thought that their traditions kept the peace between the races. From their view, changes like *integrated* schools, where Black and White children attended together, might cause violence. Some worried about other changes that might happen if White and Black children became too friendly with one another. They could not imagine a society different from the one they knew. In spite of this, in 1960 the Supreme Court decided that segregated buses also violated the Constitution.

State governments, especially in the Deep South, would not follow court orders to integrate schools or buses. They ignored federal laws. These changes to traditions and laws went against what they wanted. The changes made them angry. Sometimes, even the police officers broke the federal laws. Some racist people used violence to scare other people who wanted change. The federal government began to enforce some of the Supreme Court rulings. They used federal troops to protect some African American children who attended integrated schools. Federal troops escorted some African American adults who went to college.

America was changing, but changes came slowly. More White people, especially outside of the Deep South, began to agree with Blacks who were fighting for civil rights. Some of them were still racist but thought that laws that treated Blacks and Whites differently were wrong. Others were starting to think that Blacks might be just as good as Whites. They supported the Supreme Court decisions that made segregation illegal. They thought it was time for more changes. Some Americans who lived in towns where few African Americans lived did not think much about the problems that Black people faced. They did not see segregation as a huge problem. They did not pay much attention to it. Civil rights leaders thought that for changes to be made, they needed the help of more White leaders and voters. What could they do to help people across the United States and around the world understand the unfair laws and policies that treated them as second-class citizens?

James Farmer and the Freedom Riders of 1961

James Farmer Jr. was a leader of the civil rights movement. He thought that peacefully breaking some of the unfair laws would make people pay more attention to the problems Black people faced. People called his ideas *nonviolent direct action*. Farmer was born in 1920 to parents who had gained good educations and had great careers. As a child, he saw the racial discrimination his father and mother faced. He decided then to fight for an end to segregation. While he was still a teenager, he prepared to be a leader. He went to school at Wiley College when he was only 14 and graduated with a bachelor of science degree a few years later. He continued to go to school and earned a bachelor of divinity degree from Howard University. In his early 20s, he started the Congress of Racial Equality (CORE). This organization would fight to end segregation.

While going to school at Howard University, Farmer studied the methods used by Gandhi in India's struggle for independence. He thought that Gandhi's tactics might be used in the fight to end segregation in the United States. One of the main ideas of Farmer's plans was to use nonviolent direct action. He would choose laws that he thought were unfair. Then his friends would do something that broke those laws. They would stay calm as the police arrested them or as angry people hurt them. Farmer thought that doing this would help people across America and the world see how unfair the laws were, and then do something about it. Farmer's organization, CORE, first tried out nonviolent direct action by visiting a restaurant in Chicago that would not serve African Americans. His White friends sat in the restaurant but would not order food until the restaurant served a Black man who had come there with them. The owners of the restaurant called the police. But when the police got there, they found that the peaceful protesters had not broken any law. Eventually, the diner gave in and started to serve Black people. This little win for civil rights excited Farmer and the members of CORE. They looked for other chances to use nonviolent direct action to bring changes.

In 1961, Farmer and CORE decided to challenge the segregated buses and waiting rooms at bus stations that were common throughout the South. They wanted to show that the states were not following Supreme Court decisions. The courts had said that laws went against the Constitution when they segregated buses that traveled between states. Farmer's plan was simple but dangerous. A racially mixed group of riders would travel by bus from Washington DC to New Orleans. They would sit together not only on the buses, but in bus stations and lunchrooms along the way. The riders were warned and prepared for the violence they might face. They had to promise to stay peaceful, no matter what. Farmer did not plan to go with them, but he changed his mind and stepped onto a bus with the younger protesters he had trained.

These Freedom Riders had a safe trip through the Upper South, but as they rode into Alabama, things changed. The riders were attacked. A bus was set on fire. Several Freedom Riders nearly died. People all across the United States listened to radio or television reporters describe what was happening. Other civil rights leaders planned the same kinds of rides, with similar things happening. In some cities, the police arrested the riders to try to stop the violence other people were doing to them. Farmer went to jail. The Freedom Riders had success showing people all across America the realities of segregated buses and how bad things were in the South. Many people started to support laws to end segregation.

Farmer went on to become one of the greatest leaders of the civil rights movement. He helped organize the March on Washington for Jobs and Freedom in 1963. He served in President Richard Nixon's cabinet as secretary of the Department of Health, Education, and Welfare. He fought for equality until his death in 1999.

HISTORICAL THINKING SKILLS: SOURCING

Increasingly, students are being taught in history classrooms to engage in sourcing (see, for example, Lesh, 2011). They are learning how to consider the author, audience, genre, and the purpose of a text as they read documents. But what can they do to engage in sourcing when the source information is missing or when the perspective of the author is unclear? In this lesson, students are taught to make inferences about the source based upon clues in the text. Additionally, although the strategy of sourcing is important across all genres of text, students sometimes forget to engage in sourcing when analyzing visual texts such as photographs or motion-picture footage. This lesson gives students opportunities to engage in sourcing with traditional formats of primary sources (such as interview transcripts and a pamphlet) and with nontraditional evidence (for example, a recorded interview, a radio broadcast, motion pictures, and photographs).

Sourcing is most likely to occur when students view texts as *accounts*. As introduced in Chapter 6, an account is an intentional retelling of an event. Accounts range from journal entries, news reports, sketches, court testimony, a telephone conversation, textbooks, Hollywood-produced movies, photographs, video recordings, or any other recounting of an episode. One key feature for students to understand about accounts is that they are produced by people for certain purposes. Additionally, they are influenced by many things besides the event they describe. For example, accounts of an incident during the Freedom Rides would be shaped by the perspective of the person producing it, the audience he/she was speaking to, whether the account was produced immediately after the event or a long time later, whether it was produced for a private or public audience, and the norms of the genre in which it is produced. For instance, a Hollywood movie about the Freedom Riders would be allowed—even expected—to add fictional elements to the account in order to enhance its entertainment value. In contrast, someone testifying in court would take an oath to limit his/her account to his/her memory of the event. Even photographs, as explained in Chapters 10 and 11, are not little snapshots of reality, but rather accounts, influenced by the photographer's biases, intended audience, and purpose. Video recordings, too, are shaped by their creator, who decides, among a host of other choices, when to turn the camera on and off.

Students who view documents as accounts approach texts in a way that accommodates sourcing. They understand the importance of thinking about the author/creator, audience, purpose, and the timing of its creation. Skilled readers engage in *closed sourcing*, observing source information when it is included. Closed sourcing occurs when students gather the information about the author that appears with the document. They notice the author's name, when he/she produced it, what genre it is, and how it was published, when that information is available. Skilled readers also engage in *open sourcing* by making inferences about the author/creator's biases, purpose, and credibility. They might search online for more information about the author. During open sourcing, which generally occurs both before and during reading, readers anticipate the content of the document and notice when the content confirms or goes against their expectations (Nokes & Kesler-Lund, 2019). Good readers are more likely to pay attention to the important elements of an account after having engaged in closed and open sourcing. For the purposes of the lesson included in this chapter, students will engage in *inferential sourcing*, using the content of the passage to make inferences about the source and to judge his/her credibility. Clues, such as word choice, inclusions, and omissions, often allow the reader to determine the author's biases, purposes, and reliability.

Open sourcing and inferential sourcing are useful in an Information Age when the sources of information obtained online often remain uncertain. Further, sourcing is a vital tool for civic engagement. Whether evaluating ads for political candidates, serving on a jury, gathering online information about a controversial topic (Wineburg, 2018), or even listening to the news, knowing the source of one's information is essential to informed citizenship. Information found in campaign flyers or television ads cannot be accepted at face value but must be critically evaluated based upon the source from which it comes. Sworn depositions and sales pitches are better understood and analyzed when the source of the information is acknowledged. Because this important strategy is unlikely to be taught in other secondary classes, history teachers have a profound obligation to teach their students to consider the source when evaluating information. The lesson below is intended to give students an opportunity to practice sourcing within a historical context.

LESSON IDEAS

Introduction

This lesson could be taught during a unit on the civil rights movement or the 1960s or in connection with other lessons on civil disobedience, protest, or reform if the course is organized thematically.

Objectives

The objectives of this lesson are threefold and related to knowledge, skills, and dispositions:

1. Students will identify civil rights leaders, tactics, events, and outcomes.
2. Students will engage in sourcing with print and nonprint texts and will make inferences about a source's perspective and bias based on the content of the text.
3. Students will evaluate the use of civil disobedience as a tool for engaged citizens to promote change.

Build Background Knowledge

Begin the lesson by building students' background knowledge on the civil rights movement and the context of the Freedom Riders, James Farmer Jr., and CORE. The essays provided in this chapter under the headings "Background of Segregation" and "James Farmer and the Freedom Riders of 1961" provide a basic overview of what students will need to know in order to work with the documents that follow.

Ask Historical Questions

The background knowledge provided should lead students to the following three questions, which the document collection below is intended to help answer: (1) What was the tactical approach of Farmer and the Freedom Riders? (2) How successful was the Freedom Riders' approach, in terms of how others responded? (3) What were the immediate and long-term outcomes of their civil disobedience? Depending on the age and skill level of the students, a teacher might simplify these three questions or instead ask a single question that requires students to think about the strategy of civil disobedience.

Provide Strategy Instruction and Model Sourcing

Remind students about the strategy of sourcing. (This lesson may not be the first time that students have considered this strategy; they may have had exposure to it throughout the school year.) Tell students that sometimes it is difficult to know the perspective or biases of the author after just looking at the source information. But usually, there are clues within the text that allow the historian/reader to infer the author's bias, perspectives, and purposes.

The teacher might model for students the process of *closed sourcing, open sourcing,* and *inferential sourcing* with Document 6, a radio broadcast. Looking first at the source, the teacher might notice that the information says that it was broadcasted from New York by John Scott on a program called *The World Today.* Note that this information is *closed sourcing.* However, the teacher might realize that this basic information is not enough to know the perspectives or biases of the reporter, the news program, or its sponsors. Instead, the teacher might realize that the biases must be inferred by the content of the report. After engaging in this closed sourcing, the teacher might play the recorded newscast, pausing it from time to time when the reporter, John Scott, includes loaded language or gives clues about his perspective. The teacher might also project the transcript of the report, included below, to highlight or annotate as he/she listens to the recording. Words used during the report provide clues about the reporter's biases. For instance, Scott used phrases such as *bus-borne crusaders* to portray the Freedom Riders as heroes. Included within his report is the accusation from Robert Kennedy that the Justice Department leveled against four Alabama policemen who failed to protect the Freedom Riders from an angry mob in Montgomery, Alabama. The teacher can realize as he/she models for students that Scott's choice of content and words demonstrates that he was sympathetic to the Freedom Riders' cause.

If the teacher feels that students need more support, he/she could also model sourcing with Document 5, a photograph of a parked Greyhound bus, with smoke billowing from its door and a man sitting on the ground nearby. The teacher might notice that the source information with the photo explains that it was taken by Joseph Postiglione, a reporter for a local Alabama newspaper, the *Anniston Star.* The teacher might then think out loud about the photographer behind the picture, realizing how Postiglione's photograph represents choices in angle, perspective, lighting, subjects, and cropping. For example, the photograph appears to be spontaneous, a White man is shown staring at the ground and appears to be dazed, and his face is turned away from the photographer. At the moment, however, much was happening and a very different photograph might have been taken a few seconds earlier or later. (The teacher might search online for other photographs taken by the same photographer showing different views of the same scene). Additionally, the teacher might model contextualization by recalling that photography at the time was not like photography now, when individuals can see their pictures instantly. At the time, film had to be loaded into a camera. After the picture had been taken, the film had to be processed in a dark room before the results could be seen.

The teacher might then wonder how Postiglione felt about the Freedom Riders. He/she might realize that the choices made in taking the photograph may have been similar whether he was a supporter of the Freedom Riders or opposed them. Either way, he would have wanted the world to see what happened to individuals who violated the busing laws of Alabama—either to promote sympathy for the Freedom Riders' cause, or to demonstrate the mob's commitment to defend southern traditions and to promote fear in those inclined toward civil disobedience and reform. After modeling with one or two documents, the teacher might suggest that each of the texts in this document set is more useful when students consider the author, genre, audience, purpose, bias, and insights gained by each unique source, regardless of the source's use of printed words, images, or audio or video recordings.

During modeling, the teacher can introduce students to the graphic organizer at the end of the chapter, helping them see how they can use it to collect evidence from the historical documents. The teacher can model for students how to use the graphic organizer by completing with the students the row for Document 6. He/she can record information in the second column about the source (John Scott and John Jay, reporters for the Mutual Broadcasting System (MBS) in New York, sympathetic to Freedom Riders.) Because this graphic organizer is a worksheet in the true sense of the word, the teacher can model for students how to abbreviate and annotate in a way that will help students to later use the evidence in the documents to develop and defend their interpretive answers to the lesson questions. The teacher should also model for students how to write a brief summary of the document in the third column, explaining that this should be based upon what the document says or shows, regardless of its trustworthiness. In the fourth column, the teacher circles which question or questions the document is most useful in answering. In the case of the news report, it suggests that people around the country were talking about the Freedom Riders, primarily providing evidence of their success and short-term outcomes. Finally, in the last column, the teacher can model how to use evidence to construct an interpretation by writing how the report supports an answer to one of the questions. (New York reporters, far from Mississippi, were paying attention and broadcasting events to the world, and important national politicians such as Robert Kennedy were reacting, just as the Freedom Riders wanted.)

If the teacher senses that students are still confused about the process of analyzing each document, he/she can model the analysis of more documents and can show students how to reason through the evidence while completing additional rows of the graphic organizer.

Group-Work

Once the teacher is confident that students understand how to make inferences about the source and how to use the graphic organizer to gather evidence from the documents, then he/she can have students work independently or in small groups on the remaining documents. The teacher should remind students about their objective: to use evidence from the documents to construct interpretations about the historical questions: What were the Freedom Riders' approaches? How successful were they? And what were the immediate and long-range outcomes of their civil disobedience?

Debriefing

At the conclusion of the lesson a debriefing serves three purposes associated with the three objectives of the lesson. First, students can discuss what they have learned about Farmer and the Freedom Riders with questions such as the following:

1. How did CORE train Freedom Riders to prepare them for the experience? Did that training pay off? Why did CORE establish the policies it had about who could be involved in the Freedom Rides?
2. How did Farmer's tactics compare with those of other civil rights leaders with whom you are familiar? What surprised you about his tactics?
3. In your opinion, did the Freedom Riders achieve the purposes of Farmer and CORE? What evidence from the documents led you to that conclusion?

A second phase of the debriefing can focus on the skills associated with reading historical texts, particularly sourcing, with the following questions:

1. What did you infer about the sources of documents from their content? Give examples of content that provided clues about the source's bias.
2. Which documents did you trust the most? Which did you doubt? How did you determine how reliable they were? What role did sourcing play?
3. How can a photographer influence the content of a photograph in order to achieve his/her purposes? Why can't photographs or video clips be accepted as little snapshots of reality? What decisions did Postiglione make in order to shape the content of his photograph?
4. How is analyzing a radio broadcast different from analyzing a photograph or an interview? What are some of the special strategies you used for different types of evidence?

The third phase of the debriefing can focus on civil disobedience with the following questions:

1. How is civil disobedience different from law-abiding protests or protests that involve the destruction of property or acts of violence?
2. Why are those who engage in civil disobedience hated by some and loved by others? Why does civil disobedience polarize society?
3. What are the risks associated with civil disobedience? Why are there often serious negative consequences for civil disobedience, such as jail terms, safety risks, or hefty fines for the disobedient?
4. Why should civil disobedience be seen as a "last resort" when other attempts at reform are unsuccessful? Why should conditions be considered carefully before civil disobedience is used?

INSTRUCTIONAL MATERIALS

Eight primary source documents are included in the pages that follow (or instructions for accessing them online are given.) Students should be warned that some documents use racial slurs in describing historic events and that these racial slurs are offensive and should not be used today. I include a graphic organizer for use during the lesson. A sample poster is shown at the end of the chapter that might be displayed in the classroom to help students remember the questions involved in sourcing.

Document Set

1. An excerpt from a transcript of an interview of Ed Blankenheim, a Freedom Rider, conducted by Clayborne Carson on March 2, 2002 (Carson, 2002)

2. Excerpts from a pamphlet called *All About CORE*, written by CORE member Dan Chasan, in 1965 (Chasan, 1965)

3. The booking photographs [mug shots] of James Farmer Jr. in Jackson, Mississippi, on May 24, 1961. Courtesy of the Archives and Records Services Division, Mississippi Department of Archives and History (Farmer, 1961)

4. A clip from an audio-recorded interview of James Farmer Jr. by Terry Gross, radio host, conducted on September 17, 1985, on National Public Radio (Gross, 1985)

5. A photograph of the Greyhound bus that the Freedom Riders had been riding on, taken by Joseph Postiglione near Anniston, Alabama, on May 14, 1961. Courtesy of the Birmingham Civil Rights Institute (Postiglione, 1961)

6. A radio broadcast of a news report, *The World Today*, recorded on May 24, 1961 (This document has not been modified so that the teacher can play the original recording, with students reading along.) (Scott, 1961).

7. A letter sent from Fred Jones, superintendent of the Mississippi State Penitentiary, to Merle Nelson, mother of Joan Trumpauer, one of the Freedom Riders, on July 12, 1961. Courtesy of the Joan Trumpauer Mulholland Foundation (Jones, 1961)

8. A video recording from the *Oprah Winfrey Show*, recorded on May 4, 2011, paying tribute to Freedom Riders (Winfrey, 2011)

Simplified Evidence

Document 1: Blankenheim Interview

Carson: So why don't we start with your name, and where you're from.

Blankenheim: I'm Ed Blankenheim, and I joined the Freedom Ride from Tucson Arizona where I was going to school. I answered the call of Jim Farmer who joined the Freedom Rides on, Mother's Day of 1961. We had a very successful trip to the South until we got to Alabama. As a matter of fact, one of the [White] men who boarded the bus said, "Y'all ain't in Georgia now, y'all in Alabama." And with that, he eventually set the bus on fire which was not a good place to be at the time. They held the door shut for maybe ten minutes. They held the door shut.

Carson: This was outside of Anniston?

Blankenheim: Outside of Anniston, Alabama, yeah. . . . The mob surrounded the bus. The cops would not let the mob get on the bus. [pause] So they threw a [fire bomb] aboard, . . .

Carson: What, could you describe what it was like for you at this . . . ?

Blankenheim: Well, it was a mob surrounding the bus. They were mighty angry people. Really, really vicious. . . . They threw a fire bomb aboard and held the door closed. You could hear cries of, "Get those [racial slur] alive." Well, finally one of the tanks blew up. One of the gas tanks blew up and Hank Thomas, who was one of the Freedom Riders, took advantage of it and was able to force open the bus door, thereby we got off. When we did get off we had to run through these racists who beat us all like hell. Fortunately, well it didn't sound fortunate, the second fuel tank on the bus exploded, scared the hell out of the mob so they went on the other side of the highway and the object was to leave us there where we would be blown up.

Source: Part of an interview of Ed Blankenheim, a Freedom Rider, conducted by Clayborne Carson, sponsored by the King Research and Education Center, March 2, 2002. [Changed for easier reading and to remove a racial slur.] Found at www.crmvet.org/nars/blaken02.htm

Document 2: CORE Pamphlet

The rules for action as a guide for all CORE members. These rules are especially for people who are in action projects.

- A CORE member will check the facts carefully before deciding whether or not racial injustice exists in a given situation.
- A CORE member will seek at all times to understand the opinion of the person who made a policy of racial discrimination. The CORE member will try to understand the social situation that caused the attitude. He will be flexible and creative. He will show a willingness to be part of experiments that seem constructive. He must be careful not to compromise CORE's principles.
- A CORE member will try very hard to avoid anger and hatred toward any group or individual.
- A CORE member will never use hurtful slogans or labels to insult any opponent.
- A CORE member will be willing to admit mistakes.
- A CORE member will meet the anger of any person or group in the spirit of goodwill and creative compromise. He will submit to attack and will not strike back either by act or word.
- Only a person who is a known member of the group or is accepted by the group leader will be allowed to take part in that group action.

Source: Part of a pamphlet, *All About CORE*, describing the objectives and policies of the Congress of Racial Equality (CORE), written by CORE member Dan Chasan and published about 1965. [Changed for easier reading.] Found at www.crmvet.org/docs/coreaac.pdf

Document 3: Farmer Mug Shots

Source: Booking photographs [mug shots] of James Farmer Jr., arrested as a Freedom Rider in Jackson, Mississippi, on May 24, 1961. Courtesy of the Archives and Records Services Division, Mississippi Department of Archives and History. Found at www.npr.org/2011/04/29/135836458/a-freedom-ride-organiz-er-on-non-violent-resistance

Document 4: Farmer Interview

Listen to Terry Gross's recorded interview with James Farmer Jr., at the following webpage, starting at 11:00 and ending at 16:36.

Source: Excerpt of an interview of James Farmer Jr. by Terry Gross, radio host, conducted on September 17, 1985, on the program *Fresh Air*, recorded by National Public Radio. Found at www.npr.org/2011/04/29/135836458/a-freedom-ride-organizer-on-non-vio-lent-resistance

Document 5: Photograph

Source: Photograph of the Greyhound bus that the Freedom Riders had been on, taken by Joseph Postiglione, a reporter for the *Anniston Star* newspaper, near Anniston, Alabama, on May 14, 1961. Courtesy of the Birmingham Civil Rights Institute.

Document 6: Radio Broadcast

John Scott: This is John Scott in New York. A cooling off period is needed in the deep south according to Attorney General Robert Francis Kennedy. His statements followed an announcement from the Freedom Riding headquarters that more bus-born crusaders of the type that met violence in Montgomery, Alabama would start moving almost daily through that region. "It would be wise," cautioned the Attorney General, "for those travelling through these states to delay their trips until the present state of confusion and danger is passed and an atmosphere of reason and normalcy has been restored." Robert Kennedy warned of the increasing possibility that innocent persons may be injured. There are curiosity-seekers, publicity-seekers, and others who are seeking to serve their own causes, as well as many persons who are traveling because they must use the interstate carriers to reach their destination. In an earlier statement the Attorney General had linked his appeal for restraint to the upcoming international trip of President Kennedy. President Kennedy, who must soon meet De Gaulle of France, Khrushchev of Soviet Russia, Prime Minister McMillan and Queen Elizabeth II of Britain, and he must meet them on an unembarrassed footing. Meanwhile in Jackson, Mississippi, 12 of the Freedom Riders came to town today and got off their bus. For the rest of the story here is John Jay of Mutual Station WJQS, Jackson, Mississippi.

John Jay: The first of what apparently will be an all-out effort to test the segregation barriers of Mississippi took place this afternoon. A Trailways bus with 12 self-styled Freedom Riders arrived in this capital city of Mississippi's hard core segregation. Promptly upon arrival at the bus station, all 12 riders were hustled off to jail, charged with inciting a riot, refusal to obey an officer, and disorderly conduct. The charges came moments after they stepped from their bus. Eight negroes were arrested for entering a white men's room after reading a sign the colored area was closed. The others were arrested in front of the bus station. An estimated crowd of 200 were lined up behind a cordon of police for four blocks. Most were people who worked in the immediate area. There were no incidents in direct contrast which brought the rioting that occurred when the group pulled into Montgomery last week. The Freedom Riders were accompanied on the bus by 7 national guardsmen with fixed bayonets and 17 newsmen. The guardsmen were commanded by a full colonel. With their initial efforts finalized in arrest, the Freedom Riders have made it clear that they intend to continue their bus travel through Mississippi. A second bus load is scheduled to arrive later tonight in Jackson. The 12 are scheduled for trial tomorrow. This is John Jay WJQS News. Now back to John Scott and the World today in New York.

John Scott: This evening another group of Freedom Riding youngsters got off a bus in Jackson, Mississippi and all were promptly put in jail. Late this afternoon, Robert Kennedy's Justice Department accused four Alabama policemen of deliberately withholding protection from the Freedom Riders who faced an angry mob last Saturday in Montgomery's bus station.

Source: Radio broadcast of a news report, *The World Today*, recorded on May 24, 1961, on the Mutual Broadcasting System (MBS) by John Scott in New York and John Jay in Jackson, Mississippi. Audio recording found at www.youtube.com/watch?v=vnW-JkVmuce4

Document 7: Jones Letter

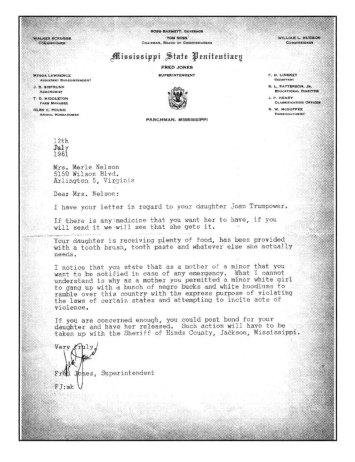

Source: Letter sent from Fred Jones, superintendent of the Mississippi State Penitentiary, to Merle Nelson, mother of Joan Trumpauer, one of the Freedom Riders, on July 12, 1961. Courtesy of the Joan Trumpauer Mulholland Foundation. Found at s3-us-west-2.amazonaws.com/static.studiesweekly.com/img/beahero/03_06_parchman_letter.jpg

Document 8: *The Oprah Winfrey Show*

Watch the YouTube video at the link below, ending at 5:12. Be aware that racial slurs are used in the video as individuals talk about historic conditions and events. These racial slurs are offensive and should not be used today.

Source: Video recording from the *Oprah Winfrey Show*, a Chicago-based daytime talk show, hosted by Oprah Winfrey, recorded on May 4, 2011, paying tribute to and interviewing Freedom Riders. Found at www.youtube.com/watch?v=nAyfoyfLsnQ

Graphic Organizer

James Farmer Jr. and the Freedom Riders

What was the approach of Farmer and the Freedom Riders? How successful was the Freedom Riders' approach? What were the immediate and long-term outcomes of their civil disobedience?

Doc	Source information (genre, author, purpose, audience, etc.)	Summary (what are the main ideas from this source?)	Question(s) Circle	Evidence suggests . . . (clues about approaches, success, outcomes)
1			Approaches Success Outcomes	
2			Approaches Success Outcomes	
3			Approaches Success Outcomes	
4			Approaches Success Outcomes	
5			Approaches Success Outcomes	
6			Approaches Success Outcomes	
7			Approaches Success Outcomes	
8			Approaches Success Outcomes	

1. What is your interpretation of Farmer and the Freedom Riders' approaches? What evidence leads you to this interpretation?
2. What is your interpretation of the success of Farmer and the Freedom Riders? What evidence leads you to this interpretation?
3. What is your interpretation of the immediate and long-range outcomes? What evidence leads you to this interpretation?

Sample Classroom Poster

QUESTIONS TO ASK ABOUT A SOURCE

1. Who created the account? What do you know about him/her?
2. When did he/she create the account compared to the event it describes?
3. Why did he/she create the account?
4. What is the genre of the account?
5. Did the creator of the account keep it private or share it publicly?
6. Who published the account and how and why was it published?
7. How did the author or creator know about the event?
8. How did the author or creator feel about the event?
9. How did people react to this account?
10. What does the content of the account show about the source?

References

Adams, J. (1815/1961). *Diary and Autobiography of John Adams.* Retrieved from law2.umkc.edu/faculty/projects/FTrials/bostonmassacre/diaryentries.html

Adams, J. (1856). *The works of John Adams, second President of the United States: With a life of the author, notes and illustrations, by his grandson Charles Francis Adams, Vol. 10.* Retrieved at oll.libertyfund.org/titles/2127#Adams_1431-10_932

Adams, J. (1909). John Adams of Massachusetts on the Boston Massacre. In Harding, S. B. *Selected Orations Illustrating American Political History* (pp. 11–23). Retrieved from archive.org/stream/selectorationsi00clapgoog/selectorationsi00clapgoog_djvu.txt

Adams, J. (1965). *Legal papers of John Adams.* Retrieved from law2.umkc.edu/faculty/projects/FTrials/bostonmassacre/adamssummation.html

Adams, J. (n.d.). *John Adams autobiography, part 1, "John Adams," through 1776, page 12 of 53* [electronic edition]. Adams Family papers: An electronic archive. Boston: MA: Massachusetts Historical Society. Retrieved from www.masshist.org/digitaladams/archive/doc?id=A1_12

Adams, K., & Keene, M. (2008). *Alice Paul and the American suffrage campaign.* Champaign, IL: University of Illinois Press.

Adams, S. (1906). *The writings of Samuel Adams, Vol 2, 1770–1773.* Retrieved from www.fullbooks.com/The-Writings-of-Samuel-Adams-volume-II-1770-1.html

American Federationist. (1908, September). Unlawful boycott. *American Federationist.* Retrieved from babel.hathitrust.org/cgi/pt?id=njp.32101045284831;view=2up;seq=120

American Federationist. (1921, April 21). The challenge accepted: Labor will not be outlawed or enslaved. *American Federationist.* Retrieved from babel.hathitrust.org/cgi/pt?id=mdp.39015034112923;view=2up;seq=178;size=150

Anthony, S. B. (1872, November 5). Letter to Elizabeth Cady Stanton. Retrieved from law2.umkc.edu/faculty/projects/ftrials/anthony/voteletters.html

Anthony, S. B. (1873, June 19). Remarks by Susan B. Anthony in the circuit court of the United States for the Northern District of New York. Retrieved from www.rit.edu/cla/statesmanship/media/ap-friday/AnthonyStanton/SBA%20speech%20before%20the%20Court.pdf

Associated Press Photo File. (1968, October 16). Tommie Smith, John Carlos, and Peter Norman awards ceremony [image]. File 16268128268630, Associated Press Images.

Barton, K. C. (2008). Research on students' ideas about history. In L. S. Levstik & C. A. Tyson (Eds.), *Handbook of research in social studies education* (pp. 239–258). New York, NY: Routledge.

Barton, K. C., & Levstik, L. S. (2004). *Teaching history for the common good.* Mahwah, NJ: Lawrence Erlbaum.

Bell, J. C., & McCollum, D. F. (1917). A study of the attainments of pupils in United States History. *Journal of Educational Psychology, 8*(5), 257–274.

Biderman, C. (2016, August 28). Transcript: Colin Kaepernick addresses sitting during national anthem. *Ninerswire.* Retrieved from ninerswire.usatoday.com/2016/08/28/transcript-colin-kaepernick-addresses-sitting-during-national-anthem/

Boston Pamphlet. (1772). Votes and proceedings of the freeholders and other inhabitants of the town of Boston. Retrieved from americainclass.org/sources/makingrevolution/crisis/text6/bostonpamphlet.pdf

Bowen, C. D. (1966). *Miracle at Philadelphia: The story of the Constitutional Convention May to September 1787.* Boston, MA: Little, Brown & Co.

Bradford, S. H. (1886). *Harriet: The Moses of her people.* New York, NY: George R. Lockwood & Son. Retrieved at www.docsouth.unc.edu/neh/harriet/harriet.html

Bransford, J. D., Brown, A. L., & Cocking, R. R. (2000). *How people learn: Brain, mind, experience, and school.* Washington, DC: National Academy Press.

Brodess, E. A. (1849, October). Three hundred dollars reward. Retrieved from harriettubmanbyway.org/harriet-tubman/

Callahan, C. (2013). Analyzing historical photographs to promote civic competence. *Social Studies Research and Practice, 8*(1), 77–88.

Callow, J. (2006). Images, politics and multiliteracies: Using a visual metalanguage. *Australian Journal of Language and Literacy, 29*(1), 7–23.

Carson, C. (2002, March 2). Interview with Ed Blankenheim, Freedom Rider. King Research and Education Center. Retrieved from www.crmvet.org/nars/blaken02.htm

CBC News. (2017, October 8). Mike Pence walks out of NFL game after players take a knee during anthem. Canadian Broadcasting Corporation. Retrieved from www.cbc.ca/news/world/pence-leaves-nfl-game-players-take-a-knee-protest-1.4346076

CBS Reports. (1964, March 18). Senators Hubert Humphrey (D-MN) and Strom Thurmond (D-SC) debate the Civil Rights Act. CBS Reports: Filibuster—Birth struggle of a law. Retrieved from www.loc.gov/exhibits/civil-rights-act/multimedia/hubert-humphrey-and-strom-thurmond.html

Cercadillo, L. (2006). "Maybe they haven't decided yet what is right": English and Spanish perspectives on teaching historical significance. *Teaching History, 125,* 6–9.

Chasan, D. (1965). All about CORE. New York, NY: CORE. Retrieved from www.crmvet.org/docs/coreaac.pdf

CNN. (n.d.) "I voted" stickers put on Susan B. Anthony's grave. *Cable News Network (CNN)*. Retrieved from www.cnn.com/videos/us/2016/11/04/people-are-leaving-i-voted-stickers-on-susan-b-anthonys-grave-orig-tc.cnn

Common Core State Standards. (2010). Common core state standards. Retrieved from www.corestandards.org/

Conkling, W. (2018). *Votes for women! American suffragists and the battle for the ballot*. Chapel Hill, NC: Algonquin.

Constitution of the United States. (1787). The Constitution of the United States. Retrieved from www.archives.gov/founding-docs/constitution-transcript

Cooper, W. (1775, February 25). Endorsement: February 1775 For the Committee of Correspondence in Rutland. Retrieved from dp.la/item/a1035e5fbf7300b2e40d073a33b58f7b

Crockett, G. (1964, April 15). If they don't watch out they're gonna ruin it [political cartoon]. *Washington Star*. Retrieved from www.loc.gov/exhibits/civil-rights-act/civil-rights-act-of-1964.html#obj281_01

Crowley, R. (1873, June 17). Opening statement at the trial of Susan B. Anthony. *United States of America v. Susan B. Anthony*. Retrieved from score.rims.k12.ca.us/score_lessons/womens_suffrage/pdf/susan_b_anthony_trial.pdf

Cushing, T., Adams, S., Hancock, J., & Phillips W. (1773, December 21). A Committee of Correspondence letter to Benjamin Franklin. Retrieved from dp.la/primary-source-sets/road-to-revolution-1763-1776/sources/11

Davis, O. L., Jr. (2001). In pursuit of historical empathy. In O. L. Davis Jr., E. A. Yeager, & S. Foster (Eds.), *Historical empathy and perspective taking in the social studies* (pp. 1–12). New York, NY: Rowman and Littlefield.

De Tocqueville, A. (1900). *Democracy in America* (Vol 1.). Retrieved from books.google.com/books?id=hS4TAAAAYAAJ&printsec=frontcover#v=onepage&q&f=false

Delaware General Assembly. (1937). Credentials of Delaware's delegates to the federal convention. Retrieved from press-pubs.uchicago.edu/founders/documents/a1_3_1-2s2.html

Douglass, F. (1868, August 29). Letter to Harriett Tubman. Retrieved from www.accessible-archives.com/2012/02/scenes-in-the-life-of-harriet-tubman-part-3/

Edwards, H. (1969). *The revolt of the black athlete*. New York, NY: Free Press. Retrieved from archive.org/details/TheRevoltOfTheBlackAthlete/page/n123

Endacott, J., & Brooks, S. (2013). An updated theoretical and practical model for promoting historical empathy. *Social Studies Research and Practice*, 8, 1, 41–58.

Farmer, J. (1961, May 24). [Booking photographs]. Jackson, MS. Retrieved from www.npr.org/2011/04/29/135836458/a-freedom-ride-organizer-on-non-violent-resistance

Foster, S. (2001). Historical empathy in theory and practice: Some final thoughts. In O. L. Davis Jr., E. A. Yeager, & S. Foster (Eds.), *Historical empathy and perspective taking in the social studies* (pp. 167–181). New York, NY: Rowman & Littlefield.

Foster, S. J., Hoge, J. D., & Rosch, R. H. (1999). Thinking aloud about history: Children's and adolescents' responses to historical photographs. *Theory and Research in Social Education*, 27(2), 179–214.

Garrett, T. (1854, December 29). Letter written to J. Miller McKim. Reprinted in W. Still (1872). *The Underground Rail Road*. Philadelphia, PA: Porter & Coates. Retrieved from housedivided.dickinson.edu/ugrr/letter_dec1854.htm

Garrett, T. (1868, June). Letter written to Harriett Tubman. In S. Bradford (1869), *Scenes from the life of Harriet Tubman*. Auburn, NY: W. J. Moses. Retrieved from www.harriet-tubman.org/letter-by-thomas-garrett/

Goldwater, B. (1964, June 18). Text of Goldwater speech on civil rights. *Congressional Record*, 14318-14319. Retrieved from www.govinfo.gov/content/pkg/GPO-CRECB-1964-pt11/pdf/GPO-CRECB-1964-pt11-2-1.pdf

Gompers v. Bucks Stove and Range Co. (1911). Retrieved from caselaw.findlaw.com/us-supreme-court/221/418.html#f1

Gompers, S. (1920a, February 14). Letter to William Quayle. *America in Class: The National Humanities Center*. Retrieved from americainclass.org/sources/becomingmodern/prosperity/text5/lettersbishop.pdf

Gompers, S. (1920b, May 17). Letter to William Quayle. *America in Class: The National Humanities Center*. Retrieved from americainclass.org/sources/becomingmodern/prosperity/text5/lettersbishop.pdf

Gompers, S., et al. (1906, March 21). Letter to Theodore Roosevelt, sometimes called Labor's Bill of Grievances. Retrieved from www.gompers.umd.edu/Bill%20of%20Grievances%201906.htm

Gorbachev, M. (1985, June 10). Letter from Michael Gorbachev to Ronald Reagan. Retrieved from www.margaretthatcher.org/document/110656

Gorbachev, M., & Reagan, R. (1988, June 1). Remarks at the exchange of documents ratifying the intermediate-range nuclear forces treaty. Retrieved from www.reaganlibrary.gov/research/speeches/060188a

Gray, M. (2012, October 16). John Carlos: Looking back at a raised fist and as a raised consciousness. *Time*. Retrieved from keepingscore.blogs.time.com/2012/10/16/john-carlos-looking-back-at-a-raised-fist-and-at-a-raised-consciousness/

Greene, S. (1919, November 1). Step by step [political cartoon]. *New York Evening Post*. Retrieved from historyproject.uci.edu/files/2017/01/Red_Scare_Grade11.pdf

Gross, T. (1985, September 17). A freedom ride organizer on nonviolent resistance. [Interview of James Farmer Jr.]. *National Public Radio*. Retrieved from www.npr.org/2011/04/29/135836458/a-freedom-ride-organizer-on-non-violent-resistance

Harding, V. (1981). *There is a river: The black struggle for freedom in America*. New York, NY: Houghton Mifflin Harcourt.

Hartmann, D. (2003). *Race, culture, and the revolt of the black athlete: The 1968 Olympic protests and their aftermath*. Chicago, IL: University of Chicago Press.

Hess, D., & McAvoy, P. (2015). *The political classroom: Evidence and ethics in democratic education*. New York, NY: Routledge.

Horton, L. E. (2013). *Harriet Tubman and the fight for freedom: A brief history with documents*. Boston, MA: Bedford/St. Martin's.

Humphrey, H. H., & Kuchel, T. H. (1964, April 19). Opinion of the week: At home and abroad. *New York Times*. Retrieved from www.nytimes.com/1964/04/19/archives/opinion-of-the-week-at-home-and-abroad.html

Imbert, F. (2016, April 20). Treasury to keep Hamilton on $10, put Tubman on $20. *Consumer News and Business Channel (CNBC)*. Retrieved from www.cnbc.com/2016/04/20/treasury-to-leave-hamilton-on-the-10-bill-put-tubman-on-20-politico.html

Jefferson, T. (1820, September 28). Letter written to William Charles Jarvis. Retrieved from founders.archives.gov/documents/Jefferson/98-01-02-1540

Johnson, A. (1864, summer). Harsh punishment of the rebels. In T. Stevens (1867, March 19). Speech on H. R. 20, the bill relative to damages to loyal men, and for other purposes. Thaddeus Stevens Papers, Furman, University. Retrieved from history.furman.edu/benson/hst41/silver/stevens1.htm

Johnson, L. B. (1963, November 27). Lyndon B. Johnson addresses congress after John F. Kennedy's assassination. *Public Broadcasting Service (PBS)*. Retrieved from www.pbs.org/ladybird/epicenter/epicenter_doc_speech.html

Johnson, L. B. (1964, July 2). Remarks on signing the civil rights bill. Retrieved from www.youtube.com/watch?v=FKfoJJA5xWM

Jones, F. (1961). Letter to Merle Nelson from Mississippi State Penitentiary. Retrieved from s3-us-west-2.amazonaws.com/static.studiesweekly.com/img/beahero/03_06_parchman_letter.jpg

Kennedy, J. F. (1963, June 11). Televised address to the nation on civil rights. John F. Kennedy Presidential Library and Museum. Retrieved from www.jfklibrary.org/learn/about-jfk/historic-speeches/televised-address-to-the-nation-on-civil-rights

Kohut, A. (2015, March 5). 50 years ago: Mixed views about civil rights but support for Selma demonstrators. Washington, D.C.: Pew Research Center. www.pewresearch.org/fact-tank/2015/03/05/50-years-ago-mixed-views-about-civil-rights-but-support-for-selma-demonstrators/

Larson, K. C. (n.d.). Myths and Facts about Harriet Tubman, and Selected Quotes and Misquotes. Retrieved from www.harriet-tubmanbiography.com/harriet-tubman-myths-and-facts.html

Lee, P., & Ashby, R. (2001). Empathy, perspective taking, and rational understanding. In O. L. Davis Jr., E. A. Yeager, & S. J. Foster (Eds.), *Historical empathy and perspective taking in the social studies* (pp. 21–50). Lanham, MD: Rowman & Littlefield.

Lesh, B. A. (2011). *Why won't you just tell us the answer? Teaching historical thinking in grades 7–12*. Portland, ME: Stenhouse.

Levy, J. (1975). *Cesar Chavez: Autobiography of La Causa*. New York, NY: W. W. Norton & Co.

Lincoln, A. (1861, March 4). First inaugural address of Abraham Lincoln. Retrieved from www.bartleby.com/124/pres31.html

Lincoln, A. (1862, August 22). Letter to Horace Greely. Retrieved from housedivided.dickinson.edu/sites/lincoln/letter-to-horace-greeley-august-22-1862/

Lincoln, A. (1863a, August 26). Letter written to the residents of Springfield, Illinois, read by James Conkling. *Abraham Lincoln Online*. Retrieved from www.abrahamlincolnonline.org/lincoln/speeches/conkling.htm

Lincoln, A. (1863b, December 8). A proclamation of amnesty and reconstruction. *Freedmen and Southern Society Project*. Retrieved from www.freedmen.umd.edu/procamn.htm

Lincoln, A. (1864a, February 5). Letter to Edwin Stanton. Retrieved from quod.lib.umich.edu/cgi/t/text/text-idx?c=lincoln;rgn=div1;view=text;idno=lincoln7;node=lincoln7%3A358

Lincoln, A. (1864b, March 13). Letter to Governor Michael Hahn. *TeachingAmericanHistory.org*. Retrieved from teachingamericanhistory.org/library/document/letter-to-governor-michael-hahn/

Lincoln, A. (1864c, July 18). Some words on peace and war. Retrieved from teachingamericanhistory.org/library/document/the-to-whom-it-may-concern-letter/

Lincoln, A. (1865, March 4). Second inaugural address of Abraham Lincoln. *Yale Law School: The Avalon Project*. Retrieved from avalon.law.yale.edu/19th_century/lincoln2.asp

Lincoln, A. (1953). Letter from Abraham Lincoln to Henry Pierce and others, April 6, 1859. Retrieved from www.abrahamlincolnonline.org/lincoln/speeches/pierce.htm

Madison, J. (1787). *The debates in the federal convention of 1787: Which framed the Constitution of the United States*. Retrieved from www.nhccs.org/Mnotes.html

Malin, H., Ballard, P. J., Attai, M. L., Colby, A., & Damon, W. (2014). *Youth civic development & education: A conference consensus report*. Stanford, CA: Center on Adolescence, Stanford University. Retrieved from coa.stanford.edu/sites/g/files/sbiybj1076/f/civic_education_report.pdf

Manning, J. J. (1925). *Labor's reward* [motion picture]. Rothacker Film Manufacturing Co. Retrieved from www.filmpreservation.org/dvds-and-books/clips/labor-s-reward-1925

Mazzei, P. (2018, March 9). Florida governor signs gun limits into law, breaking with the N.R.A. *New York Times*. Retrieved from www.nytimes.com/2018/03/09/us/florida-governor-gun-limits.html

McGrew, S., Ortega, T., Breakstone, J., & Wineburg, S. (2017). The challenge that's bigger than fake news: Civic reasoning in a social media environment. *American Educator 41*(3), 4–9, 39.

McKeown, M. G., & Beck, I. L. (1990). The assessment and characterization of young learners' knowledge of a topic in history. *American Educational Research Journal, 27*(4), 688–726.

Milligan, A., Gibson, L., & Peck, C. (2018). Enriching ethical judgments in history education. *Theory and Research in Social Education, 46*(3), 449–479.

Monte-Sano, C. (2008). Qualities of historical writing instruction: A comparative case study of two teachers' practices. *American Educational Research Journal, 45*, 1045–1079.

National Council for the Social Studies (NCSS). (2013). *The college, career, and civic life (C3) framework for social studies state standards: Guidance for enhancing the rigor of K–12 civics, economics, geography, and history*. Silver Spring, MD: Author.

Nike. (2018). Believe in something, even if it means sacrificing everything [video advertisement]. *Global News*. Retrieved from globalnews.ca/video/4428833/

believe-in-something-even-if-it-means-sacrificing-everything-colin-kaepernick-in-nike-commercial

Nokes, J. D. (2008). The observation/inference chart: Improving students' ability to make inferences while reading non-traditional texts. *Journal of Adolescent and Adult Literacy, 51*, 538–546.

Nokes, J. D. (2011). Recognizing and addressing the barriers to adolescents' "reading like historians." *The History Teacher, 44*(3), 379–404.

Nokes, J. D. (2013). *Building students' historical literacies: Learning to read and reason with historical texts and evidence*. New York, NY: Routledge.

Nokes, J. D. (2014). Elementary students' roles and epistemic stances during document-based history lessons. *Theory and Research in Social Education, 42*(3), 375–413.

Nokes, J. D. (2017). Exploring patterns of historical thinking through eighth-grade students' argumentative writing. *Journal of Writing Research, 8*(3), 437–467.

Nokes, J. D., & Kelser-Lund, A. (2019). Historians' social literacies: How historians collaborate and write during a document-based activity. *The History Teacher, 52*(3), 369–410.

Nokes, J. D., Dole, J. A., & Hacker, D. J. (2007). Teaching high school students to use heuristics while reading historical texts. *Journal of Educational Psychology, 99*, 492–504.

Palmer, J. (1775). To all friends of American liberty. *America in Class: The National Humanities Center*. Retrieved from americainclass.org/sources/makingrevolution/crisis/text8/vacommlexingtonconcord.pdf

Parker, W. C. (2008). Knowing and doing in democratic citizenship education. In L. S. Levstik & C. A. Tyson (Eds.), *Handbook of research in social studies education* (pp. 65–80). New York, NY: Routledge.

Paxton, R. J. (2003). Don't know much about history—Never did. *Phi Delta Kappan, 85*(4), 264–273.

Philanthrop. (1770, December 24). Untitled letter to the editor. *Boston Evening Post*. The Annotated Newspapers of Harbottle Dorr, Jr: Massachusetts Historical Society. Retrieved from www.masshist.org/dorr/volume/3/sequence/377

Postiglione, J. (1961, May 14). Freedom Riders stopped at Anniston, Alabama [Photograph]. File name *Anniston 40*. Birmingham Civil Rights Institute. Birmingham, Alabama.

Proceedings of the Committee of Correspondence. (1774, July 19). The American Revolution 1763–1783. *Library of Congress*. Retrieved from www.loc.gov/teachers/classroommaterials/presentationsandactivities/presentations/timeline/amrev/rebelln/proceed.html

Quayle, W. (1920, February 11). Untitled speech cited in the *Baltimore American*. *America in Class: The National Humanities Center*. Retrieved from americainclass.org/sources/becomingmodern/prosperity/text5/lettersbishop.pdf

Quincy, J. (1965). Letter to J. Quincy Jr., March 22, 1770. L. K. Wroth & H. B. Zobel (Eds.), *Legal papers of John Adams, Vol. 3, Case 63* (pp. 1-97). Retrieved from www.masshist.org/publications/adams-papers/index.php/view/ADMS-05-03-02-0001-0001

Quincy, J. Jr. (1965). Letter to J. Quincy, March 26, 1770. L. K. Wroth & H. B. Zobel (Eds.), *Legal papers of John Adams, Vol. 3, Case 63* (pp 1–97). Retrieved from www.masshist.org/publications/adams-papers/index.php/view/ADMS-05-03-02-0001-0001

Reagan, R. (1983, October 10). White House diaries. *Ronald Reagan Presidential Foundation and Institute: White House Diaries*. Retrieved from www.reaganfoundation.org/ronald-reagan/white-house-diaries/diary-entry-10101983/

Reagan, R. (1987, June 12). Tear down this wall [speech]. *The History Place*. Retrieved from www.historyplace.com/speeches/reagan-tear-down.htm

Reagan, R. (1990). *An American life: The autobiography*. New York, NY: Simon & Schuster.

Reagan, R., & Gorbachev, M. (1985, November 19). Reagan and Gorbachev holding discussions [photograph]. Retrieved from commons.wikimedia.org/wiki/File:Reagan_and_Gorbachev_hold_discussions.jpg

Reagan Speeches Suggest Lack of Strength. (1987, September 10). Reagan speeches suggest lack of strength, Soviet expert says [Reuter Library Report]. Retrieved from archive.org/stream/GorbachevVisitWashingtonSummit/Gorbachev%20Visit%20[Washington%20Summit]%20(2)%20RR-COS-BakerH-02-16_djvu.txt

Reisman, A. (2012). Reading like a historian: A document-based history curriculum intervention in urban high schools. *Cognition and Instruction, 30*(1), 86–112.

Revere, P. (1832). *The bloody massacre perpetrated in King Street, Boston on March 5th, 1770 by a party of the 29th Regiment*. Retrieved from www.indiana.edu/~liblilly/cartoon/revere.html

Risen, C. (2014). *The bill of the century: The epic battle for the Civil Rights Act*. New York, NY: Bloomsbury.

Rodrigue, J. C. (2013). *Lincoln and reconstruction*. Carbondale, IL: Southern Illinois University.

Romano, A. (2011). How dumb are we? *Newsweek, 157*, 13/14, 56–60.

Rosenfeld, E. (2015, June 17). A woman will be on the redesigned $10 bill. *Consumer News and Business Channel (CNBC)*. Retrieved from www.cnbc.com/2015/06/17/a-woman-will-be-on-the-redesigned-10-bill.html

Rutland Herald. (1873, June 26). Anonymous editorial letter: Susan B. Anthony case. *Rutland Weekly Herald, 79*, 26. Retrieved from chroniclingamerica.loc.gov/lccn/sn84022367/1873-06-26/ed-1/seq-1/#date1=1873&index=6&rows=20&words=ANTHONY+Anthony&searchType=basic&sequence=0&state=Vermont&date2=1873&proxtext=Anthony&y=15&x=16&dateFilterType=yearRange&page=1

Savranskya, S., & Blanton, T. (2016). *The last superpower summits: Reagan, Gorbachev, and Bush. Conversations that ended the Cold War*. Budapest, Hungary: Central European University Press.

Scott, J. (1961, May 24). Radio broadcast on the Mutual Broadcasting System (MBS). Retrieved from www.youtube.com/watch?v=vnWJkVmuce4

Seixas, P., & Morton, T. (2013). *The big six: Historical thinking concepts*. Toronto, Ontario, Canada: Nelson Education.

Shabad, R. (2018, September 28). Outrage from Democrats and protesters on Capitol Hill amid GOP sprint to confirm

Kavanaugh. *National Broadcasting Company (NBC) News.* Retrieved from www.nbcnews.com/politics/congress/outrage-democrats-protesters-capitol-hill-amid-gop-sprint-confirm-kavanaugh-n914791

Shaver, J. P., Davis, O. L., Jr., & Helburn, S. W. (1980). *An interpretive report on the status of pre-collegiate social studies education based on three NSF-funded studies.* (Report to the National Science Foundation). Washington, DC: National Council for the Social Studies.

Shaw, A. H. (2016). Eulogy delivered by Anna Howard Shaw at Susan B. Anthony's Funeral. In J. Daley (Ed.), *Great eulogies throughout history* (pp. 144–148). Mineola, NY: Dover.

Sheehan, J. M. (1968, October 18). 2 Black Power advocates ousted from Olympics. *New York Times.* Retrieved from archive.nytimes.com/www.nytimes.com/learning/general/onthisday/big/1018.html

Shultz, G. P. (1987, December 9). Luncheon toast by Secretary of State George P. Shultz to Mikhail Gorbachev, General Secretary of the Central Committee of the Communist Party of the USSR. Collection: Baker, Howard H. Jr: Files, Folder Title: Gorbachev Visit [Washington Summit] (1) Box: 2. Ronald Reagan Library. Retrieved from www.reaganlibrary.gov/sites/default/files/digitallibrary/smof/cos/bakerhoward/box-002/40-27-6912132-002-015-2017.pdf

Stevens, T. (1867, March 19). Speech on H. R. 20, the bill relative to damages to loyal men, and for other purposes. Thaddeus Stevens Papers Online, Furman, University. Retrieved from history.furman.edu/benson/hst41/silver/stevens1.htm

Still, W. (1872). *The Underground Rail Road: A record of facts, authentic narratives, letters, & C., narrating the hardships, hair-breadth escapes, and death struggles of the slaves in their efforts for freedom as related by themselves and others, or witnessed by the author, together with sketches of some of the largest stockholders, and most liberal aiders and advisers, of the road.* Philadelphia, PA: Porter & Coates.

Tallentyre, S. G. (1906). *The friends of Voltaire.* London, England: G. P. Putnam's Sons.

Teaching Channel. (n.d.) Reading like a historian: Contextualization. *Teaching Channel.* Retrieved from www.teachingchannel.org/video/reading-like-a-historian-contextualization

Terrell, K. (2017, October 1). Eagles Chargers: National Anthem protest by Philadelphia Eagles players [image]. File 444767232583, Associated Press Images.

Trump, D. J. (2017, March 20). Speech at Louisville, Kentucky Rally. Retrieved from *www.youtube.com/watch?v=xiAtN1ziQ9o*

Ulrich, L. (1991). *A midwife's tale: The life of Martha Ballard, based on her diary, 1785–1812.* New York, NY: Vintage.

U.S. Mint. (1981). Susan B. Anthony dollar type two deep cameo [photograph]. Retrieved from en.wikipedia.org/wiki/Susan_B._Anthony_dollar#/media/File:1981-S_SBA$_Type_Two_Deep_Cameo.jpg

VanFossen, P. J. (2005). "Reading and math take so much of the time . . .": An overview of social studies instruction in elementary classrooms in Indiana. *Theory & Research in Social Education, 33*(3), 376–403.

Votes and Proceedings of the Freeholders and other Inhabitants of the Town of Boston. (1772). Retrieved from www.masshist.org/revolution/image-viewer.php?item_id=609&mode=small&img_step=1&tpc=#page1

Warner, W. B. (2013). *Protocols of liberty: Communication innovation and the American Revolution.* Chicago, IL: University of Chicago Press.

Warren, E. (1954). *Brown v. Board of Education of Topeka. The Our Documents Initiative: 100 Milestone Documents.* Retrieved from www.ourdocuments.gov/doc.php?flash=true&doc=87&page=transcript

Wiggins, G. (1989). The futility of trying to teach everything of importance. *Educational Leadership, 47*(3), 44–59.

Wineburg, S. S. (1991). On the reading of historical texts: Notes on the breach between school and academy. *American Educational Research Journal, 28,* 495–519.

Wineburg, S. S. (1998). Reading Abraham Lincoln: An expert/expert study in the interpretation of historical texts. *Cognitive Science, 22,* 319–346.

Wineburg, S. S. (2018). *Why learn history (when it is already on your phone).* Chicago, IL: University of Chicago Press.

Wineburg, S. S., & Martin, D. (2009). Tampering with history: Adapting primary sources for struggling readers. *Social Education, 73*(5), 212–216.

Wineburg, S. S., Mosborg, S., Porat, D., & Duncan, A. (2007). Forrest Gump and the future of teaching the past. *Phi Delta Kappan, 89*(3), 168–177.

Winfrey, O. (Director). (May 4, 2011). *Freedom Rider's 50th anniversary* [Television broadcast]. In C. Carter (Producer), *Oprah Winfrey Show.* Chicago, IL: Harpo Studios. Retrieved from www.youtube.com/watch?v=nAyfoyfLsnQ

Women on 20s. (2015). Harriet Tubman on $20 Bill [Image]. Found at Women on 20s Presskit. Retrieved at www.women-on20s.org/presskit

Yates, A. (1923). Letter written by Albany's Committee of Correspondence. In J. Sullivan (Ed.), *Minutes of the Albany Committee of Correspondence 1775–1778,* 18–19. Retrieved from archive.org/stream/MinutesOfTheAlbanyCommitteeOfCorrespondence1775-1778Vol1/MinutesOfTheAlbanyCommitteeOfCorrespondence1775-1778Vol1_djvu.txt

Index

Note: *Italicized* page numbers refer to evidential material provided in the text.

About the Author

Jeffery D. Nokes is an associate professor in the History Department at Brigham Young University. He earned a PhD in teaching and learning from the University of Utah, with an emphasis on literacy in secondary social studies classrooms. A former middle school and high school teacher, his research focuses on history teaching and learning, historical literacy, and preparing young people for civic engagement. He is the author of *Building Students' Historical Literacies: Learning to Read and Reason with Historical Texts and Evidence* and coauthored *Explorers of the American West: Mapping the World through Primary Documents*. Jeff has published several journal articles and book chapters on the topic of historical literacy, literacy instruction, and teacher preparation. He has received middle school, high school, and university teaching awards and currently teaches historian's craft, building historical literacies, and teaching methods courses for prospective social studies and history teachers. Jeff enjoys hiking and traveling with his wife, children, and grandchildren.